MW00941907

Laundry Day

Rhonda Brew

Dedicated to:

Suzie Dickey, my dear friend who was there for me with love and support during my darkest hours. I hope this book can express my love for you.

Jean Wright (Grandma Jean): All my love to you for telling me to write a book. We stood in front of your burned down house where your own life story went up in a blaze!

You both have helped me to be a better person and to trust God. Thank you.

Please note: This book is written directly from my journal, which I kept throughout my incarceration. The language is a little graphic and the accounts are as they happened, from my point of view.

1.
The Arrest, CCA,
Bologna Sandwiches

On November 9, 2009, I was arrested for trafficking marijuana. I was busted at the U.S. Border Patrol checkpoint near Sonoita, Arizona on Highway 83, heading towards Tucson. I was coming from Patagonia where I have lived since the early 90's. One week earlier, my picture was on the front page of The Weekly Bulletin. There I was, standing on the roof of the famous Wagon Wheel Bar, lettering the building. It was the fourth time, over the last twenty years. I am the town sign painter and a local artist. I had also been the bartender at The Big Steer Bar for eight years. At one time, I also managed the Hot Stuff Pizza at the Texaco in Sonoita for three and a half years.

On that horrible day, I was told that I would be carrying twenty pounds of pot in my back seat with some laundry. I agreed to it because my utilities had been turned off for two and a half months. I was desperate. Twenty pounds was scary, but it was in the back seat, which was better than in the trunk.

All my laundry was separated in bags by colors and whites in the trunk. There was a lot of it, since my utilities had been off for so long. This I had done a few days before I agreed, with much coaxing, to take twenty pounds to Tucson. When I pulled out of the driveway in my "Bat Car," a flat black Crown Vic, a bad feeling came over me. I wrote it off as paranoia. The back seat looked good to me. I couldn't tell there was pot in my car, so I took off in spite of my gut feeling.

A car was ahead of me making sure the way was clear, and there was no dog at the checkpoint. There was also a car in the rear watching my backside. That was a joke!

At the check point, the officer looked in my car and asked me where I was going. He was real nice and pleasant. I told him my utilities and had been off for some time so I was going to do my laundry in Tucson. He asked me if I minded if they took a look in my trunk. I told him, "Of course you can." When they opened the trunk, I saw that my laundry had been dumped out of the bags and it was the shape of the trunk lid! My heart fell out of my chest and I thought I would pass out! Visibly I was calm, hoping to pull it off.

They started poking my laundry with a stick until it thumped against something. They had me dig that something out, probably so my prints were on it! As I was pulling out the bundle, I was saying, "How'd this block of wood get in my laundry?" It was wrapped in wood grain contact paper. As it hit the ground, I said, "That didn't sound like wood!" Their reply was, "Right, lady!" When they asked me if I wanted to waive my rights and talk to them, I said, "No, I had no idea that was in my trunk." Actually that was true; they never asked me about the back seat!

It was really embarrassing to be in the glass enclosure at the Sonoita Border Patrol Station, since I've known most of the guys for years. I used to wait on them at the Stage Stop when they came in for breakfast all the time.

I had to ask the DES (drug enforcement) guys that transported me to Tucson how many "blocks" they found in my car. They told me 204 pounds! I told them that maybe they saved my life. Actually, looking at it all from here, I think they did. AMEN.

I was only in the Tucson holding facility for a couple of days before they took me to court. There, I found my son, Johnny, his girlfriend and my grandson sitting in the courtroom.

The judge let me go home with Johnny for my pretrial time. They lived in Patagonia at the trailer park on Harshaw Road. Lisa, his girlfriend, was a total bitch to me no matter what I did for her. I watched my grandson every morning from about 7:30 am until around 11:00 am, or later. Lisa would never get up until then. Finally, I told Johnny I needed to work on my sign business. I couldn't get anything done by starting at noon every day!

Lisa turned on me after that. She even turned her mom on me, saying I was dangerous to "her" grandson. I said something to Lisa about only feeding little Josh T.V. dinners and almost nothing else. She got totally vicious after that. I moved into a tent in Johnny's driveway to try to keep the peace. That wasn't working either, so I had to go and sleep on girlfriend Suzie's floor. I told her I needed to get used to sleeping on cement when she was apologizing for only having room on the floor.

The day I left Johnny's driveway, Lisa's mother was screaming at me at the top of her lungs. It was so loud I had to leave before someone called the cops. My pretrial release agreement was that I had to stay with Johnny. Thank God that my pretrial probation officer didn't find out. She could have thrown me in CCA (Central Arizona Detention Center) in Florence until my hearing for my plea and Johnny could have been charged $5,000 for letting me leave.

I was successful on pretrial in spite of Lisa's efforts to undermine my situation.

Now you know what led up to my imprisonment. When I told Grandma Jean that I was going to prison for a couple of years, we were standing in front of her house that had burned to the ground.

The fire started in her fireplace flue and she barely escaped with her life. She had been writing her life story for many, many years, which was now gone. She looked at me and said, "Write a book!" My reply was, "OK."

Johnny took me to the Federal Courthouse in Tucson, where I pleaded guilty, my only real choice. I was threatened with 35 years if my plea was innocent. My lawyer assured me that I would lose and to take the plea of guilty, 24 to 30 months.

I turned myself in to the Marshals after the judge accepted my plea. I could have remained in Johnny's custody, but that wasn't going too well and I was tired of sleeping on the floor in the middle of Suzie's living room. Also, my time was counted as time served from this point on. So get on with the getting on!

The Marshals chained me with ankle cuffs, belly chain (wrapped around twice) and handcuffs. They put me in a large holding cell with 12 foot long metal benches on either side. There was a three foot wall at the far end with a toilet behind it. The place was cold and echoed with keys and metal doors slamming.

At first, there was only one little Mexican girl, a white girl and me. I was talking to the white girl for about 15 minutes and when I started to tell her about my family, she said, "Rhonda, don't you recognize me?" "I'm Kurt's girlfriend!" I told her that she looked different in red. I had only met her once in Kurt's room. I apologized and wrote it off as being too freaked out. No way would I think that someone I know would be there with me, let alone family!

By the time several hours went by, the cell had filled up with girls. There were 16 of us in all. Three of us were white and rest were Mexican, both old and young. Our group had women as old as 60 and as young as 18.

It had been about 3 hours when they gave us all sack lunches consisting of green bologna sandwiches, an orange drink and two cookies.

When it was time to get ready to load us on the bus, they strip-searched us one by one in front of everyone in the cell. We had to get totally naked and squat so everyone could see our assholes! They looked in our hair, ears, mouth, between our toes and under the boobs. Fortunately, I don't have any to speak of, so it was easy for me. It was terribly embarrassing for all of us. I felt bad for the fat girls. After we all had our clothes back on, they chained us up like before, only adding an extra lock-box that fit over our handcuffs so we could only move our fingers.

Our arms had to stay in the same position until we reached CCA in Florence, Arizona from Tucson. By the time we got the chains off, most of the girls were in tears. My arms were cramping before we left Tucson. They weren't going to make me cry! The time frame from the Marshals to getting our chains off was about 5 hours.

After the chains were off, we were put in a filthy cement room.

Once again, it was really cold in there. This time there was only one little bench that could sit maybe 4 people and another 3 foot wall in front of the toilet. Most of us sat on the cold floor or leaned against the cold wall. Nobody talked; we only looked at each other. We knew we were in "Hell." A couple girls were regular customers because they were letting us know what was going to happen next.

It was a couple hours before they took us to be admitted. We were chained up again to be moved down the hall. After herding us into a huge metal cage, they removed the chains again. There were several long benches, enough to easily seat a football team and their families. We sat there waiting to be called. Each of us was issued *2* bed sheets, 2 blankets, 1 towel, 1 wash cloth, a very short-handled toothbrush, a small tube of toothpaste, a sample size shampoo, a bar of soap and a comb. For our attire, we got a red, short sleeve shirt with pants to match that had an elastic waistband. They gave us 3 pairs of white socks and a pair of those plastic shoes that everyone raves about (crocks). Oh, I forgot about the sports bra and the granny panties!

After being admitted, we were deloused and showered. The walls between the showers were only 4 feet tall and a guard could see us all from above in the bubble, not to mention all the girls too.

This is March 24, 2010. Little did I know that I would be in lock-down until April. My "bunkies" names were Valerie and Kera. Valerie was a very self-important native and Kera was a 19 year old white girl, very sweet and scared. Kera was sentenced to 1 year on March 8th. We don't know where she's going because there are no Federal Prisons for women in Colorado where she's from. They could fly her anywhere in the U.S. They took her last night.

A letter came for me yesterday from my lawyer, Gretta. They slid it under the door with a paper to sign for it. My sentencing date is June 22nd at 10:30 a.m. My grandson's birthday is June 21st; he'll be 2. He is truly the light of my life. He looks just like his dad, Johnny. The sparkle in his eyes and his happy little face makes my heart melt. I am so blessed.

Right now I'm at the CCA (Central Arizona Detention Center) in Florence, Arizona. According to one of the COs (Corrections Officers), we will be locked down until Saturday. They are going through all the cells and strip-searching all the inmates (a shake-down). The sooner they can do that, the sooner we'll get out of our cell.

They have been feeding us only sandwiches with chips and a few cookies for both lunch and dinner. For breakfast its cereal with milk and a PBJ (peanut butter and jelly). As a result of this, I have gotten constipated.

Before she got shipped out, Kera gave me a pencil. If not for that, I would be waiting until next Wednesday to get one. Commissary is next Wednesday and Valerie wouldn't let me use hers. Nobody knows where I am (except my lawyer) and we can't use the phones until we get off lock-down.

Nobody here knows why this shake-down is happening, but I am sure we'll find out soon enough. Sunday is Easter, so hopefully things will get back to normal. I want to go to church. They are having it out in the yard and I haven't been outside since March 24th.

After losing 7 games of solitaire in a row, I think I'll switch up activities. My bunkie is sleeping anyway, so shuffling the cards might wake her up. The girls came by with dinner (bologna sandwiches with cookies). I haven't so much as farted in about 3 days now. They said we were close to getting shaken down now, maybe by tomorrow. We are supposed to be off lock-down before Easter and be able to have Easter dinner together (mystery meat with half-cooked potatoes and Kool-Aid). We could possibly get pudding or mystery cake to go with it, seeing that it's a holiday.

The funniest thing happened the day I got here. I was sitting with Raynalda waiting to be processed when she turned and asked me "Do you know anyone in here?" "No," I told her. "I'm not really a criminal, so probably not." Not 5 minutes later, who waltzes by but Yvette, my next door neighbor in Patagonia. Her folks moved in next door to me 17 years ago and "Polla" (Yvette) was just a little girl. As she put it, "Who does that?" They had transferred her here from Perryville State Prison. She was my bunkie for one night. They took her for sentencing and moved me to B-Pod. They put her in C-pod when she got back (high-risk inmates).

Kera had also left me a postcard that was already stamped so I could let someone know where I was and maybe ask them to put money on my books. I already spent the $50 I had when I turned myself in. That was all I was allowed to have in my pocket. I spent $49.70 on my commissary order that takes a week to get. It's cold in here all the time so I had to order a sweatshirt that cost

$12.35. What a scam! I could only get 20 minutes of phone time, 10 stamps, 10 envelopes, 2 writing pads, 2 pencils, 1 black pen, an art pad with colored pencils, Spam, a box of crackers, a box of Sweet-N-Low, 3 oz. of coffee (instant), a jar of peanut butter, an eraser and a pencil sharpener. Oh yeah, some vitamin E lotion. The water here is so hard my skin looks like a lizard! Hopefully, I filled out the order form correctly so they don't reject it. I added up the order 3 times and got the same amount so I am very hopeful since there is no room for error.

Cynthia, the first girl I met in B-pod, gave me a book to read. Her husband sent it to her, Stephen King's "Under the Dome." She wanted me to tell her all about it, chapter by chapter, so she could tell her husband. She said it was too big a book for her to read. It's really good so far.

Most of the girls in here are Mexican or Native American except for Cynthia and me. I'm white and she's black. We're like the Bobsy twins! I love her; she's a really great person. Lori, her bunkie, is pretty cool too. She's as southern as a country girl can get. Yeah, howdy!

It must have been 7am when I woke up this morning, with a rip-roaring headache. All those sandwiches with no vegetables and little to drink. We also never got hot coffee which usually helps me to be regular. I am so constipated. I feel like throwing up. It's about 8am now and they just gave us break-fast (cereal, milk, bologna, one instant coffee packet, an orange drink packet, one mustard, one mayo and bread). I turned down the bread. Valerie gave me her instant coffee in hopes that it would help me with my irregularity problem. We only have the water out of the tap, but it gets pretty hot, not coffee hot but I'm not complaining. We are fortunate to have water and a toilet.

My bunkie went back to sleep without eating. I think she read an entire novel last night. I was awakened last night about 1:30am to a guard yelling out two girls' names. She told them to "roll up," they are being shipped out. Then it got stupid! They didn't speak English. Next thing, she was hollering for a translator. One of the inmates volunteered and the whole escapade lasted about a half an hour because they had a lot of questions. The whole episode was pretty humorous, the "you had to be there" kind of funny.

My headache is subsiding a bit, and my stomach is gurgling. That coffee could be helping. I hope Valerie is sleeping when it all breaks loose. It's terrible having to crap in lock-down. The toilet is in the middle of the room and nobody can leave. At least there are only two of us, but still!

They just called pill-call, so I pushed the button for them to open the door. I asked the guard for a medical request form (kyte) for the second time. She said she would bring me one again. You have to send a kyte to get an aspirin around here. I've sent three different kytes since I've been here and not one of them has been answered yet. Eat my words; the officer is getting me something as we speak. Cool! Well, never mind my request form. The guys brought in the dogs. We all have to stand against the wall while they take the dogs through each cell. Now that the dogs are done, we are back on lock-down waiting for the next shift. They will tear through our cells searching for anything we aren't supposed to have, like extra towels, blankets, etc. and then the strip-search. After all that, maybe we'll get off lock-down.

I hope I don't have to crap until tomorrow so I can do it in private. I'm a little funny about that. When I was a lot younger, taking a crap in a public restroom or someone's house was out of the question. I had to be in my own bathroom. God please get me through this; my stomach is rumbling. Let me come through this gracefully, Amen. Enough talking shit. I'm going to read my book now. I'm almost half way through it.

So much for that idea. Valerie said the Mod Squad is already searching everyone next door, so we should be real soon. Looks like we won't be having a microwave when we are let out. Some clown had to sneak some popcorn in, while they were out of their cell to grab lunch. Apparently, they weren't able to retrieve it before being locked-down and it burned! The CO came in the pod and said, "Something is burning! Who put popcorn in the microwave? Someone just cleaned it, and now I'm taking it out of here!" Too bad 'cause we're getting off lock-down after we are all searched and everyone has gotten their commissary on Wednesday. I can't stop laughing. You know there is going to be a major "bitch session" about who ruined it for everyone, when they all do it! I can hardly wait.

I guess I'll eat some lunch now since we'll be out of here soon. My constipation is most likely psychosomatic and my headache is finally gone now.

They're here! Ten men and two women COs. They had chairs lined up by the showers where we sat waiting to be strip-searched. In the meantime, two guys went through each cell. They were looking inside the lights, cooler grates, etc., like they were looking for weapons or drugs. They pulled our bedding apart and went through everything. They took our extra toilet paper and the trash! We undressed in the shower stalls, four at a time. We lifted up our hair and they looked behind our ears, inside our mouths, under our feet and armpits. Then we had to squat and cough. After getting dressed again, they gave us back our IDs and put us back on lock-down. They are still out there shaking-down the upper tier. We are supposed to be let out of our cells when they are finished having fun. It sounds like a party out there. Wow, it's Good Friday! A Good Friday it truly is. Thank you, God for this day, and thank you for sending nice people to shake us down. Amen.

It's all quiet now. You could hear a pin drop. I'm hoping for a hot meal for dinner. Now it's 5 minutes after 5pm and they let us out, but not until they gave us sandwiches for dinner. With good news, there seems to come a little bad.

Looking around, I don't see Cynthia anywhere. Apparently they shipped her out, too. I still have her book. I guess I'm sitting at this table alone again. I don't want to say that the girls are prejudiced, but I think they are. Nobody wants to be ridiculed for hanging out with the white girl. Anyway, my bunkie, who's a native, gave me some shampoo, so time to wash my hair. It's pretty gummy right now. That was the first hot shower I've had since I was taken into custody. Kera left some cocoa butter lotion so I don't have to wait until Wednesday to help out my alligator skin. Wow, does it feel good!

Solitaire seems to be my game tonight. I won 1 out of 3 so it's time to quit while I'm ahead. There's one girl at my table, but her back is to me watching a card game at another table. Since watching the T.V. with no sound, someone has changed the channel 3 times. Maybe I'll go back to my room pretty soon. They will be locking us down for the night in an hour or so anyway.

One of the girls just asked to borrow my handbook. On the back of it I drew the Angel of Death. All the girls at her table are asking to see it. Watch, now they will want to get to know me because I'm an artist and I could do cool stuff on envelopes, etc.

Well, I got a little job already. Monica wants me to draw her boyfriend and her together. I told her to wait until I get my art stuff from commissary.

Good morning, world. I was dreaming I was working at a pizza place and was going to ride my bike home, but it fell apart when I was going down the hill. I went back up the hill and got a faded, old, red Datsun pickup and put all my stuff in the back. When I hit some bumps going down the hill, the tailgate fell open and all my stuff went flying out all over. Next thing I knew, someone was yelling from the top of the hill, "Volunteers, your breakfasts in a bag!" Hello! You are in a cell. I left here for a while. We got to eat our sack breakfast in the day room, fortunately. Thank you, God.

The T.V. is showing this gardening guy on Good Morning America and he's showing all these different flowers you can eat. It's pretty funny when there's no sound. He's just munching away.

There was a girl I met the other day in the shower stall next to me. She was a very large woman, especially naked. Her name is Claudia. She asked me what I was in here for, so I told her for trafficking. She asked me what I was hauling and I told her 200 pounds of pot. To be cordial, I asked her what she was in for and she excitedly told me she was caught with 49 pounds of cocaine. My bottom jaw 'bout hit the floor. She's only getting 5-7 years. What's up with that? I'm getting 2-4 years for pot. She should get way more, according to the scale. In fact, thinking about it, maybe its bullshit. Who would trust this woman with that many dollars' worth of coke?

I'm getting to know her now, and she's a real nice person. We've been playing cards and talking a lot. Unfortunately, she has diabetes; her bones ache and her hands hurt a lot. Poor girl, I'm going to pray for her. Going back to bed right now seems like a good idea.

So much for good ideas. Tilly just sat down at my table. She's an older native lady, not real old, (61), but older than most of the girls, more my age. I'll be 55 in May and I was born in '55. Tilly was telling me she has 24 grandchildren and 6 great-grandchildren. I told her the world knows she's here! Right now she's mad at her daughter who's watching her home. Tilly told her to deposit $3,600.00 in the bank, so she did, but in her own account! Bummer! Not much she can do about it, or more like nothing, except eat it. I gave her one of my angels that I made from our lunch bags. You can stick them on the wall with toothpaste. An angel to watch over her while she sleeps.

It's nice to hear laughing out there, everything echoes in the day room. I'd better make some more angels. I've given them all away. The girls seem to like them, silly. This would be a good time, while my bunkie is sleeping, snoring away.

The big, black CO just came and shut the cell door and said "Good morning." He seems like a pretty cool guy, but I wouldn't want him mad at me. I think they are doing count because they need beds for the new girls coming in. We'll probably get a new bunkie today now that we have an empty bed. Hope I don't have to move back to the top bunk again. If they send us someone with a medical problem, I may have to. Valerie, my native grumpy bunkie, just had a baby (C-section). When she was due, they flew her out of here by helicopter with a bunch of guys holding shot guns, standing all around. Wouldn't want her to escape! Maybe so nobody could hijack the helicopter and make the big prison break! Ha, ha.

Here I've written two pages already this morning and its only 10am. Hope my *2* inch pencil lasts until Wednesday when we get commissary. I ordered two of them and a pen. It will be nice to use a pencil sharpener instead of a Bic razor. I'm pretty excited about getting my art supplies and instant coffee with sugar substitute. Yea - yippee - yahoo - shazam - Scooby Doo!

I sent Johnny the postcard that Kera gave me and told him to give my address to all my brothers (3), and to my girlfriend whose brother is responsible for the extra 180 pounds that I didn't know he put in my trunk! They owe me some commissary, in my way of thinking. Johnny should be getting my postcard by today if the Easter holiday doesn't delay the mail in Patagonia. Maybe I'll get mail next week. I asked my son to give his brothers my address and seed me pictures so I'd have something to draw.

The coolest thing just happened to me. Shawn, the girl in the cell next to me asked, "Hey, Rhonda, do you still have that little pencil?" I said, "Sure, do you need it?" She said "No, I want to give you one." Her mouth was full of toothpaste. She gave me a brand new one with an eraser. I'm so happy! The lead is broken so I need to go back to my room and sharpen it with my razor. My bunkie kicked me out to take a crap so I have to wait. I'm hoping to kick her out soon for the same reason.

The laundry person is calling for blankets today. It's too cold in here so I'm not giving mine up. My blanket doesn't need washing anyway. They brought us another bologna lunch. I guess we have to eat the leftovers until they are gone. Someone got carried away making sack lunches!

The girl that does the laundry came in with an expanding file full of receipts for the up-coming commissary. I didn't get one. This is when I need to have faith that God didn't forget me. The girl said, "Just because you didn't get a receipt doesn't mean you won't get commissary. They may have lost it or something." Then she added, "Unless you didn't fill out the order form perfectly." Maybe God wants me to do without for another week. Look what happened to Christ! They killed him for being the son of God. They thought they did...surprise, surprise.

The best thing for me to do is focus on tomorrow being Easter, when Jesus rose from the dead. He is the most important, always. Thank you, God for giving us your only son to lead us to you.

I think I almost got into some trouble. We were watching a movie, "Snakes on the Plane". I was sitting at a table with my back turned away from the girls watching T.V. They were talking, Tilly and a couple others. I made a comment on their conversation. Big mistake! One of them got shitty with me, and stupid me, I told her it was too bad if she didn't like it. Come to find out, she's a little short on the sandwich side. Now I think she has a problem with me. Retarded people are dangerous and unpredictable. Night now she's helping Valerie to move next door with Shawn, the one that gave me a pencil. When she walked in the cell, she gave me the dirtiest look. Not good. She's a big, dumb, Native American and I'm white as hell!

There's a thrill a minute around here. My cell was empty except for me for about a half hour. Two girls moved in. One is 8 months pregnant and doesn't speak a word of English. Her name is Rafaela and the other one is Maria. Maria speaks both Spanish and English. Lori, the B-pod welcoming committee, came in and filled them in on whatever, all in Spanish.

I think the retarded girl finally forgot about me. I've been staying out of sight. She keeps circling the tables and doesn't seem to notice me. Don't think I'll be jumping into anyone's conversation anytime soon.

It seems I'm running my own little business making my sandwich bag angels. They are only about an inch and a half high. They're pretty cute. The first one took me 2 hours to make. After about 9 of them, it's down to 20 minutes per angel. Also I made some little silver crosses from the foil drink packets and two little rubber-bands. So far I've acquired 3 packets of peach cool-off, a pack of cream cheese and chive snack crackers, another pencil with an eraser and a pencil sharpener on loan. I can keep the pencil. We had bologna again for dinner. Woo-hoo, we're having fun now!

It's 10 to 7pm already and I'm sitting at this table alone again, a different table this time. I actually like it that way. I don't have to interact, but I can hear all the bullshit that's going on. A good situation to be in if I'm writing a book about the goings on in a women's lock-up. It's time to get out the cards.

Its Easter morning for 15 more minutes. They gave us bologna sandwiches again for breakfast. We heard a rumor of hot lunch. We'll know in about 20 minutes or so. I still have not taken a crap! More than half the inmates are constipated because of what they are feeding us.

I've had a pretty good time since my new bunkies moved in. Last night we had 6 girls and me in our cell. They were all talking Spanish, but I knew what they were talking about. I feel bad for thinking they are prejudiced. We just have to get to know each other better. My bunkies, Choppa, Claudia and I played cards this morning after breakfast, "King's Corner." I'm starting to have sort of a good time.

After lock-down for cleaning and count, Claudia came to our cell and asked me to do an Angel of Death picture for her bunkie. I told her she had to wait for me to get my art supplies. Looks like I'm getting a regular business going in here and it hasn't been two weeks yet. It sounds like it's time for lunch. God, please let it be hot food. We had burritos with rice, corn, and a little hot sauce, (tomato juice with a couple chunks of tomato). For dessert we got sandwich cookies and Kool-Aid. We are supposed to have meatloaf with mashed potatoes and gravy for dinner.

After lunch, Choppa and I played "Wild Rummy." We each won a game with a score of 505. Pretty evenly matched, I'd say.

I just found out that my bunkie, the pregnant one, got caught with a couple kilos of crystal meth. She was transporting it for her husband.

There hasn't been much time for me to read my book the last couple of days. Maybe this would be a good time since we are locked-down until dinner. The cleaning girls are out there singing and whistling. Now they woke up Maria. Our door just unlocked and suddenly I don't feel like reading. I've been missing my good buddies, Clint and Niki and their 5 kids. They recently moved out of Patagonia and were living in 3R Canyon in a little RV before moving in with Clint's mother in Nogales. They probably wonder why I haven't written.

What a day! I don't know where to start. Too much fun! Not really. Always have fun every moment of every day if you are able. It's our choice how we spend our precious moments. Happiness is infectious, so don't be afraid to share. Leave 'em laughing. It will cure what ails you. It sure is working on me. I keep forgetting I'm in prison. They can't take that away from me. I feel like dancing and there's no music. We're locked-down and all I hear is laughing through the whole place.

As soon as the door opens, I'm headed for the shower.

My underwear finally dried after washing them in the sink. I got some shower shoes, too. Kera left them for me. This time I'm going for a different stall. I was given the "inside," on the hot one.

So much for that idea! As soon as the doors opened, the showers were already running, all of them. I'm talking less than a minute! Wow, those girls are hard to out run! The stall I picked was one that didn't even get warm. This nice little Mexican girl stopped me. She motioned for me to use a different one. That was way cool of her for saving me. Bless her heart.

It's late now and my bunkies are snoring, but not too loudly. Earlier, all I thought about was going to bed and now I don't feel like sleeping. Sure hope my son, Johnny got the postcard and gives everyone my address pretty soon. A letter for me from anyone would be nice. It feels like I'm on another planet.

Wow, it's Monday again already and almost time for lunch. Believe it or not, we just got back from the yard. Awesome! I met a couple of girls from A-Pod, the pod for people who have jobs. Tink told me who to give my job request to her bunkie, Wetta. She said it would go straight to the person that assigns positions. I met Wetta and talked to her about work. She told me to wait until a "load" goes out (girls being transferred) and they need to fill their positions. It's after 12am so I'll continue this later. There's too much to say right now.

During lunch, Tink was banging on the door that's between the pods. She was asking for me! A girl went over and got this flattened paper bag for me from under the door. It had drawing paper, colored pencils, an eraser and a pencil sharpener. She hooked me up big time with the art supplies. I hollered through the door, "I love you. You're the bomb!"

When we went for dinner, I got a request form so I could ask for a job. I filled it out and about an hour later, Wetta came to our pod. She had property boxes for some girls. I gave her my job request form and two of my "angels," one for her and one for Tink. Who knows what tomorrow will bring. It's been pretty exciting around here lately. I think I'll do my bunkies a favor and go to bed early tonight. I'll call Gretta, my lawyer, tomorrow and see if I can get "no probation" by doing more time.

I've been hearing that once I go to prison, if I get over 24 months, I can do this 9 month drug program and get a year taken off my time. So maybe getting extra time will qualify me to get less time for getting more time. I don't want to put anyone out by having to do probation for three years when I get out. That's driving me to UA (piss test) once a week and their SEABHS drug program 3 times a week, 3 hours each for 9 months. That's a lot of rides and aggravation. Plus SEABHS does UAs also. Talk about an overkill! Give me prison time instead, so my friends and family don't have to suffer too! God, please bless them all and keep them in your grace. Thank you. Amen.

I have been tossing around for hours. I cannot seem to sleep. My brain won't stop deciphering. For instance, I'm thinking about how my grandson is not quite two yet and all he gets to eat is T.V. dinners. No nutrition what so ever! His little body is developing and growing. All his organs, his brain, eyes, motor functions, speech, coordination, imagination, eating habits, etc. He needs food that has as much nutrition as he can get or he is being deprived of a strong and healthy foundation. You are what you eat! We are only as good as the fuel we run on. Eating T.V. dinners as a regular diet is like using watered-down, recycled fuel in a high-performance engine! I don't want little Joshua to be weak and sickly like his mother and so far she is making sure of it. This issue has kept me awake so many nights. I just want to scream. I will not sleep well until I can get this message across to my son, but I don't have a stamp or an envelope until commissary next week. Johnny is always working, so he is not aware of Lisa's bullshit. She always has real food when he gets home.

It's April 5th and I've been haunted by this every night and every day since being locked-up. I promised Johnny I wouldn't start any shit with his sniveling girlfriend so his life isn't hell. But mine is! Thanks, Lisa! God's watching.

When I needed my son and my grandson the most, Lisa made sure I got none of that. When Johnny was taking me to turn myself in after my plea, Lisa sent a card for me, with my son. It said that I'm part of the family and she was there for me. F#ck you, Lisa! If she was here, I would tell her that I am not part of her family and will never need her to be there for me. Also, I would tell her to get her head out of her ass and feed that kid right. She needs to change something, and she can find it in the mirror! According to her, Johnny can do nothing right. He is an awesome father and a good provider, not to mention how fun he is to be around. She could never find a better man than my son. Maybe I can go to sleep now. I'm finally exhausted.

2.

Thirty Day Lock-down

My little business is really booming. Every day I get another little job lettering something, designing tattoos, drawings from photographs, etc. I'm working on a photo drawing now and I just finished one this morning. We're on lock-down again because Lori kicked Hanna's ass. The real truth is that Lori slapped her a few times while Hanna covered her head. It was totally lame. Hanna is the retarded girl and Lori is now a stupid hillbilly. Hanna is a real a**hole. She got 7 girls kicked out of the pod so far. Now I can't deliver my stuff until they let us out. I put the name "Yvonne" inside a heart on a card and personalized a styrofoam cup for Yvette today. The only job I haven't finished is from a photo of Monica's boyfriend. She wants me to put her in the picture with her head on his chest and his arm around her. I need to have her sit while I sketch her, and then borrow her ID to detail it.

My Bunkie, Maria is being a real jack-ass. She's a real shit starter. I hope they move her out of here! They sent me a reply to my request for a job. They said I'm on the list and will be called as soon as one is available. Tomorrow would be nice. There's going to be trouble if Maria and I are stuck in the same cell much longer. If I get a job, they will move me to A-pod. Never too soon. I promised the Officer that I wouldn't speak to her, hours ago. She keeps talking shit anyway. Things like, "Your breath stinks, I'm not afraid of you, I'm asking to move away from you, you're stupid, etc." Now she has switched to Spanish and is still talking. I'm going to bed.

Sitting here Indian style on the top bunk, I'm wondering why I gave up my bed again and took the top bunk for somebody that turns on me later! Jesus said we are supposed to carry our enemy's backpack for him and also offer him our coat while he's slapping us around. I guess that is what God wants me to do, so I'm good. I only want to do what He wants me to.

We're still locked-down, but we were able to take a shower and we already had breakfast. Man, these girls are selfish bitches! I was the first one in line for the-showers and they kept bumping me out to the back. I wonder if they think they were accomplishing anything. Maybe they are winning!

I haven't said a word to Maria since yesterday. She had complained to someone when she went to "medical" yesterday. Apparently, they told her she could move out to another pod. She feels it's unfair that she has to suffer lock-down when she had nothing to do with the fight. She was right there yelling, "Hit her again! Hit her again, that's what snitches get!" She was all proud of herself for cheering her on. Now she's frantically packing her stuff like her request is top priority for the day! Dream on, Cinderella. I don't think so.

They will never in a million years believe that I'm making her life "hell". They know I'm not a shit-starter and I've been nothing but good to her.

My crime is telling her to stop bitching. She's trouble and will never be happy unless she thinks someone is suffering because of her wrath! It's pretty humorous watching her antics from up here. She's sooo cool. God please give her what she wants, in Jesus' name.

After coming back to our cell from getting our lunch tray, my property box was opened a couple of inches. I didn't open it since this morning when I had a shower. Maria was the only one in here. What a bitch! God, please do something about her before I lose my cool. Now she has this smirk on her face. I have a feeling it won't last too long and it won't be me that changes it. It's time to take a nap and maybe things will have changed when I wake up.

Everything appears the same. However, that's not possible unless time stopped. The key word is "appears." I'm not really sure if I went to sleep or not. Maybe I was sleeping because I remember them coming to get me so I could start my new job. My job was in the serving line for chow. Any job would be nice. There's nothing I wouldn't like if it gets me out of lock-up and away from these spoiled, self-important bitches! I swear! Women are all the same, everywhere you go, not just prison! I don't really mean all of them. About 10% of them are down to earth. The other 90% think they are God's gift to the planet. How that phenomenon happened, I would like to know.

It feels like I might get some mail today, God willing. If Johnny gave everyone my address like I asked him to, it's highly possible. I sure could use some news from somewhere. Some pictures would really be nice. Johnny had a 30 day notice to move, back when I turned myself in, so I know he's real busy. Hope he's getting enough work to pay the costly move-in fees. He'll have deposits and possibly first and last month's rent, etc. Always I hope the best for him. What a wonderful son he is! I love him. Well, I'm starting to cry and I can't see what I'm writing anymore.

We got back from getting our dinner and I'm crying again. For some reason, Joshua (my oldest son) is on my mind. I can't seem to get his grave out of my head. Maybe if I draw it with the sun going down, I'll be better, but I don't know. Whatever flies, I suppose. I didn't visit his grave before turning myself in, so I'm sure it looks forgotten. Definitely it's not forgotten, nor ever will be.

It's April 12th and I just got some commissary. We are on a 30-day lock-down program for that stupid fight, so the commissary is restricted to certain items only. I got writing paper, pen, #2 pencil, eraser, 10 envelopes and no stamps. It's incredible, the incompetence. I have to wait two more weeks for stamps! Looks like I'll just keep writing this book. It's so much nicer writing with a pen instead of a 2 inch pencil. We only have 26 more days of the 30-day lock-down program.

We have been locked-down more than anyone in this place. I'm starting to think we are the experimental pod people. Nobody else is locked-down in the whole facility.

Oh, that book I was reading, "Under the Dome" by Stephen King, will have to wait. Lori took the book when they ran her out of here. She was supposed to send it home for Cynthia. Looks like I'll have to wait for the movie. I wouldn't miss it! The first half of the book was dynamite.

The day I turned myself in to the Marshals in Tucson, they had me in the holding cell, waiting to be transported to the place I'm in now. I sat next to this white girl and we started talking. She goes, "Rhonda, don't you recognize me? I'm Kurt's girlfriend." Kurt is my brother-in-law, Johnny and Ray's uncle. "Oh my God, I sure didn't. Wow!"

She was getting out as I was going in. Apparently they moved to Patagonia and Bryan knew about it. He didn't tell me either. I'm not sure why, but I'm going to ask him.

This girl ordered a picture of a naked girl on a cot, and then she backed out of the deal after I finished it. She said she didn't like it, but it was great! I think she thought it was free. I sent the drawing to my son, Johnny. He appreciates porn.

My bunkie Maria let me mail all my boys a letter using her indigent envelope. The prison pays the postage. I drew a color pencil picture of the ranch for Raymond with his letter. The first picture I did of the "Angel of Death" went to Nito with his letter. The naked girl I sent with Johnny's letter. I put them all in one envelope and Maria mailed it with her name and inmate number on the return address. It was addressed to Johnny's P.O. Box. They should be getting it by tomorrow. I still haven't gotten a letter from anyone except Gretta, informing me of my sentencing date.

I'm getting pretty tired now that I've caught up on writing my book. There was a little break in my play-by-play due to lack of paper. I'm well stocked up now so I'm good. Goodnight.

Good Morning. It's Wednesday, April 13th, 2010 and the sun is shining in Florence, Arizona. We already had our breakfast and they are running around asking for the trays, "platos." Usually Maria has her big head in the door window, but not for trays and trash. I'm not getting off this bunk to do it, when her head is two feet from the door! I can't wait to get a job or something so I can move out of here. Thank God I have another art project to do for the same person I did a skull and roses for. She loved it. It was sort of a Grateful Dead motif. Now it's an Indian dream catcher with feathers. I think it's sort of a family crest because she wants me to put her last name at the top of it. She gave me a pretty good drawing of what she wanted, another great challenge of my career.

Too bad I didn't have a photo copier to copy all this artwork I'm doing for my book. Anyway, Dee already brought me some more typing paper and she's washing a T-shirt for me. She said, "Sorry it's used." I told her "used" is more comfortable anyway. A new one isn't necessary in here. It's so I don't get so darn cold all the time. I've decided not to order that sweatshirt after all. We can't take anything with us and I'll just have to send it home when they ship me off to a federal prison.

Nothing real exciting to report except that I made a dream catcher with the top ring of a styrofoam cup, strips of plastic off the garbage bag and a cross I made from foil packets and pony-o's. It's kind of cute in a funky sort of way. Hopefully it works to catch my bad dreams from entering the universe. I thank God for the gift of creativity! I might be locked-up, but I'm doing my life's ambition, my artwork. My prayers have been answered, but I left a few things out when I was praying, like geographic location, etc. That's okay though. He has totally blessed me. Speaking of that, I need to get started with some fine art right now.

Boy, it came out beautiful (the Indian family crest).

There was a knock on the door, "legal mail for Rhonda brew." I signed the form and slid it under the door. My lawyer sent me a notice saying there will be a probation officer to visit me on the 22nd of this month, and it's the 14th right now. Gretta said she'd be there with me so to wait for her if the probation officer shows up first. He is going to ask me questions about my life, drug use, family, etc. She said to be completely honest, so I better call her as soon as they let me cut of this cell. I had to lie for the judge to accept my plea of 24 to 30 months.

We could get into trouble if I get caught lying about not knowing the pot was in my trunk. What a bag of worms! Lying down right now seems like a good idea. All this court crap gets me nervous, because it's all a lie anyway. I wish I could do time and just forget about it. Going, back to my life would be real nice.

It's 4:30pm and I'm not able to sleep. I'll be able to sleep tonight because Maria and I pulled a fast one today. They moved someone out and left her mattress outside our door. They had opened our cell door to give Rafaela a property box. Maria said, "Hurry, Rhonda, get that flat mattress off your bunk. Hurry!"

We switched them before they came back to close our door. They were talking to another girl down the way while we did our "presto-change." My mattress was so flat it was like sleeping on a cement floor with a rug on it! The one I have now is one they use for girls with medical problems. Talk about a score! Right now I feel like I'm sitting on a cloud.

They need to replace and refill our hygiene products. There's no soap to wash out my underwear and socks. If I don't get them washed and hung at the end of my bed before I go to sleep, they won't be dry to put them on after showers in the morning. Talk about hell on earth!

Boredom is the biggest issue with me, plus my arms are getting weaker. My legs are stronger because of sitting Indian style for long periods of time on the top bunk, sort of like isometrics. There's got to be some way to strengthen my arms. Push-ups are probably the answer. I'm not sure if I could even do one right now. Maybe if I do a woman's push-up with my knees on the ground. I think I'll start doing them in the morning. That's the time I feel the best and my bunkies go back to sleep after they eat. We'll see if I remember in the morning. After reading this entry I will.

They said on the 16th we will be able to make phone calls and will be able to come out of our cages for 2 hours, one tier at a time. That ought to be interesting. I'm going to play cards with Choppa like always, if they don't ship her out of here before then. That's one person I am going to really miss. Maybe we'll see each other in Oklahoma or somewhere. That's one of the places they send people doing federal time. She's got 41 months to do, so she will be there when I get shipped out. Of course, there's no way of knowing where either of us is going.

I've been thinking about Suzie, Grandma Jean and Bryan lately. Suzie's son, Alan probably went to court by now. He's looking at 106 years! My son Johnny said, "Don't they hear themselves saying that?" Serving 106 years is stupid when people don't live that long from birth! They must think it sounds cool or something.

Someone told me when we were out in the yard that they get $3,000 a month for each inmate! That's like sooo crazy! I can't even think of such a high number! My brain isn't big enough.

I started biting my nails again after quitting for 20 years. There's only one set of nail clippers for the whole facility. In order to use them, we need to give them our ID, so we don't use them longer than needed. We won't even get a food tray without it. We clip our ID on the window when we are in our cell so they can count us. They count us about 20 times a day and night. Then they times that by $3,000! That's whacked!

Writing really seems to be keeping the boredom away. It's already after 5pm. They'll be calling us for chow soon, within a half hour or so. Yippee, yahoo, we're living now!

It's funny how the light is on in our cell only when my bunkie needs it. Maria will turn it off the second she is done with whatever. She sleeps most of the day while I'm doing my artwork in the dark. She turns the light on, almost ridiculously, when I have about finished. Until then, I use the light from the window.

I can't wait to go to prison! This is bullshit here. We've been locked-down for almost the whole time I've been here for the shit somebody else did. They aren't even here now! We still have 25 or 26 days of this left. So much for my job I was supposed to get, not until the 30 day disciplinary program is over. It's so unfair. My freedom depends on whether other people f#ck up or not! Like that will ever stop happening! Other people are always f#cking up! Not a lot to look forward to. They're even holding back our mail. I haven't received a letter yet since March 25th, when I got here, except from my lawyer. Now I have 2 pads of paper, 10 envelopes and NO STAMPS! What's wrong with these people? I wonder if they get a kick out of all this. I honestly think they do. That's sick.

Well, I'm learning to crap in public now, sort of; otherwise I'd be dead now, as much as they feed us. I will give them that. We aren't hurting in the food department. I can barely eat what is on the trays, but I do. I'm on my gain weight program and someone is always giving me what they aren't going to eat. I let them think they are doing me a great favor. Actually, I'm usually uncomfortably full, just making the best of the situation.

When they opened our cell to line up for dinner, I ran down to Dee's cell and slid her picture under the door. I hope she likes how I did the feathers. They look pretty real to me. So far, she likes everything I've been doing.

Choppa's friend wants a photo drawing, so the she ran and got the photo for me before they locked our doors. It's got three people in it, so I told her about 10 bucks in commissary. She said that was fine and would like another one done when I was finished with this one.

Life can be pretty good for an artist in prison. I always heard that, and now I'm living it. There's literally a captive audience. I'm going to shut down the shop because Maria is flopping around like a fish out of water over the light being on. Now she has a shirt over her head making ho-hum sounds. I'll give her another minute before she asks me to turn off the light. Now her legs are moving back and forth and she's tapping her fingers on the wall. I think I'll tell her I don't need the light any more.

I'll start my drawings in the morning. It's only

7:30pm, but I might able to sleep on my new bed tonight without waking up at 3am waiting for the sun. If I die before I wake, I pray the Lord my soul to take. Amen.

What a day we are having! It seems like a lot has happened because I feel so excited, but I don't think anything really has. We had waffles with grits and a slice of bologna for the breakfast meat.

I drew a fire-breathing dragon for Monica next door, before they opened our cell for lunch. Now I'm going to work on the photo drawing, my ultimate challenge, besides maybe drawing someone from memory. That's the hard stuff. I told Maria I only needed the light for about a half hour, so I'd better get started.

Maria woke me up by flushing the toilet. There's so much water-pressure, you could flush a small cat down it without plugging it up. I'm skeptical about doing a "courtesy flush" when I'm still sitting on it. Maria let me draw for over an hour this morning before she shut me down. It's tough when all they do is sleep. All I do is not sleep.

I must have dozed off for a little while because I was at my brother-in-law, Kurt's, talking about what to burn for dinner. Then Bryan rode up on his bike and the toilet flushed.

Now it's 4pm, April 15th, a Thursday and I'm in a jail cell again. On the 22nd the probation officer will be interviewing me. My first visit. I think I already mentioned all this. Here I'm repeating myself when I'm writing, too. Earlier there seemed to be a lot happening, but it was just that we got to take a shower and they gave us some shampoo and a bar of soap. Also, my other bunkie got a visit from her lawyer and Marie had to go to medical. I was alone in here for almost a half hour, and it was bliss!

My drawing is turning out pretty good so far. It's blowing my mind how good I'm getting at this stuff. I think I'll continue with it even though I have light only from the window. I know Maria is not sleeping under that blanket. Too bad she has such a waste of a day. She wants the doctor to put her on Prozac for depression. She doesn't need it! If she does, I haven't seen it yet, and I've been locked-up with her for weeks now!

What a good dinner. We had baked chicken with broccoli, rice with onion, lemon cake, and I grabbed two Kool-Aids this time. I hurried back to my cell so I could deliver my drawing. I think she liked it. I did. I told her I needed stamps, coffee, creamer, sugar and lotion. Whatever she wants to do, to the tune of $10 or so.

Dee still hasn't brought me a T-shirt yet, but she did give me a mug. It's tough collecting on all this work when they have us locked-down 24-7, and are restricting the commissary to envelopes and such. Tomorrow we are supposed to be let out for a couple of hours, one tier at a time. Hopefully I can get to use the phone. Those girls are vicious when it comes to hoarding the phones! I'll probably spend my whole 2 hours ready to dash to the first available phone. There are only three phones and there are 30 girls in the bottom tier.

First I'll call my lawyer for the skinny on my situation, and then call Johnny to see what's up. After that, I'll call Suzie and Bryan to see how they are. Suzie has been through a lot since I left. She could probably use a call that's not collect. Also, I need to get my brother Jeff's phone number off of her Lipton tea box. I think I'll go to bed early tonight, God willing.

It's 4am, April 16th, a Friday. It's a little early to be up, but I had to write about my dream. It was about Willy Sanchez, for what seemed like hours. I've known Willy since 1990, for over 20 years. Then I moved into Patagonia and worked at the Big Steer Bar. Willy and his brothers called me Rhonda Brew Sanchez, after Billy Joe died.

Danny, his brother, my very, very dear friend died several years ago now. He was the only person who went to all of my son Joshua's football games. Danny would come to the bar and tell me everything that happened. Mostly, Josh was on the bench for the first two years because he was my size, but they played him his senior year. They called him the "Rubber Band Man." When they knocked him down, he bounced right back up!

They had one play in practice that David Martin, his best friend, made up called "The Fletcher." Fletcher was Josh's nickname. Josh was all proud to have a play named after him. The play was to throw Josh the ball and everyone tackle him! He never figured it out! Too funny.

Back to the dream. Willy has been struggling for his life for some time now and I wouldn't be surprised if he came to tell me good-bye. In the dream, I was trying to help him with these wires and tubes, but they kept getting tangled up and nobody would help me. I was frantic! I did all I could, which wasn't much of anything, except be there. After I woke up, I remembered that I drew the "Reaper" the day before.

Well, today is the day we get out of our cages for a

little while. I sure hope nobody messes that up. That's justification to lock up those who don't cause trouble, making an example out of us for the rest of the place. I believe it is only a test and they were just waiting for a fight to try it out on someone. In fact, they actually caused the fight situation in order to put their "Program" into effect.

This has been totally experimental, if you ask me. It has to be something like that because the people that work here, for the most part are decent, fair individuals. As I see it, they're doing time too, only they punch out and go home. For them, it will go on long after I'm gone. Bless them for all they do for those who need them.

We are the only pod in this whole place that's locked-down and you know we aren't the only "trouble-makers." We happen to be the convenient, controlled environment from which to conduct their experiment on human behavior under certain conditions.

It's time for me to brush my teeth. I've had a few chunks of my fillings fall out in the last week, and now my mouth tastes like a gym sock, or worse. I won't say it tastes like ass because I don't know what that tastes like. Thank God for that! It will probably wake up my bunkies, but I don't care. They will have to deal with it. Either that, or bad breath.

They let us out today, 7am to 9am. I didn't get to use the phone again. These girls are so selfish. Some of them took two and three turns. I told the officer that I would try again tomorrow. I don't want to start any shit.

Choppa's dad is in bad shape. Danitza save me a postcard so I could put him on the prayer chain to shrink his tumor or make it no longer cancerous. I'm sending the card to Mike and Darrell because they'll start praying right away.

I made someone a birthday card today that was pretty cute. The picture was a lady lying on her therapist's couch. Her dish rack was on the floor next to her, and she had a rag in her hand, drying dishes. Her therapist says, "I really think you need to make time for yourself!

I got a receipt for commissary today. If I accept it, I'll have 26 dollars left in my account. It's exactly the same as my last order, only it has 10 stamps. I'll never have to order another pad of writing paper again while I'm here. I'll have 4 pads, 20 envelopes, 2 erasers, 2 pens, 3 pencils, 1 large envelope and 40 minutes of phone time. 1 can always trade the writing paper for plain typing paper they give to the indigent inmates. They like lined paper better, and I get my art paper.

It's Saturday morning, April 17th, and in 45 minutes they will open the door. I'm going to make the mad dash for the phone. When I didn't get to use the shower yesterday, it was Valerie, my ex-bunkie, who kept pushing me out of the line. Shame on her. She's also the one who kept me from using the phone. They keep saving each other's place. How juvenile is that? It's like being in grade school again, only I'm the only white girl in the place. I've brushed my teeth and made my bed, so I just need to climb down, put my shoes on and stand by the door, ready to sprint! Amazing how this whole ordeal is the most important thing for me today!

I'm going to call Johnny and see how things are going, like my rent, Airstream, the Indian chair, etc., and then Suzie and Bryan to see how they are. I jotted down the things I needed to talk to Johnny about, and Suzie, too. There are still 20 minutes left before I can fly. There must not be as many girls on the top tier because there's been at least one phone empty the whole time they've been out there. I've just got to hurry up and be the first in line for everything. This is a bitch getting all anxious over nothing!

I was right. They called chow! Valerie and her girlfriend clipped their IDs on the phones to reserve them for when they get back with their breakfast. I said, "What the f#ck is that about? You don't reserve the phone in jail!" When they saw Mr. Thornton, they grabbed their IDs, kind of a dead give-away who the selfish people are. It's those same girls that are always reserving the hot showers for each other. I may have to snitch them off because it's me they always do it to. Like I said, I'm the only white girl. And being from Detroit, I'm not a sissy and I don't pull this kindergarten crap! In fact, I would never have thought of it in the first place.

When we got back, we had to go to our cells for count before we got our two hours out in the day room. I'm just waiting for the door to open again. Now we are back to fair game. Before they closed the doors, I told Valerie that she was the most selfish person I ever met, her and her girlfriend. I told her I was tired of their shower episodes and that I am starting to take it personally. I need to call home, damn it. And get a hot shower!

I don't think we are going to get let out until after 11am or so. I need to focus on something else. Maria is cleaning the shit out of the room. I asked her if she was going to clean the ceiling, too. She said that in state prison they do. When it's your turn to clean, you do the ceiling, walls, floor, and everything. Everyone takes two showers a day. Nobody wants to smell bad.

She said they also don't segregate the population in state prison. You get thrown in with people that could kill you while you are sleeping and could care less, because they aren't getting out of there, ever!

They finally opened the doors way early this morning. I called Johnny. "Is this Juanito Rojo Zapato Grande?" "Simon," he said. He hasn't handled anything yet. I told him he'd better not lose my trailer or I'll.... He said, "I won't trailer lose. Well, you know what I mean." He was in a hurry to get to Fire Class. He told me that Fred Roberts wanted my address, so I told him to give it to him.

After lock-down, Danitza ordered a drawing. She wanted a heart with a ribbon saying, "China & Danitza." I made one like it for Johnny and Lisa.

It's Sunday afternoon and I finished Danitza's artwork. I wrote Fred a four page letter and decorated an envelope to go with it. I put an iris on the envelope and did his name real nice in black pen. I was thinking of another cool thing to put on an envelope (a heart with barbed wire around it).

They just called pill-call, and both of my bunkies take pills, so no sleeping now. The metal doors are slamming and everybody's talking. It really echoes when they talk out in the day room. I think I'll do an envelope for Suzie before chow.

This is getting so old, being locked-up in this room when I did nothing wrong to deserve it. It's like they are trying to train us like dogs in a kennel. There is no one else being put through this, so there's got to be something more to this than meets the eye. Probably more than meets the imagination. Many girls have asked for grievance forms, but nobody will give them one. They are supposed to do so. I've also heard from others that when family calls to check on them, they were told that nobody is locked-down! So they are lying to our loved ones about not mistreating us. We're screwed! Well, I'm calling my lawyer in the morning about my interview with the probation officer. Supposedly, the questions will be about my life. My lawyer better be there, I don't want to go this alone.

It's Monday, 2pm and we got our two hours out in the day room. I got a nice hot shower and Choppa and I are playing "Wild Rummy" like always. We even got to eat lunch at the tables. It's difficult eating in our rooms, especially when they serve soup. They pour it in the tray, and it's easy to slosh it all over.

Maria has been selling more artwork for me. She had me show off my envelope for Fred. I had an order for two more envelopes before we came back to our rooms. Boy, what a good nap I had, too. Usually I don't sleep in the day too well, but today I fell right out.

Maria and I were discussing what to charge for envelopes, maybe a candy bar or something about a dollar. Two sodas cost a dollar. A candy bar and a soda sound really good right now. I sure would like a letter from someone, too. I don't think anyone misses me. It's now Tuesday evening. We finally got commissary and I finally got my stamps! I had four letters to mail and I forgot to take them with me to chow so I could mail them. I was having a severe blonde moment. I still get those a lot even though I went grey.

I did a picture of Mickey and Minnie Mouse doing the "Hot Dog Dance" for little Joshua. I stuck the letters to be mailed in the window so the girls collecting the trays might mail them for me. There's one for Garland, Suzie, Johnny and Fred Roberts. If I had more addresses, I'd have more letters to send. Maybe by next week somebody will send me a letter. I'd really love that.

Maria had me laughing so hard I was choking! She colored her lips blue. Not her whole lips, but outlined them real dark all the way around. She was talking to me and then I looked up at her! Oh my God, the Prozac isn't working! Every time I looked at her, I started laughing again. She went to chow that way and nobody said a word except Choppa. She was laughing like me. Everyone else acted like she was normal. Who are these people?

It's been a pretty nice day today. I picked a book out of a pile of books in the day room, "Battlefield of the Mind" by Joyce Meyers. I heard her preach on T.V. once and I thought she was great. I'm already on chapter six. She writes through her own experience and is an interesting writer. I think I'll read some more before they turn the lights out. That will be soon.

It's hard to believe that I was so excited about getting stamps that I forgot to mail the letters. I have been waiting four days short of a month!

The officer doing count just took my letters for me. She's a sweetheart. She came to my room when I couldn't stop crying. I swore I saw my son Joshua on the toilet with a shotgun in his mouth. It was 12 years ago, but it happened all over again in front of my eyes. Must have been lack of sleep and being locked-down so long. She told me whenever a thought like that comes in my head, think of something else really quick. We can't let depression grab hold of us like that. Satan loves that shit! Well anyway, she definitely is a good person.

Good morning world. It's Wednesday, April 21st. Tomorrow I get my first visit from my lawyer and probation officer. I'm sure I'll be glad to see them. They will be my first visitors. Last night after the officer mailed my letters, she came back and slid a letter under the door for me. It was from Fred.

What a nice guy. I like Fred. He saved a stray dog from starvation in Nogales a few weeks ago. He named her Hazel. Fred says she gets along great with Molly, his Great Dane. You could land a small plane on Molly's back, she's so big. That's the first letter from a friend that I have received. I had a hard time sleeping, thinking about Fred and everybody at home.

Today we get out of our cells for 4 hours instead of 2. The top tier is taking their 4 hours first. I need to call my lawyer and take a shower. Other than that I have no plans except to finish Monica's picture. They locked us down when I was only half done. I only drew her boyfriend from a photo. I'm to have him with his arm around her and her head on his shoulder. I'm going to use her ID for the most part, but I may have to have her sit for me in order to finish.

It's time to read some more of my book. I need to stay tuned in to my program of eliminating the devil's strongholds in my mind. I want to be closer to God.

Never mind the book! They let us out for 2 hours. I took a shower, called my lawyer, played some rummy with Choppa and drew Monica, real life. I think I did pretty well. It looks like her to me. Anyway, I finally got that one done. I'll give it to her after we get called out for dinner. Tomorrow I start another one. This girl wants me to draw her and her five kids! I asked her why she only had five. I told her my charge was usually around $10, but I may have to get a little more for six people! Kids are pretty easy to draw. Actually, it's all easy when I can get my head wrapped around it.

Around 3pm tomorrow is the video interview with the probation officer. He is going to ask me questions about my life and who knows what else. I am to be perfectly honest. If he asks me about the pot in my car, I am going to tell him that I didn't know who loaded my car because I wasn't there. Also, that they were going to catch up with me if I made it through the check-point. That's all I know. But, if I say I didn't know the pot was in my trunk, then they wouldn't accept my plea of guilty. They have to believe that I knew all about it.

I decided to write Fred a letter and I also wrote to my lawyer. I asked her if she could get me more time instead of probation when I get out. I explained the strain it would put on Johnny and family if I had to do the SEABHS program. I'm hopeful she can help me with my request. God willing. I wrote Fred a five page letter. I get writing like I'm talking to him. He's someone I can be totally honest about everything to, because he's a real friend.

The book I'm reading says I really need to pay attention to what I'm thinking and doing so "Satan" doesn't win by controlling my thoughts, causing confusion and doubt. I believe all this writing I'm doing is advantageous in seeing what my mind is thinking. Good stuff!

It's almost 6pm, time for chow. I'll remember to mail my letters this time.

It's Thursday, April 22nd. I was able to take a good little nap after breakfast, only to be woken up to them shaking-down the cells. When the officer came to our cell, she told the other COs to go to the next one because we were searching ourselves. We were, too! We went through everything and threw away anything that should not be there. They never came back to search for themselves either. I took it as a compliment.

I keep thinking about the story of Peter when they were out in a storm at sea and Jesus walked up to the boat on the water. At first they were terrified like they'd seen a ghost. Jesus told them to have courage because I AM, and they calmed down. Peter said that if YOU ARE, then call me out to join you on the water. Jesus did, and Peter stepped out of the boat and was walking on the water with Jesus. The wind and the sea started to frighten Peter and he began to sink. He hollered for Jesus to save him, and he did. Jesus reached out his hand and held Peter up from sinking while he stepped back into the boat. The storm then ceased. Oh, why do you doubt, ye of little faith? I feel like that is me at times. I don't ever want to doubt or have a lack of faith. I know God is there and won't let me sink.

I drew a picture of Jesus out of my mind's eye and gave it to Maria. She hung it up and now he is looking at me on the top bunk.

I just got back from my interview. I believe it went

well. The whole thing was actually enjoyable, like having a visit. Ernesto seemed to be a pretty cool guy. Gretta looked tired. She worked all day in Tucson before coming to Florence for my interview. They told me I could write a letter to the judge before I am sentenced. Well, now that's done and life goes on. I thanked God for quieting my brain so he could do his thing so beautifully like he does.

I am pretty hungry and it's only 4pm. Maybe I'll read my book some before chow. I really love this book about keeping aware of the Devil lying to my mind and trying to derail my train.

I hope I get a letter tonight. It feels like there's one on the way. Pretty soon my brothers are going to have to call Johnny. I bet Greg already has. I feel good today thanks to good people, especially since I've started working on my thinking instead of my thinking working on me.

I don't know why I have to keep asking to have the light on as early as 6pm. Maria says the light is making her too hot. I told her that fluorescent lights don't give off heat, so it only seems hot. No comment. She likes to be the alpha-girl! Whatever blows her skirt up is okay with me.

Tomorrow is Friday. I don't know what that means, other than time is flying by, one day at a time. "Three hots and a cot" is no joke!

We are always looking forward to the next meal. Pretty crazy, but that's how I tell what time it is. You wouldn't believe how much junk food these girls buy from commissary. I don't know how they can eat so much! What they give us is already too much to eat at every meal. Of course, the majority of the girls in here are overweight. The officers, both men and women, are for the most part, huge! Some of the fattest people I've ever seen work at this facility. We're talking 300 pounds of woman, in uniforms, men too! Only one out of ten is a fairly normal size. I'm not just the only white girl in our pod, I'm one of the ten girls under 150 pounds and that's out of 60 girls. They say obesity is a disease, but you have to eat to get fat. Seems to me that obesity is a symptom. Here I'm doing my best to put on a little weight so I don't disappear. God has blessed me that way. I don't have to concern myself about eating too much.

I never have to be concerned about anything, for that matter. God has taken very good care of me all my life, so my mission is to never worry because he will not let me sink! I want to be like Christ and never doubt the Lord. He has never let me down and I've never had a reason for not believing in him. I pray that God keeps my loved ones in his grace. The Devil can't have them.

My heart feels good tonight and I'm going to retire, hopefully until morning. Sweet dreams, my sons. I love you.

I don't feel like taking a shower or calling anyone on the phone today. I'm relieved that my interview went so well. Just chillin' is all I want to do. I'll play cards if Choppa feels like it, but right now she's the only person that I will put my pen and paper down for. She makes me laugh all the time. She's just waiting to get shipped out of here. She's hoping for Connecticut, and I hope she gets it. It's beautiful there, especially in the summertime. Choppa is originally from California and I don't think she's been too many places. Time to brush my teeth and watch a little T.V. or play some solitaire.

We got to eat our lunch at a table today. Yeah! It's a good thing, too. We had soup poured right in the tray again. Everyone loves the artwork I've done for them. I enjoy it when my customers are happy. It's Saturday night. No mail until Monday or Tuesday.

I'd love a letter from Johnny, Ray, Nito, Mike, Greg, Jeff or anyone. Maybe all of them! Tonight I feel like sleeping, so that is what I am going to do. I want to dream sweet dreams of those I love, beautiful things, people and places and God.

It's Saturday night now. We had 4 hours out of our cells today. I took a shower and taught Choppa how to play 10,000 with dice I made out of bread. One was made out of toilet paper, because I didn't have enough bread dice. We decided the toilet paper ones were better because the bread ones chip a little bit.

We lost a dot off one of the fives. It was fun. We needed a new game. Choppa and I have been playing Rummy forever! She kicked my butt every game! I made more TP dice, so now we have a set of 6. They are very quiet.

After dinner an officer came to the door and pointed at me to come with her. She opened the door and said, "We need you to get ice for the pod." I told them I'd love to do something productive. They just laughed. The officer said they were wondering who to get to do it and they both thought of me. That makes me feel good that they can judge character when we are locked-down all the time.

I really want them to give me a job. I have to wait for this 30-day program thing to be over with! Supposedly we'll be back to normal on Tuesday. That means I'm in line for a job if they didn't throw my request away. If I get a job, they will move me out of here and into A-pod. That would be a blessing for me and Maria. Especially for Maria. She's so jealous of me that she can't see straight! Everything she liked about me to start with, she hates me for now. That is the way it often goes for me. God has gifted me in many ways, and for that, I am thankful. Others tend to notice my blessings and forget to be thankful for their own. I am seeing and understanding more, and the importance of not giving up! Especially in these days of trouble. I'm not going to help the Devil win this one. He sure is dangerous and a total pest.

It's another beautiful day outside my window. I'm pretty hungry this morning. I was thinking of eating the cake I saved from last night's dinner. Now that I'm awake, Maria has decided to be quieter. She has been banging around, rustling plastic bags, tapping on the wall and the metal part of her bunk, gargling extra loud and long, and just really making an issue of herself.

She doesn't talk to me anymore, not since her pen pal wrote me a letter. That is so silly. The guy is a 27 year old cowboy whom she has only written one letter to. We never meet our pen pals, even if we are in the same facility. He wrote to me to say he's looking for a pen pal that's more my age and is not an asshole. I can't wait to get a job and get away from all this jealousy stuff. She's doing her best to get to me, and it's working. I want to kick her ass! Now that's what Satan wants me to do, so I won't. Heaven help me. My patience is wearing thin. Don't let me sink into the stormy sea.

We get 4 hours out today. I had $2.75 on my phone time, so I tried calling Clint and Niki. There was no answer, so I called my son, Nito. All the boys were there together. I got to talk to all of them, even Joshua, my grandson. He is so cute. They were all glad to hear from me and that I sounded happy. I am happy! That was the best $2.75 I ever spent. Johnny still hadn't given his brothers their letters yet. They're still in his glove box! He's doing it now. If I hadn't called, they still wouldn't have them.

Anyway, we are locked-down again and I have a lot of artwork to do. I'll do that right away so I don't have to pay any attention to Maria and her bullshit.

It's the next day, evening. I was a little too busy to write this morning. I hadn't slept more than a couple of hours last night. Maria was snoring so loudly I couldn't sleep for several hours. Plus, I think I have restless leg syndrome. I can only lie in one position for a minute or two before I have to move. This goes on for at least an hour every night. Part of it could be that I sit cross-legged on the top bunk all the time. Anyway, this morning I'm pretty hungry and it's only 4 pm. Maybe I'll read my book some before chow. I really love this book about keeping aware of the Devil lying to my mind, and trying to derail my train.

Anyway, this morning I was a little crabby. Maria was cleaning the room again at 7am after cleaning it yesterday. She makes as much noise as possible. When I walked by her to leave the room, after brushing my teeth, I said, "Life's a bitch!" Then I went and sat at a table and was putting the dots on my toilet paper dice. I knew Choppa was going to get up and want to play something and I wanted to be ready. The bread dice were totally falling apart. I went back to the room to get the artwork I had for somebody and said "excuse me" because Maria was standing in the way. She grabbed me and threw me down on the cot and locked the door. She was yelling at me saying I called her a bitch! I told her I didn't and she kept saying I did. She kept shoving me, but I managed to push the button for an officer. Nobody answered! She was saying how she was going to get me out of her room today!

Last night Maria said she wanted to do something to deserve to get locked-up for, if they didn't let us out of our cells pretty soon. I didn't realize she meant me! Well, here come the handcuffs! They locked us both in shower stalls in D-pod, (they're cages). They were still wet, too. Then the officer was asking what happened. Maria told her I called her a bitch and I never brush my teeth, and that I blow gross horrible breath in everyone's face. Also, that I never take a shower or wash my clothes, that I smell all the time and I don't ever wipe my ass. She said I was nasty! I couldn't believe what I was hearing. She kept going on and on with the lies. "She hates me because I'm a good artist" is what I told the officer. I told her she had some real jealousy issues. I mean bad!

I'm so glad she is out of my reality! I prayed for God to help me because my patience was wearing thin. It was a miracle that I wasn't locked in solitary confinement for 30 days, and the pod could have started the 30-day program all over again, too. Enough of that subject!

We just finished dinner and now we are all coloring.

Well, I'm writing and they are coloring. Maybe today I'll get a letter from someone.

Wow, I slept well last light! My legs quit jumping around and I went right to sleep. I woke up a lot to pee, about 3 times, and went right back to sleep again. I have a little bit of a headache, but I think it's because I ate cookies whenever I woke up, too much sugar.

This is Tuesday, April 27th. My glasses are broken, but the lens is staying in the frame, barely. Today is commissary, so I'll use the red tape off the commissary bag to fix my glasses. The tape is red and so are my glasses. That's pretty cool. It's 8am and they haven't let us out yet. Mr. Thornton comes back to work today, so who knows how the day will go. God willing, the pod will be off restriction. I pray that Maria's little stunt yesterday doesn't ruin it for everyone. I think she has been locked-up too long to think straight. Well, it's in God's hands, and I know he will do what is best. He always does. My bed is made, teeth are brushed, and I'm ready to take a shower ASAP.

We just finished breakfast. We had to go half a tier at a time and back to our cells. I spilled my juice in half my tray and the rest on the floor. The cup just went topsy-turvy...toilet paper sucked most of it up off my tray. Thank goodness nothing got on my waffles or in the syrup, so I was able to eat it all. Looks like we aren't getting out at all today! We were so close to making it through the 30 days.

Anyway, I'm going to decorate an envelope for Ocael this morning. I haven't written to him yet. Printing would be the best way to write to him in case he doesn't read too well. My writing can be a little hard to read at times. I have to write fast to keep up with my thoughts. I did his name all fancy on the envelope, but spelled it wrong. He'll love it. I sure do miss him. The rainy day at the graveyard, when we saw two rainbows appear before our eyes, is the picture I put on his envelope. God, I pray you keep him in your grace and keep him from harm. AMEN.

I didn't get any mail yet. Too many people have my address! I need to write my brother, Jeff. He's been on my mind a lot lately. Also, Clint, Niki and the kids. I miss them all. What a gang they are! Taz is another one I need to write to. Tomorrow I'll work on doing all that. Today I made a Mother's Day card for Grandma Jean with a matching envelope. I put a yellow rose with a bud on the card with pretty lettering. Inside it said, "A mother is not a person to lean on; she is a person who makes leaning unnecessary." There was a short note inside telling her and Clare I love them, and I'm writing that book she told me to write. I've got about 50 pages so far.

The girls and I have been talking a lot today. We seem to get along pretty well. I had been moved to another cell since the incident with Maria. Both of my new bunkies are from Mexico. Angelica is from Mexico City and I don't know where Miriam is from yet. I'm done with my letter writing and the only artwork I have going right now is the Angel of Death for myself. This one is in pencil. Pencil seems to be my preference lately. My photo drawings are in pencil. I seem to have better control of the realism. I'm almost finished with my book that I am reading, so that will be my focus. There's another book by Joyce Meyers called "My Big Mouth" that I want to read. Ginger has it in her room.

Looks like we are in phase two again, (2 hours out of our cells a day). That's way better than back to phase one. This 30 day lock-down program stinks! They must have modified the program a bit, because the way it was written, we should have to start over again because of Maria and I. Thank God! By the grace of God go us.

They locked us back down when we still had 40 minutes left because some girl was visiting a friend and she was in the wrong cell. I didn't know we couldn't visit someone in their room. There were 4 girls in my room a while back and they didn't have a problem with it! I really don't understand the mentality of it all. I'm starting to think they are enjoying having a pod they can push around. We are at the mercy of the officers on duty. Some of them are mean as hell, and others are God's gift to the planet. I trust in the Lord, so there it is. We aren't suffering, by any means.

I'm getting a lot of "getting to know Rhonda" time. I'm liking myself better and better, thanks to the spirit inside me that's calm and giving. I'm appreciating others a lot more, too. Not focusing on me makes it possible to notice others. It makes me more in a position to do more for them, paying attention to what they are going through. I detest being selfish. I already know I never have to be needy. God's always had my back and I wish I had noticed that fact a lot sooner. However, I'm thankful that I see it now. Maybe I had to go through all that "stuff" so I could see better. It takes a different action to produce a different result.

Joyce Meyers has been working a miracle in me. I can feel it and I have no clue how big it is. All I know is that I have this tingling feeling in my chest, like when my parents took me to the Shrine Circus for the first time. That was probably the very most exciting thing of this magnitude that happened to this little girl. I feel like I could cry writing "this little girl." Maybe that's what is going on. I'm finding that little girl who believed the world was wonderful and loved everyone and everything. I danced and laughed all the time. I would laugh so hard back then that I thought sometimes I was going to die. I would be hurting so badly from laughing so hard and long. I would have to leave the table every night because of laughing so hard. I'd go lie on the couch in the living room holding my chest and trying to stop. As soon as I could almost stop, the laughing would start again. By the time the laughing would stop, I would be on the floor under the coffee table, hanging onto the leg, totally breathless and hurting.

When I thought it was safe to get up and go back to join the family at the table, I would take one look at my Dad and it would start all over again. This happened every night at dinner for several years. I'm not sure when it stopped. My oldest son, Joshua, and I had an episode like that in the trailer I live in now. We were listening to "Lunch Lady Land" by Adam Sandler. We were both in tears on the floor laughing. I pray that I can always re-live that memory. Johnny and I have had a few of those too. I love laughing until my guts feel like they are falling out. It makes everyone else laugh too.

I drew a picture of my grandson today. It's a picture of a kid playing his guitar. I swear it could be my grandson in the future. The face looks like the attitude he has now, all happy and sparkling. In the picture he's playing the

Gretch that my son Josh used to play. The guitar originally belonged to Shannon's grandfather from Lochiel. Shannon let Joshua use it, but he never gave it back. The grandfather was livid!

Shannon was the one that gave me the letter from Joshua saying he was leaving for Washington State. I was working at the sandwich shop when be brought me the letter. I never saw my son again.

I saw Shannon just before I turned myself in. He had a couple kids, and he named his boy Joshua. I told him I had the Gretch and it blew his mind. He asked how I got it and I asked if he wanted it back. He said, "No!" He got in so much trouble over that. Apparently, Joshua stole it from him, sort of. He refinished it and painted the sides red so Shannon didn't recognize it. Josh didn't hide it or anything. It had been 12 years since I had seen Shannon. I need to ask Johnny if he still has his number and address so I can write to him.

I'm all lettered out at this moment. I need someone to write to me so I can answer them instead of telling them everything. Maybe tonight I'll get a couple letters, in English this time!

We had spaghetti for dinner tonight; still no salt! They did put garlic in the butter, so I put some on the spaghetti, the green beans and the bread. It's about 7pm I turned in my laundry on the way to dinner and forgot to mail my grandson's letter. It's in the window in hopes that the officer will mail it for me. The only action left for the day is hoping for mail. I'm pretty tired this evening; I didn't get any sleep last night. The girls next door sleep all day and party all night. They were really whooping it up last night, laughing and singing. They're looking "tore up" this morning in the breakfast line. I don't hear a peep out of them right now. They are resting up for later.

It's Friday, April 30th. We were up early yesterday and I wanted to sleep, but I had to get up because the door was open. This morning, though I was still tired and wanting to sleep, they woke me up over the intercom to go to medical. Nothing like "Rhonda Brew get up" over a loud speaker. So much for sleeping in again. They took me to the library to get my blood drawn. I asked them what it was for. They were testing for syphilis and gonorrhea. I told them I don't need to be tested for those, and the girl said "OK." I said, "Really, I can say no?" She told me to sign a paper refusing and that's it. I got up for that? I'm still asleep writing this. Now they are calling chow. I'm still wearing my "way too short" pants. I had to tie the elastic to the material in a knot to hold them up. The elastic in my underwear is coming off too.

They'll be opening the door pretty soon, and I'll have 2 hours to do whatever. After a shower, I'm going to put some clothes on that fit a little better, clean the room and find out from Choppa what's going on.

I wrote Suzie a letter last night with a little poem about life. I told her that I was bothered by her comment regarding her being hurt because I was "screwing up" on my last day of freedom. I wasn't screwing up; I was getting screwed up! Well, I didn't hurt her. She decided to feel that way all on her own. I'm alright with myself and so is God. I hope my letter gets my point across that I'm making. If not, she's going to think I MADE her feel bad for CARING! If I have to, I'll explain it again until she gets it. Sometimes her way of caring is destructive to herself and keeping her sick. I pray that God can help both Suzie and Bryan somehow to change their direction, like he is doing for me. I thought I could help, but it only drags me in. They need to find some kind of happiness.

Choppa was sleeping so I couldn't talk to her. She went to medical yesterday because her left breast was hurting. I hope she is alright; she is my best bud. Choppa has a huge heart and is totally down to earth. She does her best to leave them laughing. God bless her.

I found a little booklet on the book pile. It had cool lettering, sort of a diploma style or Christmas fancy. I may need it later for the holiday season.

It's been a couple days since I've written anything. It's Sunday, May 2nd. I was going to call Uncle Mike (my brother) but I only have a few dollars on my phone time. Danitza wanted to talk to Darrell if I get through. Darrell and Mike live together. Darrell is paralyzed from the 7th vertebrae down. Mike takes care of him and Darrell takes care of Mike. Danitza knew Darrell on the outside. She also hadn't talked to her mom in a long time. I told her she could have my phone time if she wanted it. We could always call Mike and Darrell later.

I took a "hot' shower and made myself an extra cup of coffee. Raynalda and I were sitting together watching T.V. when I showed her my shower shoes (size 13). They hung out behind my heel about 4 inches! She asked me how to get a pair. I told her she had to do a request form for them, but I would be happy to do it for her. I had to send a "kyte" for some underwear, anyway. Then somehow we got talking about our regular shoes; hers were too big, mine were too small. I said, "Remember when we were checked in together in the beginning? I think they could have gotten our shoes mixed up." I went to my cell and got my shoes. I had just washed them too, in the shower. She tried them and they fit perfectly. Imagine that! We traded shoes and now we are both happy!

Right now I've got a sock full of ice to hold on my mouth. I still have fiberglass coming out of my lips. It's been several years now and it's still coming out. I should be dead; God really loves me a lot, because I'm still here now. I'm sure He has plans for me, so I will survive whatever the Devil has in store. He sure likes to mess with things, but that's nothing new. Wow, my face and my mouth feel better now. Thank God for ice and hot water. AMEN.

I talked to Johnny on the phone yesterday morning. He was on his way to Patagonia, and then to Sonoita for his fire schooling. He was in the emergency room at the hospital in Nogales until well after midnight that morning with Lisa. She came down with a bad flu all of a sudden. Johnny said she had stuff coming out of every hole. Man, she sure gets sick a lot! I'm a little confused about the girl. Is the Devil working on her? She's sickly and devious. She's never happy, no matter what you do for her. In fact, she's down right hateful. I know Johnny loves her with his whole heart and he's being tested hard. They sure did make a beautiful little boy.

My roommate, Miriam, was looking to marry an American man so she could re-establish her citizenship. She wants her kids to go to school here instead of Mexico. I called my brother and told him about it. He actually said he would think about it. Maybe they could stay married long enough for the paperwork to go through, then get a divorce. He's supposed to be sending a picture of himself so she can see what he looks like. We'll see how fast he sends one. It may show us if he really wants to do it.

I got another letter from Samuel Cordova, Maria's pen pal. I guess he's my pen pal now! I told him about Maria trying to fight with me and almost getting 30 days in the hole. I also told him how jealous she is of him writing to me, and hates me for being an artist, etc. I haven't gotten a letter back yet.

Fred wrote to me again, and this time be told me a little about himself. What a story! He had been married for 37 years and has three daughters. When he got divorced, he just walked away and left everything. His wife had left him an insurance policy so he would have something, but his daughters sued him for it and won! He says they are witches! He sure did get the shaft. I think the world of Fred. He got a job as a court appointed advocate for foster children. It pays nothing, not even gas money, but he loves it. He gets attached to the kids he checks on in their foster homes. What a good thing to do with your life.

I have so much to be thankful for; I can't even count that high! Higher and higher than the sky. My kids are the most wonderful thing that ever happened to me. I love them so much. I would do anything for them to be happy and healthy. I sure would like some photos of them so I could show my new "friends" how neat they are. Also, I could lie in my bunk and daydream about what a miracle they are.

I'm trying a new craft idea, making beads out of bread. I'm using the inside tube of an ink pen to form the bead around. So far, I have about 10 of them drying out. The dice I made earlier are hard as a rock. That's what gave me the idea. It's all still in the planning stage. Next is to figure how to make them different colors. After the color, they'll need to be dipped in coffee creamer to make them shiny. That's what they use on drawings. Whatever is coated with coffee creamer mixed with a tiny bit of water dries shiny.

Monday, May 3rd, 6am. I got up, brushed my teeth, went downstairs, found my laundry bag, came back to the room and went back to sleep. Screw two hours of freedom! I was already free to sleep until breakfast. Angelica had to "roll-up" today. They are taking her to another detention center, probably Tucson. Maria had to "roll-up" today too. Everybody was cheering! I guess they were happy for her. Ha, ha. I believe they are shipping her to a federal prison in California. There she will do four more years. She already did four years for petty theft with an assault tacked on. That was state prison. The four years she has to do now is for illegal entry from Mexico. She had gotten deported after she was released from state prison. I guess she just couldn't stay away!

Angelica only has about 40 days before she gets sent back to Mexico City. She took Miriam's sweatshirt with her when she left. Just another user! Miriam has court tomorrow and that was her best shirt. They cost $12.35 and Angelica never did get any money on her books, so Miriam paid for her stay.

I wrote Bryan today and put a real cool deal on his envelope, a flaming heart with a butterfly sitting on it. Of course, I did his name real fancy, too. It was the coolest lettering I ever did! I want him to know how I feel about him. I think about him all the time, every day. I want him to take care of himself so he will be there when I get out of prison. I took the bunk on the floor since Angelica left and I traded my f#cked-up pants for her good ones. I'm sure they are too short, but they have to be better than the ones I have. At least I won't have to tie them on. As long as she returns what she was issued, it doesn't matter what condition they are in.

I have 6 cents in my account, so I ordered two 3 cent envelopes for the next commissary. Tomorrow I will get the stuff I ordered last week. I ordered $5 phone time (20 min.), 10 stamps and a big envelope to send my book home (this one). I was thinking of saving the stamps for the big envelope so I could send everything home when it's my turn to go. If nobody sends me any money, I have to cover my own ass. Now I have to find out how much it would cost to mail the envelope with at least 100 pages in it. I'm going to start getting it together now and continue adding to it, so I am SO ready! This getting caught with my pants down would be for the birds!

Good morning, it's Tuesday, May 4th. The officer just stopped by my door and said, "Just one?" I told her that Miriam was at court. The officer is finding housing for the girls in the little boats. They have been out there for a couple of days now, in the day room. At least they get to watch T.V. Whoopee!

I cleaned our little table area in our cell. It's about one foot by 16 inches, sticking out from the wall. There's another lower table the same size that's supposed to be a seat. We use both of them for table space. The top one is in pretty bad shape (rusted and peeling), so we cover it up with an opened up brown paper bag. I changed the bag today and wiped everything down. We get 4 hours today, the top tier (ours) gets the 2nd shift, so I still have a couple of hours before they open the door again. My plan is to sweep and mop before Miriam gets back from Tucson. She had to be shackled with the hand-cuffs, leg irons, belly chain and the "black box" so she couldn't move her hands, very uncomfortable! Miriam's a real soldier, so she'll be fine.

After a while you don't notice the chains. That's what they will do to me when I go to court. Not very attractive, but it keeps the cops out of danger from us attacking them or trying to escape! I heard they get $3,000 a month for each inmate. If that is true, we are more valuable in prison than being productive on the outside!

It's kind of nice being by myself with just God. It's so peaceful and calm. My shoulders aren't feeling all tense. I did a couple rounds of pushing from the wall, standing about two feet away, like a push-up standing up. I need to do more and get into a routine of it. I don't like sitting here getting weak.

Today we are really getting 4 hours in the day room. Right now they had us go back to our cells to do commissary. Afterwards, we should get our remaining time. It doesn't always happen fairly, but I'm grateful for the time we do get out of our cells.

I have a lot of work to do now, two drawings for one girl, and two for another. That will keep me busy and positive. I love doing artwork all day, every day! Thank you, God. You always knew where my heart was, I'm in heaven.

Besides the orders I just got, I'm drawing the Virgin of Guadalupe. She was on the wall of this cell when Miriam moved into it. I took down the old one and am doing a new one, only beautiful.

The book I'm reading now is another one by Joyce Meyers. This one is called "Eight Ways To Keep The Devil Under Our Feet." It's very good. I like the down to earth way she communicates, good stuff.

I just called Johnny and he likes the idea of sending me money. I told him to get together all the money from the people that want to help me out so he only has to pay one fee for Western Union. He said he would. I told him I just spent my last 6 cents on two envelopes.

Miriam made it back from court and the judge was good to her. She got 6 months, the least she could have gotten. I'm happy for her. She just got done telling me the story of the Virgin of Guadalupe. Wow, I'm glad I asked. I finished the picture of her and put it where the old one was.

Heather just gave us a Mountain Dew for the coffee we loaned her yesterday. We're not suffering. It's Wednesday morning and we already had breakfast. I was able to deliver the drawing I was working on. One was a little boy with a diploma, wearing a cap and gown. The other was a bouquet of roses in a vase with water. Everyone really liked the rose picture and I got a few more orders, only in different colors.

3.

A-Pod:
The Working Pod

Now it's Friday and I have a job! They moved me to A-Pod, the working pod. I have the top bunk again. This pencil is almost too small to write with, but I don't want to climb back down to get a pen out of my property box.

My job is getting ice for all the pods and picking up the trays and trash after every meal. Right now we are in lock-down for count, but I need to go to work pretty soon. I imagine someone will let me know when and what to do.

Now I'm in a cell where my two bunkies don't speak English! What an adventure! I hope they get my mail over here without any problem. Actually, I hardly get any mail. Suzie and my Spanish pen pal send me letters. I think I'll work on my art projects until I figure out what's going on.

Well, I managed to successfully do my job tonight after dinner. I don't think I'm confused any more. All I have to do is eat my meals and when I'm finished wait for the food servers to get back from work. Then we go and collect all the trays and garbage from each pod, then scrub out the garbage bins after dumping them.

The girls in this pod are a little more hard-core. They seem to treat me just fine, though. Not too many white women around here, either! Looks like I need to make some dice. The girls want to play 10,000.

Heather from B-pod was also transferred to this pod. She told me she didn't know anyone, so she's hanging out with me. I told her she's the only one I know in here, too. In casual conversation she told me she is a paranoid schizophrenic with a depression problem. Wow, the medication must be working!

We're all sitting here watching a really good movie, "Avatar." I still don't have any ear-buds to listen to the sound, so I read the captions.

Today Holly and I did the trays and trash by ourselves. We did good. It's lock down time and I just noticed that I have mustard on my sock. I already knew it was on my shirt and pants. We should have left before the lunch ladies did so we could get aprons and gloves. We are going to do that at dinner.

My bunkies are sleeping, so I think I'll take a nap, too. I don't really want to. Maybe finishing my Dracula book is a better idea. I wish my kids would write me a letter. They are so wrapped up doing their own life; I'm an after-thought.

I was able to get a couple aprons and two pair of plastic gloves before the dinner shift. We had much less slime on us after work. We are locked-down until 9pm when they let us out in the day room until 10:30 pm. I need a shower real bad and I have no shampoo. I guess a good rinse and clean clothes will have to do.

Shannon let me borrow her ear-buds, but she said to be careful with them. They're real touchy because they were made with spare parts. This is the first time I get to actually hear the T.V. since I've been here. They are supposed to issue us a pair of ear-buds when we are checked in, but as you can see, they don't always do what they are supposed to do, only what they feel like doing.

Choppa is gone! She got shipped out on May 5th to Dublin, in California, or so I heard. Way back when we were playing cards, our points kept being all 5s. I told her she's probably going to get shipped out on May 5th, 2010. She laughed like it was a joke! The day she left, she had lunch bags tied in her hair and was dancing around wearing a sheet around her waist. She was a pretty good dancer. Choppa sure made me smile! I hope I see her again.

It's Mother's Day! Yippee! I haven't received one thing from my boys since I've been here. All the other girls are saying the same thing. What's with the kids? They are way too busy for such nonsense. Eat my words! I called Johnny, and he was trying to visit me for Mother's Day. He was too late! Hopefully, he thinks to put money on my books. I ran out of phone time talking to my grandson. He's the bomb, the most precious thing on earth.

Johnny gave me some very disturbing news. He said that Raymond was freaked out! Ray was drinking with his cousin, Zach, or maybe second cousin, and they both got pretty wasted.

When Raymond passed out, Zach stole Ray's keys to his car, and took it for a cruise. He got in an accident, totaling the car and was killed! Oh my God! Raymond is freaking out and I'm stuck here with these little children trying to act tough. I told Johnny to take care of his brother. We don't want to lose him, too. I'm writing him a letter, but I'm not sure what to say.

I want him to read the Study Bible that my brother Greg gave me. He really needs to know Jesus. He also needs to know that pain from emotional trauma will let up with time. I want him to write me a letter so I can understand where he is at, maybe answer a question or two he might have.

I just mailed off a letter to Raymond. I included a drawing of my own hands praying with handcuffs on. I hope he likes it. I told him how the Devil puts lies in our head causing us depression, anger and all the negative, destructive thoughts that we think are our own. All along he is whispering in our heads. If our thoughts are not of love and positive things, then we should pay attention to why! We need to pay close attention to what we are thinking and saying. We don't need to help the Devil to destroy us! We need to think like Christ.

My roommate, Maria, gave me her T-shirt, boxer shorts, and her sweats because she is going to prison real soon. It made me cry. We hugged each other for a long time. When I got back from work this evening, there was a tray of cookies and a carton of milk on my bunk from the girls. They work in the kitchen. Marlena and Maria serve the trays; Molly and I clean them up. We collect them on a cart and the guys clean them for us. We also collect all the garbage and the guys take it out.

Michele is going to be released in about 8 days now. She taught me to play Canasta.

I'm feeling more comfortable now that I have sweats and a T-shirt. I don't have to wear my reds all the time. It feels more like a pajama party that I can never leave!

I was supposed to get my hair cut today, but I had to go to the visiting room to see my lawyer. Too bad it's not that easy. First I had to sit in a closet-size room with four young Mexican girls that didn't speak English. Of course they had to introduce themselves and ask me what I'm in here for!

It's difficult to communicate, especially when I don't feel like talking. I'm polite, so I do my best to help them feel comfortable. They were all nervous. I was so relaxed I could have fallen off my chair. I told them God wants me here, so no sense in being tense over it. It's not so bad in here that there's any reason to be nervous. It's all a state of mind, and there is a lot to be thankful for when we think about it. Try saying that to four girls who don't speak English!

My back is hurting, so I'm going to lie down and let my body rest.

Good morning. It's Tuesday. My bunkies are gone and I'm locked in the room. There are a lot of girls in the yard, so I missed recess again. Boy, they get out early! All I want right now is a cup of coffee. Marlena gave me some sugar, a soap dish and some coffee this morning. I said, "Is it my Birthday?" They both laughed. Now they are at work serving the breakfast trays. When they get back, it's Molly and my cue to go to work. I really would like to get out of this room.

My pen is running out of ink, so I hope Arlene gets me my pens and the stuff she owes me before it runs out. I may have one more letter I can write before it's gone. I do have pencils, but it's not the same.

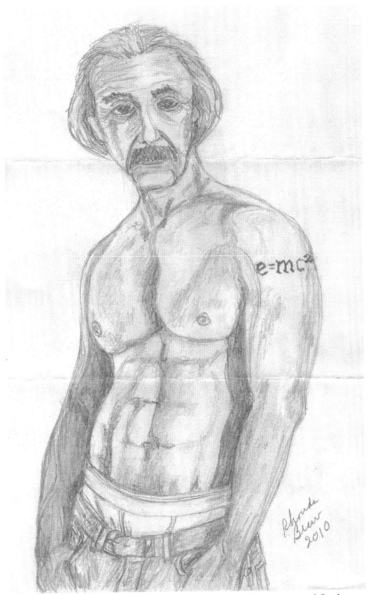

I'm working on a new picture for myself, in pencil. I'm copying it, actually. The picture is over my bunk and I really think it's cool. Einstein all buffed out with no shirt on, with a tattoo on his arm (E=Mc2) in old English. I'll send it to one of my boys to save it for me.

Here I am again, in the cell waiting for "Line up for chow!" For some reason, I don't always hear them say it. I think we are supposed to automatically know. Eat my words again, there she goes.

They gave us three slices of bread on our trays. One of mine was a crust. I was going to throw it away when Wetta said, "You can't throw that away, that's the lucky bread!" You're supposed to offer everyone a piece of it. That took about ten minutes to ask them all. Only two people said no. It made me laugh and I threw the rest away.

I got a letter from my pen pal tonight. He asked me if there was someone who needed a pen pal that was cute. He's a lot younger than me, so I will try to find him someone more his age to write to him. He also has a buddy, Kevin who would like an Asian girl to write to.

It's tomorrow! It looks just like today! We haven't had breakfast yet, but the commissary girls are here already. I didn't get anything yet, they said maybe because I changed pods. I only ordered my two envelopes for 6 cents. If they charge tax, I'm ass out! Hopefully the girls in B-Pod hook me up with what they owe me. We shall see.... They are all good girls.

I was thinking of whom to send my Einstein to, maybe Bryan. I know he would love it. It kind of reminds me of him, real smart and totally gorgeous! People tell me that Bryan is homely, but not to me.

Boy, I slept hard last night. It's rough waking up this morning. The girls were watching Joyce Meyers on T.V. I finished Maria's picture of her son (a different Maria) and she loves it. Looking at it from here, I got one eye open farther than the other. After I get off work, I'll fix it for her. It's nice to have my own coffee for a change. Ginger gave me a little container of coffee and some envelopes yesterday. I really could use a couple stamps. Some lotion would be nice too.

Tonight Paula is going to show Molly and me the sewing room, and tell us the ropes of the seamstress's job. I really like Molly and I hope we work together through this whole adventure. She's like my favorite kind of people, fun and always smiling.

It's Thursday night, May 13th and Mary Frances just got transferred to our pod. I've known her for years, along with the rest of her family. The rest of the family is out on bond, but she goes to court on Tuesday. They will probably let her out. She's in Heather's room. Mary and Heather are both nice people, so it ought to work out.

I'm going to talk to Ms. Padilla about the seamstress job. Molly and I both want to sew instead of doing trays and trash. Padilla said they are out of thread, so maybe in the future.

Heather gave me a few stamps so I could mail a few letters. One was for the judge to go with my pre-sentence report. Another was for Bryan and one to send Johnny a letter telling him not to bring little Josh to sentencing. The judge frowns on little kids being in his courtroom. People use little kids to influence the judge to give a lesser sentence. If Johnny doesn't visit me here with Joshua, I won't see him until I get out of prison. The photos will have to do.

Man, I'm tired tonight. I've been sleeping pretty good these last few nights. My legs are getting big! I'm getting an ass too! My arms are getting stronger, too, from lifting those garbage bags. It seems to be good for me because I'm sore. I ought to look pretty healthy by the time I go to court. I still need my hair cut, my nails cut and some lotion. That should about do it for taking care of myself. I guess I could fold my laundry before we get let out for the last time this evening.

Friday morning. Last night while we were watching "Driving Miss Daisy," Michele and Yoli gave me a little bag of popcorn. Later, they gave me 4 pairs of socks, 3 T-shirts and a plastic soap dish full of Kool-Aid packets. I told them "That's so cool," and I mentioned that my birthday was this month. They looked at each other and said "We should have waited." I told them that it's OK, they'll think of something, ha, ha, ha.

It seems as though there's an extra pair of pants in my laundry bag. My stuff doesn't have creases, and the bag was tied in a knot. I always tie the cord around the top of the bag a couple of times. It looks like there's a laundry fairy in my life. These girls really hook me up. Now all I need is a letter, maybe today.

Maria and I are up early. Marlena is gone to court and they woke us up over the intercom: "Maria Chavez, you have ten minutes." They got the wrong Maria. Now we're both up and ready to go whenever. I made coffee, but I really need to nuke it. The tap is pretty hot, but not coffee hot. I don't have any idea what time it is and feel like lying back down. There go the door locks; we can get out now.

I'm back from work and wow, can I sling some trash! Those bags get heavy, dude.

I started math class today, I don't know why. They are doing fractions; I guess it can't hurt to refresh my memory in that area.

It's Saturday morning and I feel like I'm bigger. They tell me there are hormones in the juice. I asked why they would do that. It's because they keep us from getting horny. If that's true, I don't know, but I think they are making me put on weight. My boobs are growing some too. This could be good. I've noticed that my hair and fingernails are growing incredibly fast too. Maybe hormones are what I've been missing.

God's so great. He's got me in a place where my body can repair itself from all the damage I've done to it. I'm getting stronger and healthier than ever.

I wonder how my beautiful family is doing today. A letter would be nice. I'm excited about getting some photos. They should be calling for chow soon, so I'd better brush my teeth. Later... it was a pretty OK breakfast, oatmeal and eggs, with salsa and tortillas.

Mary Frances told me the "Wild Boys" taco wagon I lettered, is parked at her house. I painted it to look like a circus wagon. Now, it needs to be re-done since they sold it. Mary was telling me that I was probably set up, so a bigger load could get through! I'm not real happy.

We've been locked-down since yesterday morning. They said it's an emergency lock-down, so it's the whole place. The only people getting out are the line servers. They have to get the food trays together to feed everyone. Yesterday, Molly and I got out because we were tray porters. Someone had to collect the dirty trays and trash. Today, they're using styrofoam trays, and the COs are collecting the trash.

It sure does feel like Sunday, all sleepy and relaxed. So far, I finished my math homework, Molly's 3 envelopes and the sketch of her and her husband from a photo. She's going to let me pick what I want from her next week's commissary. I'm out of money except for the $7 a week for working. I get $8 this week because I worked as a recreation porter for an hour. Usually it's a dollar a day, not a dollar an hour. Here comes lunch delivered. Oh God, what a mess! There are two trays a piece. There's menudo in the bottom tray with rice and a tortilla, salad and cookies in the top tray, with a piece of wax paper between them. I got three meals, two for my bunkies. It will be nice when this emergency situation is over.

Somebody keeps trying to open my door. They must have to go to the bathroom. There are still a couple of girls out in the day room in plastic "boats"; they haven't been assigned rooms yet, so they don't have a bathroom.

I need to remember to get the nail clippers. I think I could about "free-climb" the building pretty soon. It sounds like my bunkies are on their way back. There's a lot of slamming of metal doors. Everything is metal around here, except the cement walls and floors. Oh yeah, the shower area is all ceramic tile, and the sink and toilet are porcelain. The mirrors are metal with a piece of chrome sticky paper over it. Good idea, actually.

Realizing how repetitious my journal has become, I must stop writing for now. Maybe in the re-write I'll be able to make it more interesting somehow.

When they called pill-call, Molly was able to get her envelopes and drawing of her and her husband. My bunkies insisted on seeing them first. They all went, "Wow!" It makes me happy that my artwork makes other people happy, a double happy.

Marlena just save me a picture of her husband that she wants me to draw. She's all giggly, hoping I will. Of course I'll have to say yes. She's all excited now, like a little kid. I was going to write in my journal, but I finished Marlena's picture first. She is so happy. Now it seems I have BBQ chips and some Pepsi. She keeps looking at the drawing saying "Oh, Joe...." Her husband's name is Jose Louis.

A couple guys were just running around the day room on a lift. I wish I had one of those for my business on the outside. It goes straight up about 20-25 feet, and you drive it from the bucket.

We don't get to see guys very often. I'm not sure why, but it's a big thrill when they come around. They don't even need to be good looking. What's up with that? Speaking of guys, Fred hasn't written me in a while. No letters have come for me in a while, ever since moving to A-pod.

Johnny said he sent pictures and money, but neither one has arrived yet. I don't really care about the money. It's the photos I'd really love. He said there was a picture of them and one of their house.

It's time that I write a letter to Nito and maybe he can give me the low-down on what's going on with him and Ray.

Last night was bad! I got a headache and threw up in the middle of the night. Marlena gave me an ibuprophen this morning. That lunch meat they serve us is not handled properly. It spends too much time in the "unsafe food zone" (40 degrees and up). I'm not going to eat it anymore. I'm still not feeling that great!

We're off lock-down and I'm back to work again. I'm happy now. I don't like being locked down for days; it seems to affect my whole world. A headache is the first thing that happens, and then I have trouble taking a crap with other people in the room.

I got a little commissary from Arlene in B-Pod, there's more coming at dinner time for the artwork I have done. It's never what I ask for. I got vitamin E lotion, two hot and spicy soups, one pack of popcorn and some jalapeno cheese dip. I asked for stamps, two black pens, lotion, coffee, sugar and etc.... We'll see what's in the grab-bag this evening. It definitely keeps things exciting. That makes me feel like taking a nap.

I got my hair cut this afternoon, the Rod Stewart look. I said I loved it, not bad for a prison beauty shop cut. In a couple weeks or so, it will be perfect.

I got a letter from Fred today. He wrote in cursive; now I see why he was printing. The letter was written on his old stationary from when he was a vice-president of a bank. He sent me a couple extra pages to use for drawing paper. I like Fred. He has been sick for about 10 days or so with flu symptoms. I'm glad he's OK now. He's pretty cute for an "old" guy. I guess not really that old. I'll be 55 in a couple days. Johnny and Raymond's dad is 14 years older than me, so there's not "that" much difference.

The girls in B-pod gave me commissary today, a couple Snickers bars and another photo to sketch. I finished a sketch and Birthday card for Lynette's son. I've been getting all my art orders done right away, as soon as I get them. Molly wants me to do a couple more envelopes by tomorrow, and Becca wants me to do a picture of an Indian Chief, in full headdress, on a bandana and something else (Detroit) on another. That will have to wait until later. She doesn't have the bandanas yet.

I almost finished the Stephen King book, "Dark Tower". I imagine I'll get some reading time in tonight. God please watch over my loved ones, AMEN.

I talked to Johnny after work this morning. He said, "Would you like me to telepathically connect you with Ray?" I said "Sure!" "Hello," Ray says. He was in the truck with Johnny. Those guys crack me up. Right when Ray was telling me about him talking with my brother Greg about releasing funds for him to go to school, the phone cut off! I only had 79 cents in my phone account. Ray told me he was OK and not to worry about him. I sure love my boys. Thank you, Jesus, for letting me know how they are. I love you too.

I think it's Friday night, because we had chicken for dinner. There are a lot of girls in here right now. When Molly and I collect the trays and the garbage, we go into all the pods. There are six pods (A-F). D-pod is where they put the new people to delouse them, give them a mattress, a bag of bedding, a bag of hygiene products, etc.... There are so many girls that they have mattresses between the tables in the day room, and the whole floor is little "boats" lined up like sardines.

They moved several girls into our pod, even though it's supposed to be for the working inmates. They don't have any place else to put them. I imagine they will be shipping several girls out of here to prison soon.

I wrote to Keith Barth today, asking him to write a letter to my sentencing judge, so I could include it in my pre-sentence report. I also wrote to Nito asking him to write and send me some photos. I wrote a few other letters too; now all I need is stamps. I'm always on the hustle anymore, but that's what it's about in here.

I'm going to save a few weeks' pay ($7 a week), so I can purchase a $12 pre-paid box to send home my stuff when it's my turn to go. I sure can't count on any money coming from the outside; I've never received any yet. Looks like I work for postage; that's the only thing that is really important, other than black pens and colored pencils.

I keep getting hand-me-downs from the girls, 5 erasers, about 50 colored pencils, two black pens and I have no idea what people owe me for artwork. It's gotten to the point that I'm happy with whatever they give me. They never give me what I want anyway. I just tell them how many dollars' worth of commissary I want for each project.

Father's Day is coming up, so I ought to do a couple envelopes ahead of time.... I have one now; that's good enough. If nobody buys it, I'll send it to Johnny with a picture of him and Josh or something. Maybe I'll get those photos that Lisa is supposed to send. I'm pretty tired tonight, so I'm hitting the hay. Goodnight and God bless everyone, and I'm thankful for this day.

4.

Happy Birthday!

It's my birthday. It's May 21, 2010 and I'm 55, born in 1955. I think that's pretty cool. I forgot about it because I thought it was Friday yesterday.

Michele finally got to leave this morning, real early. Instead of going home, she has to do 6 more months. She left me shampoo and hair gel for my birthday. Yoli gave me an extension cord to plug my ear buds into. Now I can get farther away from the box by the T.V. The buzzer just went off for the door, so I'd better get out there before someone comes to drag me out.

The whole pod, except for Tink, Brittany, Shannon and I, are standing in line waiting to go to church outside. We're watching cartoons. The service is in Spanish. Looks like they decided we are on pod restriction, after they all were in line for over a half hour. Kelly asked me if I was going to math class. "No," I said. "It's my Birthday!"

I just gave Shannon, Yanaba's address; she's already writing to her. I'm hoping they will make good friends and I won't have to worry about her. Shannon, that is.

Well, I'm locked in my cell and I'm pacing like I do every time I'm alone in here. My bunkies are at work serving trays. Before every meal, we get locked- down until they call, "Line up for chow". I pace until the doors unlock. Right now I'm not, because I'm writing about it.

That's all I have to say besides being disturbed by the envelopes Tink was drawing. She drew a skull on one and a hypodermic needle on the other. Right away, I thought about Bryan. I know the road he's on, and only God can save him. I can't save him. I'd only get dragged down with him. Between Suzie, me and Bryan, Grandma Jean sure knows how to pick us. We all need saving. I need to write her a letter.

Tuesday after commissary I should have some stamps. It's a good thing, because my letters are piling up.

I wonder what we are having for lunch today. Some of the girls have the menu memorized. I don't know what day it is half the time, and the other half, I'm not always right. It's all one day; it just gets dark and light a lot. That means for me. This day has been 55 years long! My life from this perspective looks like it hauled ass, and while I was living it, my life seemed to crawl. I want to live to be 200 at least, this time.

Paula made me a necklace for my birthday out of bread. It's awesome. It looks like it's made from bones, and turquoise. What the girls come up with around this place is unbelievable. They thought my toilet paper dice were pretty awesome.

I heard metal doors slamming, so it's almost time to line up. They already called "special diet," so any minute now.... I'm pacing again. The door hasn't opened yet and as soon as I set down my pad and pen, I start pacing. Maybe that coffee shot had something to do with it. Woo-hoo! We're flying now! When I get out, I'm going to use coffee shots as a tool to get me buzzed legally.

They need to let us out. I don't like being locked in a closet. I'm so thankful that God has blessed me with gifts that make it possible for me to do this as long as I have to, AMEN.

Some time has passed and I'm locked in my cell again, waiting for chow! Molly and I were playing Canasta when they made us go to our cells. There's never enough time to do anything. They keep interrupting our free time. I won't be able to do what I want and relax until after work; then its lock-down time at 8pm until 9pm, and then it's lock-down for the night at 10:30pm. Like I said before, I'm blessed to be able to occupy myself during those times when we aren't sleeping; in fact, that's when I get my artwork projects done, so I'd better stop complaining. God is helping me to keep up.

I went to return a Stephen King book to Shannon, when Tink and Shawnee stopped me. I handed them the book and sat at a table. I think they are plotting something for my birthday. I know those guys. I'm going to forget about it again, so I don't ruin any of their fun. That's a real crime, ruining someone's fun. People don't know how to have fun like I remember as a kid. I had a lot of fun, all the time. I still do, every moment possible. It doesn't take much for me to enjoy myself. I keep hearing Tink laughing, and she's in a cell at the other end of the pod.

We're having fish tonight, patties. They are usually pretty terrible! Maybe we will witness a miracle and they will be good tonight. The rice is great; someone knows how to make it right. The guys do all the cooking and I try not to think of gross things they could be doing to our food.

What a Birthday! Those girls, I love them. It's probably going to take a whole couple pages recalling yesterday's goings on.

Days later.... It's Monday, May 24th, only 5 days until my son Raymond's Birthday. He'll be 20 years old, hard to believe. We will get out one more time this evening, but I feel like going to bed instead. I'm tired. I took a nap before lunch too. My brain feels over-worked or something. I'm in sort of a spin. There's been a lot of enlightening in my life lately. I think I'm re-booting. On that note, I'm putting on my sweats and getting under my blanket.... Ten minutes later, I'm playing cards and watching "Grease" with John Travolta. Now I'm going to bed. I have a couple art orders to do, but I think they will be waiting for me in the morning.

Mary gave me a stamp after hearing me tell someone how I have to hustle for stamps. Mary's a nice person. She sat between Tink and I during the church service yesterday so we wouldn't screw around. Tink was licking her Body of Christ before we took communion. Mary was telling her to quit it. Tink said that God gave her the sense of humor and knows she loves Jesus. "I'm sure Jesus doesn't mind if we lick the wafer, as long as we aren't mocking him. AMEN." It was cool because I got a Bible and the service was really good. I totally enjoyed the chaplain and his wife.

Back to the stamp, I'm not sure which letter to mail with it. Maybe Nito will be the lucky one.

Tuesday morning. I'm not sure why I have such a hard time waking up in the morning. I feel like I've been drugged. It takes a lot of coffee to get me going.

We are on lock-down and breakfast is over. Molly and I just finished with all the trays and trash. I still feel all dragged out. I'm normally pretty jazzed, but I'm progressively feeling complacent. I don't like feeling this way, totally relaxed and spaced-out. Girls keep telling me that I look tired.

I think I'll' read my Bible for a while before starting my drawings or letters. As for my birthday, I have chosen not to disclose the goings on, other than these girls made me cry. They gave me new underwear (I didn't have any). Shawnee gave me some longer pants (reds); my pants have always been way too short. Paula made the necklace out of bread and they made two cakes. All the girls signed two cards and we laughed for hours.

I got a card from Lisa today with a couple photos of Joshua, and one with all of them sitting on the motorcycle. I drew a picture of my grandson, and it turned out better than anything I have ever done. I love that kid so much. I'm sending back the drawing with the photo, and asking for more pictures.

Molly just brought me a pad of paper she got two with her commissary. She didn't have enough money to give me what I wanted for the artwork. I really don't care about it. She didn't get her phone time either, so I'm going to let her use part of my $4 worth of phone time to find out if her husband is going to put money on her books. I'm hoping at lunchtime, B-pod will have some commissary for me.

I have a birthday card order for a 7 year-old kid. She wants a flying unicorn princess. Samantha wants a photo drawing of her and her daughter. I already did her mom and step-dad. I drew my "Grim Reaper" for Tink's birthday; she loves bones and skulls like I do.

I'm waiting for the door to open so I can go to the party! I'm going as a pirate! Tink gave me a bandana for my party hat and I made an eye patch with paper and attached a string to it. When I was doing the trash, there was a box of pumps that are used for gallon jugs. They were throwing them away.

The top looks like a bird with a beak, like for hand lotion. I put one in my sock, so I could bring it back to my room. I wrapped toilet paper around it so it looked like a bird body, a parrot. I put a rubber glove over the whole thing, and tied it at the bottom. The fingers of the glove were like tail feathers. I colored it green with magic marker, made the beak orange and put eyes on it. The tube was long enough to attach it to my sports bra at the shoulder. It was a parrot sitting on m*y* shoulder. Tink colored triangles on my socks to look like A-A-A-ARGILES.

What a party! We had a lot of fun. We played pass-the-egg on the spoon and pin the penis on the guy. Tink liked her presents, the drawing and the skull I made out of bead for the end of her pencil. It had a French wee-wee mustache and a goatee.

Good morning, it's Thursday. We have a new bunkie "Rosie." Maria rolled-up yesterday. She was pretty freaked out by it all, ever since I moved in. She and Marlena were always crying and praying, singing and crying. I told her to have some fun and things would be better. Don't be afraid; God's got our backs. It breaks my heart to see them crying all the time. I cry now and then, but I'd rather be laughing. Laughter is contagious and healing.

Raymond is 20 years old today. Time goes so fast; it seems to fly. I find it hard to believe I'm over 50! I feel barely 30. Gravity seems to work us over pretty good.

I found out what happened to my pen pal. He's

practically a celebrity around here. He's the reason we don't have inmate office clerks anymore, and we also got locked-down for 4 days (with pay). He got jumped by about 40 Mexicans. They split his head open *(2 staples)* and cracked a couple of ribs, but he says he's fine!

A couple days later.... I called Nito today, and he said he just got a letter from me about 10 minutes ago. He liked the way I lettered his name. That's about the only cool thing about the letter. I didn't know what to write because he never wrote to me to let me know what was going on. He said he was going to take a bunch of pictures with his digital camera for me. I called Nito when I couldn't get a hold of Johnny. I wanted to wish Raymond a happy birthday. Now, I don't know what to write about all of a sudden; everything is so repetitious.

Right now I'm sitting in the day room watching a cute Santa movie, and I finally have some good ear buds. The extension cords I got for my birthday make it more enjoyable, because I don't have to be so close to the T. V.

We had my favorite dinner tonight, baked chicken. They gave us broccoli with it and a side of rice. It was way too much to eat. I had to give my cake away. I finished work for the day and am in my sweats now. Looks like we're going to play cards. The game sucked! Nobody was paying attention, and neither was I. I had a stomach ache from eating too much, and I was lifting really heavy bags of garbage. That last bag was when my stomach really started hurting. I need to take a hot shower when they open our doors at 6 pm. That will give me an hour and a half to get in there.

Can't tell what time it is because our clock stopped

working. That's funny, I was imagining an alarm clock floating in space, like in Alice in Wonderland, about an hour before I looked up and the clock was gone! Creepy! Our whole existence revolves around that clock. It's back on the wall now, but not working.

I've got a couple photos to do drawings for someone, but I'll start tomorrow. Earlier today, I drew my trailer on an envelope. I'm missing being home. I was home in my mind while I was drawing it.

I got caught on the can again! Every time I sit on the toilet lately, the CO comes by and looks in, or opens the door on me. My bunkies are laughing every time! There are hours in between, and still my timing is impeccable!

I'm starting to feel more inspired, not thinking things are so boring. Every now and then, I get caught up in the ho-hum of it all, instead of making my own fun. I just got word that I'll be getting a bag of coffee next commissary for the photo drawing I did last night. I'm going to ask for stamps on the next one. My money is starting to stack up some, since I don't order anything. Thursday when we get paid, I'll have $21 on my books. By next Thursday, I'll have $28, and so on. I want to have a couple bucks in my account for when I go to prison. Traveling with no money is for the birds.

The door just unlocked, but I don't feel like taking a shower. I may just read my werewolf book and go to sleep. Morning is better for a shower; the water is hot!

Good morning. I got in the 4th shower stall and it kicked my ass! Between the water pressure and the scalding hot water, I am totally blown away! They already called "special diet", so we should be in our cells.

However, I'm not.

There's a deal on T.V. about a Playworld for kids, a good place for child molesters to hang out. There's also a huge oil spill in the Gulf. Not really a spill, but oil is shooting out of the ocean floor for about a month now. They have attempted 2 or 3 different ways to stop it, but failed. They have another plan, but they don't expect to start it before August. This is Memorial Day, *May* 31st. The hurricane season is coming up, and that means giant waves will be covering land masses with oil, not to mention the polluted waters and poisoned sea life! People ruin everything they get their hands on!

I just found out the reason for us being locked-down this weekend. Outside, they were protesting the new immigration law. They figured we might have an uprising. Right! Like we give a shit in here! They are giving us too much credit, like we are into world affairs or something! The things we care about in here are what's for breakfast, lunch, dinner, hot showers, the micro-wave, commissary and mail! That's about it! Oh, let's not forget phone time and getting our hair ironed.

We're locked-down now that breakfast is over. I have two photos, one of an inmate and one of her parents. I'm attempting to bring them together in a picture. I'm getting totally frustrated by it all! The pictures are too small to see. I'm unable to differentiate their features. It bothers me to think I can't come through when others are so counting on me. I swear, these girls think I can do miracles! God willing, she has a couple more photos of her folks. The one of her is a good one. I'm feeling better just writing about it. I showed her what I drew so far and she likes it. Her mom needs a little more work, but she wants it no matter how it comes out. She said her folks will really love it.

Now that I'm no longer stressed out over it, I'll be able to do a good job.

They'll be calling us to line up for chow any minute. Lopez, the CO, didn't make us lock-down. That was cool of her.

After lunch, I finished the drawing. Jessica cried when I gave her the picture. Her father died, and I had his arm around her in the drawing. She gave me some coffee to go with my Sweet-N-Low; they don't have sugar. I think it's so we don't make hooch! Syrup, fruit juice, and 6 bread balls in a soda bottle work just fine. It takes about a week. You have to sleep with it so it stays warm from your body heat. It's has a little kick to it.

We're watching funniest home videos. I still like that show. We just played the worst game of Spades ever, 102 to 247. Screw that game!

They locked us down for the last time tonight before bed time. Hopefully I can get something done before they open the door. My bunkie, "Rosie" wants me to do some cool thing on a post card for her boyfriend.

It's June 1st, 2010 and I'm up before anybody this morning. My teeth are brushed and my coffee is made. I will never drink coffee the same after being in here, like 3 heaping "sporks" of coffee per 22oz of water with 2 packs of Sweet-N-Low.

After watching Joyce Meyers, I want to look up Ephesians 1:17. Now the news is on. They are talking about the oil problem in the ocean. Seems they are attempting to use robotics to replace the system. Also, they have an oil tanker that can suck up about 400 gallons per minute. Good luck with that! I'm sure many people are out of work, and many lives will never be the same again over it.

They made us lock-down before breakfast again. It all depends on what officer is on duty. There are only a handful of us in here because a lot of girls are already at work. I guess I'll work on an "I miss you" post card for a while. I finished it before the door opened. Now I can get two stamps for it at breakfast. I've decided that Molly can square up with me by giving me ten dollars in postage stamps. That way I won't have to be kissing ass for stamps, at least for a while.

I know better than to let this lock-down bullshit bother me, but it does. It's so unnecessary! I am totally wrong about what I just said. The average mentality and the childish behavior of the majority of inmates makes it necessary. There's a total lack of social education and etiquette. I'm glad I mentioned my frustration because now it's defused. Roll with it; ain't nothin' but a thing.

Sitting here in my cell, I'm realizing it's already June 1st. My sentencing is on the 22nd. I need to be ready to mail everything home, just in case they ship me out right away. They usually keep people up to 6 weeks or so after sentencing, but I'm not going to assume anything at this point. For instance, I've been waiting all day to go outside. It's after 4pm now, and they just ordered us to lock-down. I'm getting pretty tired of this crap! I think things will be better in prison, so I'm really looking forward to my sentencing. It will have been three months that I've been here at that time.

Rosie just moved out of our room, and moved in with

Michele, the one who knows too much about Patagonia. The girl claims to be "tight" with Frank, whom I've known for years. He's not tight with anyone. He's my brother's friend, and he barely answers his phone or his door either.

Frank doesn't do anything, and she acts like she knows something. I think she's just fishing. I wish there was someone I could write to, maybe Bryan, and let someone know there's a girl talking shit about Frank in lock-up. Maybe it's not really my business to care about it at all.

It's time to play solitaire and plan for dinner. Our new bunkie doesn't speak English, go figure. I have a feeling we are going to be locked- down all night. "Special diets" people have gotten their food and are staying in their rooms. The officer has 4 girls in the shower area stripping down to be searched. I don't know what's up, but I hope we don't have to. We might, but I'd rather not.

The officers are pretty nice, most of them anyway. They are like babysitters in an adult daycare center. I don't think I would like their job very much. They will still be here when I'm long gone.

Here's a new one. They forgot to feed me dinner, and I'm the only one. They didn't realize that I was locked-down. Everyone else's door wasn't quite shut, but mine was. They were very apologetic and gave me a sack lunch of bologna, cookies, milk, and a fruit cup. Sometimes shit just happens! Everyone knows how much I love a good bologna sack lunch!

Marlena came back from work and told me we would be locked-down for three days. Two girls in D-pod got caught with drugs. Marlena saw them in cuffs on their way to the hole. I don't know what they do around here for drugs. They throw us in the hole for 30 days for everything else.

Well, it looks like I'll have plenty of time to write letters, draw, or do whatever I feel like. First, I'll finish my werewolf book so I can start another one by Stephen King.

I'm sure I can keep myself busy enough. I have plenty of paper to write my book and the chaplain gave me a Bible, so I'm set. This will give me a chance to get my affairs and paperwork in order. I really need to write my "peeps" some letters. I ordered 15 stamps and 10 envelopes for next week; also, B-pod owes me some stamps. Valerie, my ex-bitch bunkie, owes me for a Mother's Day card, too. It would be totally perfect, if I got some mail this evening. Whoever sends me a letter first gets one back. Terry Otto wrote to me the other day, a good buddy from Patagonia. She's only here seasonally. She's a fire fighter, and normally lives in Missouri.

Terry came to Patagonia and found my place abandoned. Here she had brought a movie camera so see could film some of our comedy stuff. What a disappointment to find me gone. Until we meet again. I love Terry; she's a total character. I need to write and let her know what happened, that I didn't lose my mind, or maybe that I did.

I hear some commotion out there; maybe its mail-call. No, it's "platos and basura" (trays and trash), my job, but not until lock-down is over.

There's a picture of a fallen tree that's now a stump, with the roots lying by the water, like driftwood. I really want to draw it. It has seen hundreds of years, and plenty more to come.

I just did a rose with a shadow on an envelope for Suzie. I realized, too late, that the envelope was upside down. It's real pretty. I'm sure she'll like it anyway.

I'm sending the envelope with my trailer on it to Bryan. There's a letter in it, of course. He's supposed to be watching it for me, so I think it's appropriate. I really need to write to Fred; he's probably wondering what happened to me since it's been a long time since I wrote. No stamps! It's getting kind of late for them to be bringing any mail, so I guess I'll read my book until Marlena and our new bunkie want to turn out the light.

Good morning. Really, it's about lunchtime. They are doing commissary right away, so we stay in our cells until our name is called. They won't be calling me because I have nothing coming. Hopefully, those who owe me will pay up a little bit! I could use the stamps. I have been doing a lot of art on envelopes, but not many letters. When I get stamps, I'll write.

I got woken up this morning by Marlena telling me they were searching the place. They got us all lined up in the day room while they ran the drug dog through the rooms. We had to stand inside this cage while the dog smelled us. Nobody got "red flagged." Tink's room got turned upside down, and so did Wetta's. They didn't find anything. Apparently, they piss-tested Tink, Shannon and Shawnee. That's a shock! I didn't think Shawnee did anything except listen to music and jog. The door just opened, so I'm going to see what's up.

I scored big time. Heather gave me a bag of coffee and 5 stamps, Samantha gave me a bag of coffee and 2 stamps, Rosie gave me two stamps and Angela gave me 1 stamp. What's funny is Heather didn't owe me anything. I gave her an envelope I just finished, the moon shining on the ocean waves.

Later...I did the "hot dog dance" in the lunch line; we had hot dogs. I used to do it with my grandson after the Mickey Mouse and Goofy show. After lunch, I did another pair of converse tennis shoes on an envelope for Patty. Now Lynette wants a pair of red ones.

I sent Suzie and Bryan a letter. The rose went to Suzie; my trailer envelope went to Bryan. He said he was making a box for my artwork, so I sent him the Einstein picture. Einstein's head, on a buff body, with a tattoo that says $E=Mc2$. I didn't know how to symbolize that on a typewriter.

I just got a receipt from the CCA that my brother put $100 on my books. My balance is now $114. That's the first money I've received since I've been here. It looks like he gets the ocean scene with a thank you letter. I hadn't sent him any cool drawings yet.

I'm sitting here on my bunk, doing the lock- down thing.

Now I have the money in my account to mail all my stuff home. I have to mention Jack-Jack in this book, in case I haven't already. She's the bomb, I call her Fred Astaire. It sounds like tap dancing when she walks around in flip-flops. It makes her laugh when she makes me laugh!

Saturday morning and I almost just blew Kool-Aid through my nose! Tink said, "I wish I was free," and for some reason, it was incredibly funny! We are sitting at the table coloring and drawing together, like always.

People come to our table and order stuff. Tink and I do different styles of art, so there's no conflict whatsoever.

As usual, we are waiting to line up for chow. Molly, my work partner is no longer a tray porter. She's now the "photo-shoot" girl. I'm training a new girl, Jessica. She's doing good, but she doesn't like "yucky" stuff on her. Too bad there's no avoiding getting yucky. I'm getting 15-44 cent stamps and 10 envelopes this commissary. My new balance is $107.11. I like that number.

My new help is working out fine. Now we are watching a movie; it's pretty good. It takes place in the end of days. This man and his son are survivors. They made it to the ocean, but now they are both sick. On the way, everything they had was ripped off.

Next day... I've done some pretty great artwork and I just found out that I could possibly get it photo copied. Now I need to find out the process for doing that. The officer in the bubble said I had to talk to the case manager, who is on vacation.

I'm still here watching T.V. and feeling real tired of being here. I'm not going to get depressed, but I am on the low side. I want to be home, even without utilities. I no longer care about them. Getting a letter or two from home, or maybe a photo would help my attitude. I know what my problem is, putting up with people all in my business. I'm used to being alone. There's no such thing here. I'm alone right now in my cell, but in 5 minutes, they're going to be lining up for chow. After that, Jessica and I will be doing the trays and trash, one more time. I sure would like to watch a whole movie tonight.

I'm done working for the day and feeling much better.

Tink and I have been talking art. That always makes me feel better. Like Tink says, I'm finally coming out of my box. I've been stuck on realism, like my photo-drawings. My new project shows a big chunk blown out of the earth in space. There's water flying off the chunk because it was ocean property!

Think I better go lie down now. I keep getting pains in my chest on the left side. It feels like a bubble or a pulled muscle, a pretty sharp pain, stopping me in my tracks when I take a deep breath. The pain is like where my liver is. If I go down, at least it's documented, not that it would matter. Too bad I don't have phone time to call my kids. I don't think God is going to take me just yet. I have a feeling there's something more he wants me to do first. If not, I appreciate the life he gave me and I love my wonderful children. I lived a good life in spite of myself. I think I would miss this place, so full of surprises. Surprises keep us on our toes. Here comes that pain again. Now it's going away. It all started yesterday, June 6th.

It seems that Angelica #2 knows Patagonia a little. She got caught with a load on the Sanctuary Road, but got out of her car and ran. They didn't catch her then; she made it to the lake and slid down a mountain, where she stayed hiding for about 12 hours.

She didn't know she was at the lake until her Mexican friends found her and got her out of there. She said she went to the Market and got something to drink once. That was the only time she had ever been to the town.

I sure would like a bag of potato chips. I feel like eating a whole bag. Wetta just gave us the commissary form and said we had two hours to fill it out and turn it in. Looks like I can get that bag of chips after all, next week.

I thought I was finally going to get my hair trimmed when out of the blue came pod restriction. That means we can't leave the pod, and the beauty shop is out in the hall. They do that shit all the time. That's one of the reasons I'll be glad when I get to go to prison. Things in prison are more consistent than here at CCA.

There's an antsy feeling in my stomach, like I'm waiting for something to happen. The only thing that's keeping me sane is my artwork and reading books. It keeps me from thinking too much. Today while we were getting our shampoo refills and other hygiene products, I talked to Ms. Dunigan, the pod manager. I asked her about photo-copying my artwork for the book. She said she'd check into it; usually they only do legal stuff. Apparently, they have never been approached with the idea before. I told her about the book I was writing, and she asked me what it was about. I told her it was a play-by-play and she couldn't imagine that there was anything to say. "It's all drama to me," she said. I told her I might send her a copy when it's finished. "I hope so!" she said.

It's Saturday morning, and I got off work early for a change. I have 5 minutes to sit at a table before they lock us down. I have no idea how much time has gone by since my last entry. I got a letter from Suzie and Bryan. It's the first letter I ever got from Bryan. Some boyfriend!

As usual, I have a lot of artwork to do today and tomorrow. A lion in the grass on an envelope for Molly and a Betty Boop full page. Also, a photo drawing of two married women. That one is under the wire, because nobody needs to know their business. Love is love as far as I'm concerned. I'm also working on another drawing for me. My son Raymond is the keeper of my artwork and my book. He's the one I trust to keep it all together.

There's this new girl that seems to use the people I am close to, to get close to me. I don't like it! I like to be left alone when I separate myself from the general population. She knocked on my door and just came in when I was reading a book. She said she was bored and just sat on the toilet (like a chair). Of course, I could no longer read my book. I told her I like to read when we are locked-down for meals. She said, "Oh, we're locked-down? I'd better get back to my cell!"

She lives in the same cell as the girl that knows too much about Patagonia. I really don't care if they are snitches or cops as long as they leave me alone! I don't want any friends. Tink and Shannon are good enough for me, and let's not forget Molly and Jessica, my work partners. The rest can find something else to do besides bother me.

Since I've been doing art in the day room, I've picked up a lot of jobs. I'm swamped, to put it lightly. I think it's time to make a list of requests or I'm likely to forget a lot of orders. It's lock-down time and I hope the girls clear out of my room pretty soon. I really need to pee. We all need to be in our cells at lock- down, so they will be going in and out while I'm on the toilet, right by the door. Well, f#ck it! I have to go too bad to care. I lucked out; nobody whipped the door open on me this time.

I wrote down the jobs I need to complete. So far I have 8 orders.

I've got a huge underground zit coming out on my face, actually, 2 of them. I never get zits, but I'm getting them now! On that note, I'm going to read my book and go to sleep.

Monday, June 14th, 2010, only 8 more days until my sentencing. Yippee, yahoo! That's much closer to the end of this adventure. The prison adventure, not the total adventure that goes into infinity and beyond, according to Buzz Lightyear.

I've been cranking out the artwork the last couple of days: Hello Kitty, Betty Boop, a lion in the grass and names in hearts. Now it's Spiderman, cowboy boots, sculls and my own stuff. I've been making patterns to make it easier for Tink and me.

Tuesday, June 15th. I just mailed Raymond a letter with Spiderman on the envelope. Now my plan is to get some of my orders done before I get bitched at because Father's Day is coming up.

What a day I've had. It started out with waking up to "last call" for laundry, then I heard them call for Rec. I flew out of bed, threw my laundry bag in the bin, got my shoes on and brushed my teeth. I ran to the door for Rec. and they shut the door in my face. I waited for them to open the door again; they didn't. The girl in the bubble says, "Sorry, nobody goes to Rec. once the door closes."

She's the one that operates the door, so I don't think she's sorry at all. I'm out of coffee, so I filled my cup with ice water and sat down to watch T.V. We watched the news and Joyce Meyers.

If Tink hadn't come to my room, I would have missed lunch. They told us to lock-down for lunch and I never heard them say to line up. I had to run to make the lunch window. As I was heading back to the pod, the COs shut the door so I couldn't get back in the pod. I was 10 feet from the door and they were right there. I had to turn around and go back through the Sally Port and they didn't open the door for me for at least 10 minutes.

They obviously had a good time f#cking with me today. None of them had to do what they did. They chose to. They also had no gloves for the tray porters all day. When we were done, they said, "Oh, you don't have any gloves? There's a box of them in D-pod."

This is the first page of a brand new pad of paper. For some reason, I always loved a new pad, it's so perfect. The edges aren't curled, no impressions in the paper yet, and it's never been flipped through. As I fill the pages, I stick them in the back of the pad between the cardboard and the last page. Maybe this time I won't do that and the pad will stay the way I like it. Its June 17th, and I have 5 more days until my sentencing. Hopefully, Keith Barth will have written me a character letter for my Pre-Sentence report. He said that he would, so I'm going to trust that he did.

It's a different day. The doors aren't shutting in my face today. I also had plastic gloves for doing my job. Father's Day is coming up, so I'm going to do this "racy" picture for Johnny. I thought I would do a Father's Day thing for Bryan too.

I'm hoping for a letter from someone so I know where to send my stuff. My plan is to send everything to Raymond. I think I'll read for a while before starting my art projects. Things ought to get more interesting soon.

I just mailed my first big envelope home. I mailed it to Suzie and Bryan since there's no word from Raymond yet. I signed a release of funds to cover the postage because they don't have a scale to check the weight. I have two other large envelopes left, and a lot of stamps. Also, there are several small envelopes so that I can mail whatever else needs to go now. They could ship me out of here any time, even before my sentencing, like they did to Brittany. They sent her to Wilmot in Tucson before her sentencing.

Poor Tink. I just woke her up for pill-call. She just had a tooth pulled and it was abscessed. They gave her antibiotics and pulled it right then. She is in a lot of pain. I thought they were supposed to get the infection taken care of first, before pulling the tooth. I never heard of pulling it while the infection was in full bloom. I hope they give her pain pills to go with the antibiotics, but most likely not!

Once again, they stopped the movie before it was over and removed the disc from the machine. I wonder if we'll get to watch part of another movie, two for one!

This evening I plan on cleaning the trash out of my property box and organizing what is still good, so I can just walk away and the girls can do what they want with it. It's time to write everyone a letter and let them know what's up.

Good morning, It's Saturday, June 19th, 2010. My sentencing date has been changed to September 13th, 2010. I got a letter from my lawyer at about lunchtime. I had just written to everyone and told them I was packing up to leave. Now I have 3 more months to do in here. By the time I get sentenced, I'll have 6 months' time served.

Every now and then, I think about how I don't have to

be in here yet, but knowing that I chose this makes it better. I can't blame anyone for anything, even accidentally. I'll be glad I did this time when I did. I have to be here for Tink and a couple others. They are also here for me.

Alan, Suzie's son, got 26 years. They took him to Wilmot prison, that's where Tink's ol' man is doing time. I need to write a letter to Alan, "piggy-back" style. I'd have to do it through his mom. We can't write directly to each other. Alan can't get mail from an institution. Plus they read the letters, so it has to be written in third party. It's going to take some thought to do that. I have a couple photo-drawings to do, so I can be thinking while I'm drawing.

Nito sent me some of his drawings that were pretty cool. One wasn't finished, and he asked me to help him with it. It was a scull with a guitar through his head. Between the two of us, it became a great creation.

I'm not sure yet, but I think someone may have stolen my ear-buds. We have a lot of new girls in here, so who knows? I find it hard to believe someone who lives here, and knows me, would take them. I put them on the chair by the outlet and now they are gone. I don't like thinking that someone is stealing.

A few days later.... Nobody stole my shit. Moddy put them in her room to keep them safe. I sort of knew that. It's lock-down for lunch and all hell is breaking loose. Wetta had herself SEGD (solitary confinement) because she was afraid of getting her ass kicked for being a snitch. She got a couple of girls thrown in the hole, and ratted on a couple others for selling drugs. The COs are running around here trying to violate anyone that Wetta put on the list.

Apparently, I'm not on there, for good reason. I never do anything except my artwork, my job and play cards now and then. I write a lot of letters. These girls behave like a bunch of children in a day care center! This is freaking prison? What is wrong with them? They all point fingers at each other. Nobody can own their own crap!

All they do is blame each other. I used to hear that shit on the outside, like, "I wouldn't be such an abusive asshole if it weren't for you!" or "You are the reason I'm always pissed off!" Everyone decides to react or not in any given situation. Reacting is having no control over yourself. Thinking first, before acting on any issue, is being in control of yourself. Others push buttons and we decide to let them or not!

They let us out for lunch, but not until being lectured! We are to get along with each other and we were reminded that we are in prison. We are not children. We have children of our own, for goodness sake.

Like I said, the COs were looking for a way to lock us all down. They don't have to work as hard that way. Life is easier for them when they don't have to deal with us, even though it's their job. You can tell they enjoy the drama; in fact, I believe they keep it going!

We're watching a pretty good movie with Clint Eastwood. He's getting quite old these days. We get to watch the last part, after lock-down, maybe. I started a new book, "Servant of the Bones".

That movie was really something. It had me in tears. Everyone was messing with me about it, asking if I was OK. Of course I'm OK! A good movie that brings tears to my eyes is one I will remember. That's the good stuff. Sometimes I feel like banging heads together. They just don't get it. Now they are staying away from me, thinking I'm upset. What a bunch of crap!

When I was a young, I went to see "Love Story" with my friends and a guy that I liked. They ruined it for me, making fun of me for crying. People can really suck!

They did mail-call; no mail for me. Actually, I do get more mail than most.

Dinner was over and I was done working, when E-pod decided to put their trays and trash out in the hall. We had already taken everything down to the kitchen pick-up area. I went out there and got the COs to help me decide how to rectify the situation. They told me to bag the trays and double-bag the trash. One CO found a little cart and I loaded the trays and trash on it. She ran it down to the kitchen for me. That took 20 minutes to handle, not bad for an emergency situation for a tray porter!

The girls are making a birthday cake for Paco; she's 34 today. My bunkie just showed it to me. They even put her name on it. It blows my mind how these girls can make cakes out of cookies, fruit, granola and whatever else they can dream up. I just got off the phone with Johnny, and let him know about my sentencing. He told me, "Hey, I thought I saw you on the side of the road, picking up garbage." Ha, ha. He cracks me up.

I got to talk to my grandson today; he's two. It's his birthday. I asked him how he was doing, and he said he was stoned. I'm sure it only sounded like that. He's just learning to talk. Johnny said he heard it too, but they don't get stoned, so that couldn't be what he said.

My glasses broke again today, so Tink hooked me up

address of a church that provides reading glasses tes. She also gave me a post card to send to them. I had to fill out a request form so I can receive them.

I'm getting tired of this place. I keep getting caught up in the seemingly random, chaotic zones. It's irritating that the people are like puppets in a puppet show, and nobody can find their script. They respond best to input that resembles rumors or gossip. Other than that, they have deaf ears. Isn't that freaking special? The funny part is they are not aware of it and it's not their fault, entirely. They don't know they can be different. There are not enough years in my life to school them. I need to focus on those most important to me, like my kids, their kids and a select few friends that I may acquire on the way.

I may get asked to paint a mural for the inmates to get their photos taken in front of. I told Molly I'd do it if Tink could help me. We make a good team.

I'm wondering if Fred has forgotten me. I haven't received a letter in a long time. He's been talking to Suzie a lot. Maybe she knows what's going on with that. Maybe she jumped on that action. God knows she could use a man in her life.

Speaking of men in our lives, Bryan and I were good for a couple years, but then things went all to hell! I still care about him, but he is a lost cause. Only God can help him now. He never writes to me and he's screwed up all the time on pain pills.

The town of Patagonia sent me a card. Really, Skye sent me the card and he had everyone sign it. He works at the Patagonia Market. I'm writing him a thank you poem he can post at the store. I'm mailing it in an Angel of

Death envelope. He likes that kind of stuff. Tink is working on the poem.

Well, it's almost dinner time, so Tink, Molly and I are getting all of our artwork together to photograph it. Mr.Thornton already has our request form to do a mural on the wall in the hall. The photos are to show that we are capable of doing something real nice. We've done some pretty impressive pieces.

We just got off lock-down and I was sort of waiting for Tink to climb out. They just called mail-call and Tink got two letters, so I woke her up. I didn't get any, so I called Johnny to see if he mailed those photos that he said he would. He mailed them yesterday, so I should get them on Monday's mail-call. He told me to take notice to the order of them. He had put them in their order on purpose. I'm sooo... looking forward to it. Yippee, yahoo!

The movie tonight, "The Book of Eli," with Will Smith, looks pretty bad-ass.

Next day.... Saturday. We had waffles again. That's probably still my favorite. I have just finished one of the most frustrating jobs I've ever taken on here, drawing a soccer ball with six-sided figures surrounding a five-sided center. It totally sucked! I'm going to offer her one of my T-shirts since I think it came out kind of lame. The girl said she loved it, so all is well. The girl is pregnant, and the soccer ball does look cute on her T-shirt.

At lunchtime, I'm delivering an Angel of Death and I'm going to ask for some chewing tobacco. That's like gold around here. That and coffee are the most valuable possessions besides sugar and stamps.

I'm not sure what to do today. Tink said I could look

through her color book for ideas. The movie today is "Clash of the Titans", a very old movie with Pegasus, Medusa, the Kraken, Perseus and Zeus. It's time to lock-down for an hour or so, nap time. My body is totally sore, and has been since I've been here. As soon as I woke up and went to make myself a cup of coffee, the CO yelled, "Lock-down for chow!"

They let me finish heating my coffee, which was totally out of character for them. Now that we are locked-down, I'm fighting sleep again. I don't want to miss chow, or be late again and have the door shut in my face. They love this shit, pushing us around. Don't dare react or you are in trouble, either hand cuffs or in the hole, or both.

A couple of the COs around here love the power they have over our so called freedom. They may be officers, but they are still women. The nice ones are the older ones, more mom type figures. There are a lot of girls that deserve to be f#cked with, the "want to be" gangster lesbians! Then we have the girls who are "gay for the stay," who have a man on the outside but are gay in here. Creepy! I don't want anyone to touch me!

It's nearing the end of the day and I was thinking of going to sleep when Molly and Tink talked me into a game of canasta after the last lock-down. I was telling Molly how irritated I was getting with this place. I usually spend my days alone and I only like hanging out with people for a little while, then go back to doing my own thing. It's like going somewhere with a bunch of people. I ride with them and I can't leave until they do.

I need to pray about changing my point of view. I

have awhile to go yet, so I'd better change my attitude about being here. I'm really not suffering; in fact, things are better than ever. Now Tink and I will be painting murals on the walls in here. That will be the coolest thing that could happen to us.

Writing about the blessings ought to help me in my quest to stay happy. It's up to me to get happy because nobody is going to do it for me. I know better to think any different about the subject. Happiness first, then good things come, not the other way around. May I not forget to smile each day when I wake up, or when I lay my head down at night. I pray that I live a long and healthy life so I can be around while my children are doing their lives, and their children's lives. What a wonderful thing that will be. I'm feeling better already.

I went and played cards with the girls and told them what I was thinking about. They are a great bunch of girls.

The Mexicans were having a birthday party and dirty dancing with each other. They were giving each other lap dances until the COs came into the pod. They all started singing a church song in Spanish. The CO told them to quiet down or they were going to lock us all down. Their lesbian behavior is what I get sick of! Women do not turn me on, and these girls are by no means beauty queens! It gets pretty disgusting at times. I've seen quite a few things that I never want to see again!

It's quarter 'til 11pm, so they'll be slamming the door any minute. There's time to read a few pages of my book before the lights go out. I've been pretty burned out, even after taking a good nap today. Tink thinks we need some iron. The multiple vitamins on commissary don't have iron in them. I guess canned green veggies are the only source of iron we have.

Happy Sunday! I almost started a fight over the T.V. this morning. I picked up the controller after lock-down and someone said, "We were watching 'Myth Busters.' It's sort of a Sunday thing." I said, "I didn't know there was a regular Sunday thing!"

There isn't a Sunday thing anymore! I got my way and gave the controller to someone who would look for a movie for us all to watch. After she found a movie, I set the controller back on the table where I found it. I may have thrown it down, sort of, so nobody wanted to change the channel again. The situation defused on its own. The movie we are watching is "Sleepless in Seattle," with Tom Hanks and Meg Ryan. It's so romantic!

I was thinking about the most productive thing I could do to help me through this "out of place" feeling. I decided that my book, the one I'm writing, is the focal point because it is about life right now. It's necessary to have weird times so I can write about it, and do artwork to go along with it.

Monday morning. It's not even 8am, and I've already been out in the yard, had two cups of coffee, got my reds in the laundry and had to borrow a pair of red pants to go to breakfast. We can't go out of the pod without our reds on. My tennis shoes are too big and I keep tripping on rocks out in the yard. Maybe they have shoes in the laundry that will fit me. I could trade them out.

I'm sitting at our table and they haven't told us to lock-down. Cool. I almost have enough artwork for a photo-shoot!

The coolest thing happened to me when we were doing the trays and trash. Ms. Dunigan said to me, "You seem to be happy to be in jail!" I told her, "I'm happy to be anywhere." I told her that when I was a kid, I thought people were supposed to be nice to me if I was nice to them. What a rude awakening! I told her that life is only a pile of moments, just like this one, and I'd rather be enjoying it! I already know that people aren't going to be nice to me, so I forgave them already. This gives me the freedom to be happy. They can't make me angry knowing they are going to try. Unbelievable. I got stuck in the Sally Port at shift change.

Little did I know, I had a surprise waiting for me back at the pod. When I got back to the pod, I had to go to the toilet, so I just breezed by everybody and into my cell.

When I came back out, Tink had a hairnet on, doing artwork on an envelope. Then she looked up. Oh my God, she was made up with a clown face! She's really something; what a good friend! Earlier, I had drawn a picture of myself with a wind-up key on my back and a thought cloud with a clown face in it. She was being the clown I was thinking about! I really love her. Too bad I couldn't be bi-sexual, so it wasn't so awkward, but I just can't do it. Nothing personal; women don't turn me on.

Tuesday afternoon, the COs have been really nice to me today. It's sort of creepy! They are even making conversation and shit. I wonder if it will continue. Later today, Molly is going to take pictures of Tink's and my artwork. After she does that, I can deliver all of it to my customers and family. I also have another girl for my series to send to Johnny. I need a large envelope so I don't have to fold it.

I didn't realize how long it's been since I made an entry in my book. I don't know where the days went. It's Sunday, July 4th. The letters I've been writing have been like writing my book. It's annoying, writing the same things over and over. I'm still getting a lot of work, same ol' same ol'.

I'm tired of this place, the conditions, the "gay for the stay" girls and all the girls in general. They are all a bunch of weekend lesbians, feeling each other all the time, playing with each other's hair and looking at me with flirty eyes. I want to punch them in the face! They act like children, and there's no lack of drama! I guess there's more to write about with all this action. I really am looking forward to prison.

There is a girl glaring at me right now. She's just a kid. Like I said, I'm ready to go to prison, or maybe home. This girl thinks that I think that I am perfect, whatever that is. Her behavior is very annoying to me and I let her know about it. She has a real problem with criticism. Every time I turn around, I know she has been watching me. The look on her face is like throwing daggers. Too bad for her that I really don't give a shit about it, other than an annoyance.

I have been feeling sorry for myself lately, instead of counting my blessings. I think looking at the pictures Johnny sent me would help to cheer me up a little before I begin again. Happy 4th of July! God, please help me to get happy again. We're locked-down, so I listed all the artwork that I need to do. Quite a bit! I'm thankful for that. God blessed me with something to focus on, besides crap!

Monday, lunchtime. I just finished a photo-drawing and gave it to Molly to give to Mary for a bag of coffee. I was just asked if I could put two people together in a drawing. One person is dead, so it would mean a lot if I could put the two together, like a photo that was never taken. I feel like I am doing something very important for people in here. It gives me chills!

News flash! The girl that was annoying me is now my work partner. Jessica, my old partner, is now a mattress porter. We'll be working together in about 2 hours or so. I hope she doesn't bring any drama to work with her. God has a funny way of handling things. I'm a lot happier today than I was yesterday, too.

Tomorrow Tink goes to court. She will probably get released. I'm happy for her and her kids. She tried to give me her mattress earlier today, but I said no. I'm not taking her stuff before she's even gone! There's a possibility that she will come back. They will have her "roll-up" about midnight or so, in order to get to Tucson in time for court. There's the bus ride and the long wait in lock-up in Tucson. She'll be lucky to get a sack lunch tomorrow. God willing, she won't be back.

Tuesday, 11am. Tink was standing there when I opened my door. Looks like her court date wasn't for today, or they screwed up. They changed the date, or Tink didn't know the correct date in the first place.

Joyce Meyers gave me some inspiration today. She was preaching about holding fast to your joy, no matter the changing circumstances. Funny, I was telling Tink and Patty I was tired of waking up pissed off! It's me that needs an awakening, not my situation needing to change.

My attitude needs adjusting. By changing from within, the world will take care of itself.

Angela did good on her first day of being a tray porter. I sort of thought she might. We had fun, believe it or not!

I have a funny feeling going through my body, like a mild rush, especially when I just wake up or roll over and whenever I make sudden movements. It's not normal for me at all! I think there's something in the juice that's causing it. I don't know what they are doing to us, but they are doing something. Who's a better candidate for experimentation for the pharmaceutical companies than people that are incarcerated with no choice? Anyway, God has my back, so whatever will be, will be.

I was talking with Moddy last night about how it seems that time is flying fast lately. She agreed. The days are measured by the meals and before we know it, it's time to eat again. After dinner, the day comes to a close and then it starts over again. The weeks are measured by commissary day (Tuesday) and Friday, being the last day of the week we can get mail. Monday is mail-call day, after a long weekend.

The temperatures outside have been record hot all over the country, but we are not affected by that. I miss the hot sunnier weather. I never liked air conditioning much. That's all it is now. I guess it would be pretty miserable in here without it. There would be all these women complaining, non-stop bitching! They act as if they are all princesses or something. There's not a "ho-bag" or a criminal in the bunch! What a crock of shit. They are all too cool for this place. Wait until they get to prison. Whimpering and whining won't go over, I imagine. I am surprised everyday about the goings on around here.

Well, I'd better get back to my artwork before I get behind. The girls better start paying me, or I'm going to quit doing shit for them.

We're locked-down right now for an hour. I've been on my bunk for 10 minutes and my bunkie, Eva, hasn't stopped rattling off in Spanish for one second. She barely takes time to breathe. There's all the expression in her voice of a soap opera! Talk about dramatic! Why are these Mexican girls so dramatic? Another funny thing about the Mexicans is if they witnessed a horrible crime on the outside, not one of them would say a word. In here, they snitch continuously on Americans and are also very rude.

Tink asked me today, "Why, if Mexicans want to be here so bad, do they hate Americans so much?" I told her that maybe it's because Arizona and other southwestern states used to be part of Mexico. They seem to want what we have and would like to boot us out. I can almost never get into my room because it's always full of Mexican girls. They don't even get off my property box so I can climb onto my bunk unless I tell them to. They just sit there like it's their room and I am an inconvenience because I need them to get out of my way. Enough of that; it's starting to sound like I'm complaining. To be honest, I don't really care! I've had to live with way worse conditions. It's not my job to teach them manners. They have no respect for Whitey!

Tink finally got in touch with her lawyer. Her court date was changed to Thursday, July 8th. This day is flying by like crazy. After lock-down, it's mail-call. I could really use a letter. I got a letter from my son, Nito. He signed his name "Nito Wham Beanie Zapato." I love to hear from my kids. I guess Nito's dad is being a real asshole to Nito, and he's getting angry about it. I just called him and told him not to kick his dad's because he could really hurt him. That kind of thing could put my son in prison, Nito concurred. I gave him a riddle to think about, but didn't give him the answer. He thought that was pretty cool.

Tonight is Tink's last night here, possibly. I don't think they'll be bringing her back. They might, but I doubt it.

It's been a pretty nice day. I did a little artwork, a couple people gave me back commissary and now we are watching funniest home videos. Work is going well and Willie, the CO in the bubble has been joking me all day. I appreciate that kind of thing. I asked her for two pair of gloves and she gave me one glove. Ha, ha. I asked her for one bag and she gave me a little bitty one. She makes me laugh. I told her "I don't know if anyone appreciates you, but I do."

It's Thursday afternoon, and business as usual. I finished a real cool dragon envelope for Moddy and a nice anniversary card for Michele, the girl I thought was a snitch way back. She was asking too many questions about Patagonia and was naming names, like Frank Lopez. Nobody knows Frank, but he was arrested in the "sweep" in Patagonia and Sonoita.

I am holding my glasses together with stamps, it looks pretty ridiculous, especially when I wear them with my totally taped together headphones. Quite a sight! I would like Molly to photograph me this way but she can't bring the camera into the pod. Maybe I'll stage it in the hall like I'm sitting at a table. A photo ticket costs $1.55, so if I don't order commissary for a few weeks the ticket won't cut into my balance. I don't want to go below $100 and I have $89 right now. I need to lay off ordering anything until it builds past my goal. It won't take too long at $7 a week. I think lunch is ready; it smells like burned chicken.

I sure hope my new glasses come soon. The stamps holding these together block my peripheral vision on the right side. It's like having a sticker on my lens.

Tink isn't here, so they must have taken her to court. The burned chicken turned out to be slop, slop, slop, sloppy Joes! At the next lock-down I'm starting a new book by Stephen King, "'The Talisman." I miss you Joshua, my son.

It's Friday, 7am, the coffee tastes extra good this morning. My stomach was hurting last night, so I went to bed early. I was woken up by the intercom, "Hurry and come out in your reds. You have garbage to do!"

I'm done for the day after my trays and trash, following dinner. They no longer want anyone working after 10pm, so the chemical girls don't take out the garbage anymore. Nobody informed me of this change, but they don't have to inform me of anything. I'm an inmate.

We're off lock-down until 3pm and I just finished getting the garbage out of here. I had to do some brain-storming at work, and the COs liked my ideas. I can solve a lot of problems that they don't need to deal with. They are having me do some audit posters for them too.

It would be nice to get compensated for the task, but it wasn't an issue. I said I would help regardless.

The movie today is "The Time Machine." I love that movie. We finished the audit posters, but Tink and I acted like we weren't done at the last lock-up so we could stay out in the day room.

Saturday morning. I'm finished with the breakfast trays and trash and now Shannon and I are watching Sponge Bob.

July 10th, Raymond has been on my mind a lot these days. God, please keep him from harm and warm his heart with your love. This is a crazy world and he is a new explorer, as you know, and I love him so. Nito has his father to deal with. Help him to be a loving and compassionate man that he is becoming. I don't want my children to suffer because of my poor choices in life. Help them to be the wonderful, loving guys that they are and no matter what lies ahead, be their guide. AMEN again.

Sunday, July 11th. Tink and I have been doing artwork all day. She's taking a nap right now and I'm getting ready to take a shower. I believe it will be fantastic.... It was. I feel like the old me went down the drain. I'm feeling younger and calmness has come over me. It seems like my wrinkles are disappearing, but that's probably because I'm not wearing my glasses.

I called Johnny to see how everyone is doing. He said, "All is well." I called the Ranch to talk to Ray, but there was no answer. Johnny said that Nito was helping Ray a lot. I think that's good. Nito's dad is such an ass. The less he's around him, the better. It would be nice if Ray would write me a letter. My glasses are supposed to be here on Monday, and then I can enjoy seeing without them falling off or coming apart.

Wednesday. They called for Rec. again and didn't let us out. That's dirty pool! I just got back from breakfast chores and Angela, my work partner, was running around spreading the news that they were cancelling Rec. altogether. The CO told Angela that a couple girls were screwing around in the yard, thinking they weren't being watched so they were cancelling Rec. forever. It was all a bullshit story to see how fast the news would spread. Like I said, Angela had to be the first to spread the news. Too bad she looks like a fool. Rumors start so fast around here your head could spin. It's amazing that they are never true,

Fred wrote me a letter and put money on my books. He really is a sweet guy. Fred would enjoy a relationship, but it's too scary for me at this time in my life. I'm still messed up about how my last relationship ended up! I didn't want the good lovin' to end, but it takes two to tango.

Wow, it's Thursday already. I finished a lot of artwork and it feels good. I don't know what's going on, but my body keeps tingling all over, several times a day, and intensely.

There's about 20 minutes before count, so I'll color until then. I slept a lot today and I want to continue but I have to get up for mail-call.

Fred sent me another letter. He wanted to know if I

got the $90 he sent me, also about what the visiting hours were.

Sunday, July 18th. I had the craziest nightmare ever! I was glad to wake up. Everything everyone said happened, right when they said it, and nobody would shut up! They all kept on talking about this and that and how right they were. Nobody would shut up long enough to notice that they were making the shit happen by talking about it. They just kept jabbering on about being right.

They had it all backwards. Nothing would be happening if they would all shut up! Now, wrap your head around that one!

5.

Get Me Out of Here!

I want to get out of here! God, please get me out of here today. AMEN!

Monday evening, this is pretty interesting news. We are going to be transferred out of here because they no longer have a contract to house women in this facility. Thank you, God.

We are watching "Avatar," one of my favorite movies. I got a letter from Raymond today. I was sleeping and everyone started calling my name. Usually I'm awake for mail-call, but I forgot about it today. He sent me one of his first poems. I cried when I read it the first time. I'm not sure why. I think maybe the deepness and the closeness to the bone of it. He's seeing without understanding, but a total knowing. Raymond is such a man for being so young. I'm definitely going to put it in my book. I called the Ranch again, but Ray was babysitting for his half-sister's daughter's son, Andrew.

Commissary is tomorrow. Hopefully, Tink gets some clasp envelopes, so I can send my stuff home. They will most likely ship me out in a week or two. I already found out she didn't order the envelopes, not until next week. I have 3 of them; hopefully they will suffice.

Well this is the last entry in this part of my journey. I'm sending everything to Raymond. The photos Johnny sent I'm sending back to him. When I get somewhere, he can send me some more. When I go to sleep tonight, I will be ready to "roll-up."

They are organizing our transfer to FCC, only a couple blocks down the road, but they have to inspect all of our property boxes and our persons before they can think about moving us.

I just mailed off everything that I have accumulated while being here at CCA, Florence. It's July 21st and I have my pad of lined paper, and a few pieces of typing paper to draw on. I already sent off my color pencils and turned down my commissary order for more.

I have a card for Raymond that is already addressed and stamped, so whatever I write, I'll put in the card and mail it as we are leaving. I sent everything to Raymond, partly because there are some pages that I don't want Lisa to get a hold of. I may not feel the same about her now, but it's necessary to keep my writings.

It's a major growing up period for me. All I saved to occupy myself with is a black pen, a pencil, a sharpener, and an eraser. Nothing I can't live without. I will have to throw it away when we leave. That is why I have the card to send to Ray. I told everybody I wasn't doing any more artwork until we are relocated. Molly talked me into drawing Elmo on an envelope in his PJs. She got me a picture to look at and borrowed some colored pencils, so I did it for her. She gave me half of her Pop-Tart. I told her that was plenty since it only took me 15 minutes! I think I would do anything for Molly. I swear, she looks like a relative of the Indian that I painted on a chair for Johnny and little Josh.

Its 5pm, and of course we are locked-down. I'm going to read my book, "The Talisman." I need to finish it because it belongs to CCA.

The latest news from Willie, the CO, is that for sure we are moving. We have to be out of here by September 4th, so they will start moving us this weekend.

Now I'm covered. I'm doing envelopes for stamps; they won't let me quit! I'm not getting any more commissaries, so my balance grows $1 each day. What a rip off! Franko did pay Tink and me for the posters we did for the audit. We got $7 each, so my paycheck is $14 this week. Moddy gave me a bag of potato chips, Michele gave me a Three Musketeers bar and so did Marlena. Isabel gave me a bag of coffee, Patty gave me cream cheese and chive crackers and Molly, of course, saved me half of her Pop-Tart.

This is the last lock-down until tomorrow, so I'd better get reading my book. I love Stephen King. His stories can be more believable than reality at times!

Shannon fixed up some headphones for me, and Molly, Moddy, Tink and I played canasta while watching "Legally Blonde." Patty came over to our table and was really upset. Angela and Tanya are making her crazy. They are young girls with no respect. Somebody is probably going to kick their asses before they are done doing their time!

Thursday morning. The COs are taking forever to escort us down the hall. They make us stand there and wait, for sometimes half an hour to forty five minutes with our trays and trash. It takes about five to seven minutes to roll the carts down to their destination. I think they enjoy making us wait while two or three of them are just standing there in the hall bullshitting with each other. We only needed one escort when I heard they get paid

$27 an hour, plus benefits.

I got up early this morning. I got my teeth brushed and made my bed before they opened the door. Finally, I made it to the yard. Molly and I jogged around the yard three times, and then she said "Let's go!" We took off running. Molly is a full blooded Native American and is in really good shape. It feels good to know I can keep up with her. I saw Mary out in the yard and she asked me what she owed me. I said she owed me nothing.

I think Tink is a little pissed off at me because I barked her about always talking about having sex with girls. Everything always comes down to sex with her. I told her I was tired of hearing about it. I told her the flesh thing is sooo not deep! It cheapens every conversation that I have with her. I love Tink, and it doesn't matter what her sexual preferences are, but I don't want to be constantly hearing about it! Sexuality is a private issue with me, more of a sacred, deep place inside my heart. All this exploitation of sex has diminished the importance and closeness people can share with each other. Now it's a meat-puppet smorgasbord (bring a dish buffet). Sex without love is Satan's way of winning and I won't be part of it. If there's no love in it, then I don't have sex. I've spent a lot of years without it. I like keeping it special. It's time to go back to reading my book.

The door just buzzed open, but I'm not going out there. It feels good to sleep lately, and I'm really missing my inflatable bed at home.

We have a new unit manager and they are playing by the book! It is lunchtime and they are feeding us, one tier at a time. I'm on the bottom tier, so we are first. We get our trays, come back to the pod, set our trays at our tables, go to our cells and lock the door. The top tier is next to get their trays and come back to the pod. They let us out and we all sit down together after our food is cold. Someone told me they do it that way so no one gets an extra tray. I can't wait to get out of here! The top tier is back, but our doors are still locked. What a pain in the ass!

Angela is playing sick, so I have to keep finding someone to help me with the trays and trash every meal. Right now she is playing cards with Jack-Jack, acting like a little girl, swinging her ponytail around and talking baby talk. I have a hard time not reacting to her crap. She's going to prison and I don't know how her behavior is going to fly in the pen. She is the one who is totally disrespecting her bunkie, Patty.

It must be raining because the T.V. is out. They could play a movie on the DVD player. We don't know why they won't. I don't know why about anything really.

I just took the greatest shower ever. It ranked up there near the top, anyway. It was hot and the water pressure was outstanding. It feels so good to be clean.

I was talking to "Big Mary" about her tattoos. They are really beautiful. I'm thinking of getting sleeves to cover up my scarred up forearms. The pigment's all splotchy and I have several scars, mostly from a dog fight.

I talked to Nito; he said he is doing real good. Ray showed Nito the "Einstein" picture. They both think it's bad-ass. Nito said he was mailing me a letter today or tomorrow, so I should get it next week sometime.

I'm sitting here with Shannon while she's drawing her "cups" for art class. She helped me do my job today too. Shannon is a cool person; I like her a lot.

After dinner Molly got Angela to help me with the trays. Now she's walking around like she has cramps. Jessica said she would help me instead. It was a lot more fun working with Jessica. Angela is not cut out for the job, maybe no job! She's a spoiled little sissy!

My plan is to turn this extra weight into muscle, plus it felt good to run. I just noticed that I had my headphones on and there was nothing on the T.V. Ha, ha.

I don't think I mentioned that during work after lunch, I managed to cover myself in vanilla pudding. They had no aprons and the stacks of trays had pudding running down the sides. My pants and shirt were covered in pudding. Willie, in the bubble, was laughing and they all got a big kick out of it. Fortunately they washed our "reds," and I was able to take a hot shower.

July 23rd, only 52 more days until my sentencing. I no longer can wear my glasses; they are beyond fixing. I can see what I'm writing, only it's blurry.

Saturday, lunchtime. It seems like all we do around here is eat. I want out of here.

Sunday. I've been in a weird mood lately. I have no tolerance for anyone, only a couple people, Molly, Moddy and maybe Tink. It must show somehow, because people keep asking if I'm alright. I tell them that I'm daydreaming. I just really want to get out of here.

I noticed they haven't mailed my box of shit yet. They're sure taking their time doing it.

We have art class tonight and I was supposed to draw something to take to class. I didn't know what to draw, so

I drew an aerial view of me sitting at a table drawing.

It's bedtime and Tink, Molly, Moddy, Patty and I had been playing canasta. The art class got cancelled because the art teacher, Joanne, an old lady in a wheelchair, got fired. I don't know what happened, but we just started the class two weeks ago and the girls were doing really well. Everyone is disappointed. I could teach the class, but I don't want to.

I have a feeling my bunkies are going to do the tired, wanting to sleep thing so they can turn the lights out early. She's already looking up here to see what I'm doing. Well, goodnight. Tomorrow will be 49 more days.

My shoulder is really bothering me today. The top bunk is probably the cause of my shoulder not getting better. It never has a chance to heal all the way. Some days, it's hardly noticeable and then I'll make my bed and screw it up again.

The nurse will probably see me some time tomorrow. They don't usually do that much for us around here except give us ibuprophen. A bottom bunk would be a good place to start. I don't think my bunkie would like that, but she's young and in good shape. I might go lie down until dinner. I finished a five person photo drawing for Marlena today. She cried. I guess I did a good job.

Wednesday morning. My shoulder is still aching. For some reason, I can do my job with no problems. I seem to be able to sling garbage bags, heavy ones, into the bin and lift stacks of trays. Relaxing is what I have a tough time doing.

Joyce Meyers' message this morning was a good one. It was about grieving the Spirit by being afraid (showing no faith), being idle, and using stupid and destructive words when all words have power. We will pay for everything we have said in the end. Please forgive me.

I'm getting that "all over" tingling again. I sure wish I knew what was happening to me. When I came back in from working, the commissary people were doing our pod. Tink tried to give me a drumstick as I was going by, but they said "No!" That means she'd better give it to someone else because it's melting. We can't share our commissary in front of them.

Everything is against the rules around here. I can't wait to go to prison so I can cut my nails, blow dry my hair and have colored pens. I'm sure there will be disadvantages, but the advantages will outweigh them. I can't believe they wouldn't let me have a drumstick! Ice cream orders have to be eaten right away.

They have pool tables in prison, I've heard. I'm sure they are for minimum security inmates. A person could die from getting "beaned" with a pool stick or a ball.

I finished "The Talisman," so all I have to concern myself with is getting my art orders done and writing in my journal.

August 6th, Thursday. I've lost track of time and it seems to be more difficult for me to stay in the up-beat! I know that happiness is a frame of mind, so I continuously fight that pissed-off feeling. Lately, my mood of indifference is even bothering me. I really hate being locked- up with these women that act and talk like they are little girls. I haven't gotten any letters in a while and I haven't felt like writing any either.

I am so easily disturbed. Maybe the pain I'm in has something to do with it. I saw the nurse and she gave me

400 mg ibuprophen, which I take every day.

Samantha and I are watching a concert on T.V. Carly Simon and James Taylor are just what the doctor ordered. That didn't last long; it was public television. After a couple of songs, they started campaigning for money. Sponge Bob was my next choice.

It's lock-down time, so nobody had to suffer through my Sponge Bob show for more than a half hour. I feel a little better after talking with Samantha about feeling mean. Apparently, she has been feeling that way too. Shannon had been telling her she needs to chill out.

Earlier, I was sitting at my table watching T.V. after a nap when I realized that Mary and Lisa were trying to get my attention. I took off my headphones and asked what they wanted. They asked me if I was alright. I said "Why, don't I look alright?" They said I looked a little down. I told them I just woke up, and maybe I'm tired of being here. Mary said, "Imagine how I feel being here 19 months!"

Why the hell did they bother me? F#ck! It's that kind of shit that I am sick of! God, please get me out of here! The Devil is working overtime in here, and so is God!

I just wrote to Bryan and Suzie and I'm sending them a couple drawings of my art table at home, one in color and one in black and white. I'm not sure what to do with my artwork when I get home, maybe have a show. Clint and Niki will be important in such an endeavor. Clint is my computer wizard.

Lately I've been getting into the soap opera, "The Young and The Restless," because it's on. I just remembered that I'm supposed to be doing a photo shoot. I'm not sure if I want a picture of me, or my art with me next to it. I only have one photo ticket.

I got a letter from Katie today; she's so cool. I wish she was my daughter-in-law, or I used to anyway. Now she's my wonderful young friend. Katie is someone I can communicate my deepest thoughts and feelings to. She's doing OK, taking care of her two kids by herself. She hadn't mentioned Nefi, the father, in her letter at all.

I sure hope we move soon. I could use a change of scene. It's Monday, August 9th, only 35 more days until sentencing. I've heard that we need to be out of here in two weeks. We are only moving across the street, but it will still be a change, and the bus ride won't be that long. We will have to wear all the restraints, including the black box that holds our wrists. They really do the over-kill on the chains! I will appreciate my freedom tremendously, whenever that is.

My dreams lately are about home. None of them are disturbing, like the one last night. Everyone was undermining whatever I was doing. I need God; that's all there is to it.

I sent off a letter to Isabel in town hall. It's in regards to them suing me for a $500 water bill. I knew it was only $140 when they turned it off. I asked her to check for a leak or something. I told her I could never afford a $500 bill when I get out of prison. Hopefully they will be kind to me. I also filled out a medical request for ibuprophen; hopefully they will be kind to me also.

I miss my boys! I wonder how Raymond is doing. He hasn't written in a while. Nito either, the little six foot stinker. Johnny finally sent me a real cool letter some time back. I only have $1.50 of phone time left, so I'm saving it for when we move.

Unbelievable! I just came back from work after lunch and Tink had switched mattresses with me. Hers is like a twin bed mattress. She also gave me some potato chips and ear plugs. What a friend! It's been so long since I had a real friend, that I forget they did shit like that.

I still didn't sleep all that well; I tossed and turned all night. My shoulders are still achy. I'm still up early enough to make it to recess this morning. I woke up early because of the dream I was having. I dreamed that someone was killing us with tainted laundry soap, food, flowers in the room. Just everything was tainted with something that was fatal when exposed to moisture. I was running around trying to stop everyone from poisoning themselves, but nobody would listen! It was a living Hell!

Last night I had a real wild dream about fishing. I was fishing in a little boat and I caught an albino, giant catfish, the size of the tank I was fishing in. It had a baby the size of a human. The tank turned into my cell, and the fish capsized my boat which turned out to be my mattress. It kept wrestling me in the water and I was keeping the mattress between us to keep from being eaten. I had to watch out for the baby at the same time. Water was escaping out of the crack under the door. I was desperately trying to grab the crowbar at the bottom of the tank to open the door, but the baby fish kept getting in the way and I had to keep coming up for air. Finally, I woke up. The fish must have been my bunkies! Marlena was the big one and Eva was the baby. Apparently, I was fishing from the top bunk.

Later... I made it to rec. It was nice. I jogged around

the track at least three times and Molly and I took off running, for only 30 or 40 feet. That's all I had in me today. I tried throwing the basketball at the basket and my shoulder went into instant pain; I almost couldn't stand it. We thought it would help to loosen me up.

I drew a self-portrait that actually looks like me. I used the photo that Molly took of me the other day. She's really good; she captured "me." I think I'll send the photo to Fred. I'm sure he would like it. I'm sending the portrait to Suzie to keep for me.

I'm sitting here wondering what to write about. It's August 12th, 2010, and I don't know what to say. "The Young and The Restless" is on. I was watching that show when I got my first sign job in Sonoita. It was the summer or 1986. I remember doing the scale drawing of a 12 foot, double-dip ice cream cone. I used a cone box as a model to draw from. Talk about underbidding! $350 for a 12 foot, 2 sided, ice cream cone, installed! My husband, Dale, wanted to kill me! We almost paid them to make them a sign. That was one of the worst sign blunders ever.

Sunday, August 12th. I was standing in the hall with my plastic apron and my latex gloves on when I looked up and coming down the hall from nowhere was Annette from Patagonia. She told me she was going home soon because she was caught with only 30 pounds. We couldn't really talk because the Warden was in the hall too.

Johnny sent me some pictures and I couldn't get one of them off my mind. I love it. The picture is of Johnny and little Joshua holding hands, standing in the water watching the sun go down over the mountains across the lake. I drew the scene on an envelope. I'm going to write a nice letter to Johnny just so I can send it to him. He's so wonderful. I love my boys more than anything on the planet. God has blessed me with more than I ever could have hoped for. I feel the sting in my eyes and the lump in my throat when I think about it. Those are the things that are important in life.

August 18th. Jack-Jack goes to prison today. We're happy for her. They will probably send her to Dublin in California. I have a feeling I'll be seeing her again. The girls are coming in from the yard and I just finished a photo-drawing. I don't know who it belongs to. They all talk to me about drawing at one time or another. I figure, by leaving it on the table, the owner will magically appear.

I've been out of balance the last few days and I asked God to help me several times. He helped me get this far. The word is, we are moving to the other facility around September 4th. I have a feeling it will be way sooner.

I have been staying away from people as much as possible, so their mouths don't interfere with my life. It's something that's nearly impossible to avoid completely. I've been doing a pretty good job of only drawing positive energy. God is helping me a lot with that. The picture I just drew is bringing me positive energy.

I keep reading my Stephen King novel, "Under the Dome." I believe I'll finish it before they ship us out. I started the book back in March, but only got half-way through it before I had to give it up. Ridiculously, the book went full circle and landed in my possession again. Now I'm on page 747; the book has 1072 pages in all. Something wonderful is going to happen when I finish the book!

Thursday, August 19th. Only 24 more days until my sentencing. Hopefully we'll be moved to FCC by then. I got my requests for character letters all out in the mail.

I finished envelopes for the art teacher, two lions on a big yellow one and two fish in the ocean on a small white one. They were angelfish in the seaweed. Now I have two Angels of Death to draw, one sporting a basketball and the other with a black cloak holding a sickle and the world. They can wait until tomorrow, for now I want to read my book....

Lock-down is over but I don't feel like leaving my bunk right now. I've been doing a lot of thinking and a lot less talking. The spoken word is powerful, and I figure it's time to take it very seriously. I have to think about what I am saying before I say it. The only way for me to do that is to stop talking!

I'm staying out of the social banter that seems to be harmless, but I'm not so sure about that anymore. Every word holds some kind of power, be it negative or positive. In the day room, conversations are flying everywhere, all the time. I feel like I'm getting sucked into a reality that I don't want. I don't really what the same things that other people want. I don't want to talk about how other people are, or care about the latest rumor or gossip.

The things that concern me are about the ones I love and the ones that care about me. There are a lot of people that I pray for and daydream about, how they will be blessed in God's time. I want to be more like Christ, not more like people.

I imagine a few girls are wondering what's up with me. This all came over me at once. I felt that standing back and watching from a distance was the best way to deal with this insight. One of my favorite people here, sorry to say, never stops talking. If she's not talking, she's singing out loud to a radio that no one else can hear, because she wears ear phones. If the words spoken today are making tomorrow, I don't want just anything being said constantly. I become totally involved by being in the immediate vicinity.

I can no longer use politeness as an excuse to let someone else manifest my reality. Others don't have control over themselves, for the most part. The majority of people seem to blame their state of affairs on someone else, or something else, and let's not forget the Devil or even God. Looking in the mirror would be more accurate.

Tink was the one I was referring to earlier. After I talked to her about what was up with me, she went and got a Joyce Meyers book to show me where she talked about choosing the people you hang out with and setting boundaries. It referred to being caring and good to people, but not getting tangled up in their circumstances. Some people don't really want our help; they want to drag us into their reality, sucking up all our energy.

The really funny thing is that "my friend" is one of the worst at not paying attention to what she is saying, most of the time. She's dangerous and doesn't see it, only in others. She means well, but she's not well. The beautiful thing is she wants to be better. She is seeking out information to do that. She wants to do what God wants her to do, and so do I. I still don't feel that I am controlling my life very well, I need guidance. Staying at a distance is my way of dealing with me for now.

Well, God has answered my prayers. Tink is in transit, on her way to prison. Maybe she can grow in the spirit without me, and I can do the same. We will meet again.

As I was walking into the pod after work this morning, I had this thought that Tink better check to make sure she is on the transit list. Before I could say anything, she came running over to tell me she was in transit.

I believe that God has the Feldmann ranch situation well in hand. Mildred and Lloyd built that place on prayers and the grace of God. Dale, my ex-husband, is a good man and so are his brothers. Somehow, the brothers need to agree, but that is a miracle waiting to happen.

I have to hurry and read "Under the Dome." I'm on page 853. Tink says she wants to read it, but she's leaving on Sunday. Maybe she's the fastest reader on the planet!

Lock-down just got over, and once again I don't feel like getting off my bunk. I have artwork to do, but I don't feel like doing that either. My ass hurts, my leg keeps going to sleep and cramping, so lying down for a bit is my next trick! My bunkies are asleep, so I think I can pull it off... taking a nap.

My timing is excellent today. I walked out of my cell after waking up and Ms. Thornton yelled, "Lock-down for chow!" She's real loud too. I guess I'll read 'til "Line up for chow!"

Another shift down for the day, and they are playing a movie. Ever since Tink found out she was leaving, she's been acting like a total juvenile! I don't know what to think about her. I wonder who's talking to me when she seems to understand deep things, and then proves that she doesn't! It's very annoying and a little confusing. I'm glad she's leaving; I'm tired of dealing with her wishy-washy bullshit! I think I'll start sketching my art projects while watching the "Italian Job."

It's 3pm (lock-down). I finished the Angel of Death sporting a basketball for Peanut. She's going to love it. She's at class right now, but I'll see her after lock-down. They just called for "Visitation" porter, so Tink has to go to work. Back to my book.

Sunday morning... nobody is awake yet. It rained last night real good, so it's that rainy day feeling. I had a hard time sleeping; my arms and shoulders ached and then I kept dreaming about having to play dead and to teach others how to survive. Survive what? I don't know. We were taking care or kids we didn't know, doing a lot of running and playing dead. Later I dreamed we were being burned by a giant magnifying glass. I was running around in a fire-retardant suit, telling people to get under cover, and nobody would listen! As soon as they would say I was full of shit, they burst into
flames! Everyone was telling me I was nuts, and you know the rest. I was the only one left standing, and then I woke up.

Jackie told me about a dream she had a week ago about her, me and Moddy. We were standing outside in L.A., California. We were looking up in the sky and a pyramid, like in Egypt, is flying by with jets under it and then blows up! The Eiffel Tower goes by and also blows up. People are panicking! There were huge white clouds that turned into horses with helmets. The horses were hundreds of feet tall and came roaring towards us, pulling a chariot full of hot lava. The lava was creeping towards us, melting everything. It was moving very slowly as we were backing away from it.

We were in front of a shoe store, so we ran in and

Jackie said I picked a pair of knee-high Dockers (cranberry color) and she put on a pair of moccasins. The lava was coming in, so we went into a room that looked like a sound room with a window. The lava came roaring through the window, then everything turned black and she woke up.

It took her a while to go back to sleep, having to walk around the cell, make some coffee and sit there a while before she could sleep again. The whole thing sort of sounds like a movie I might have seen. Jackie left a week ago on her way to prison.

Happy Sunday. Marlena just gave me some ibuprophen. She heard me moaning up here. I think it's August 22nd; only 22 more days! My teeth are brushed, my laundry is ready to go, and I'm lying here until they unlock the door.

It's 8pm; we were watching a movie when they shut us down for count. They never played the finish of the last two movies we were watching. I was hoping to see the end to this one.

I tried to call Johnny tonight, but no answer. I wanted to tell him we are moving on Saturday and I need him to write a letter to the judge for me right away. No time to procrastinate; my lawyer needs it before my sentencing.

We get to take one property box with us to FCC, across the street. I told my bunkies that I want a bottom bunk when we move. Eva is going back to Mexico in a few days, anyway. Jessica is going to be our bunkie when Eve leaves. I finished "Under the Dome" and gave it to Tink. I hope she has time to read it.

We can't take any books with us that don't belong to

us. They are shipping our property boxes on Friday; we'll take our bedding with us in a bag on Saturday. They said we will have the same bunkies, the same room number and the same pods. It sounds like an organized move. We shall see! I've never seen too many things go down the way they were planned. It ought to be interesting to observe!

Looks like I'll still be wearing red to court. I bought a T-shirt to wear underneath. I was hoping for a different color when we moved; red is federal for woman.

Rosie gave me a couple of post cards. She wants a 6-pack of Budweiser on one of them and a bouquet of flowers on the other. I have one more high-heel with the ball and chain to do. Someone always wants one more of those.

It's Monday 9am lock-down. I've decided to get all my ducks in a row today, throwing out all the trash I've acquired, returning library books and making the envelope to mail to Raymond. I'm sending the picture of my cell from the top bunk before anyone sees it. It's totally against the rules to duplicate or draw anything about the facility, for security reasons, they say.

I hope Ray is putting my book pages in order for me. He's probably doing better than I would. He's like that. I miss my boys so much. Maybe I'll get to show them how much I appreciate them when I get home.

I'm going to pay close attention to the company I keep. Like my dad said, "You are who you hang out with," and my mom said "You are who you eat!" She was a clown; I'm so much like her. I hear her voice when I'm talking, especially when I laugh. I also have her attitude. If I answered the phone at my folk's house, her friends would think I was her. At my mother's funeral, her best friend, Ruby Berryman, heard my dad and I talking in another room. She was freaking out, thinking it was Mom. I thought she was going to pass out!

We're finally packing up to move across the street. We are supposed to have everything moved by Friday; that's what they told us anyway. We are never supposed to know the exact day for security reasons.

It's 3pm lock down. Rosie's post cards are done and I drew some praying hands with a rosary hanging from them, with a ribbon that said "In Loving Memory of Aaron," for Moddy. I started a new book, "Walking by Faith" by Jennifer Rothschild. She is blind. Our feet will tread our heart's pursuits.

I keep thinking about taking piano lessons when I get out of prison. No mail for me today, I really thought I would get some. I want Bryan to write me a letter!

We finally got to watch a whole movie today, "Saving Private Ryan." They actually didn't lie to us this time!

Well, it's time to load up our property boxes with our stuff. We are only allowed two sets of "reds," one to wear and one in our box. We will most likely be issued another set when we get to the other building.

6.

They're Moving Us To FCC

Tuesday morning, August 24th, 9:30am. Rolina and I finished our first shift and now they are doing commissary. I didn't order anything this time, but everyone that owes me will be paying me, paying up today. Of all of the COs that are here, I think I'm going to miss Ms. Lopez the most. She's real cool. She doesn't take shit from anybody and she tells it like it is with no hesitation. I find that credible. I think she sort of took a liking to me too. Every time we walk by each other, she says "What's happenin', Brew?" I say "Not much, Lopez." An inmate heard me say that I would miss her. She looked at me and said "That's so gay!" I told her "I'm not going to miss you, faggot!" I don't know how she took that, but I bet I find out at lock-down. She's all gangster and shit! I hope there are no problems. If there are, she's not as cool as she acts.

As I figured, there was no problem. Christina is the girl's name. She enjoys acting all gangster and totally slutty, always talking about having sex with several women and men, always sticking her tongue out, gesturing that she likes to lick things! She grosses me out! She's going to be old before her time, tore up from the floor up! Then there's a girl from Wilcox, Velvet. My sister-in-law, Ann, asked me to make sure she was OK. Christina is her bunkie. What a couple!

We just got back from breakfast shift. "Molly

McButter" helped me this morning because Rolina had a family visit today. She got to use the visiting room with the phones instead of a speaker in the window.

I'm watching the news before we get locked-down; they're getting so tough at the border crossings. There is a huge increase of illegals coming into California by water. They apprehended over 240 boats this year so far and the year isn't over yet.

Excuse me, last year it was 240 boats. It is 800 boats this year so far.

Anyway, it's lock-down time again. I'm really going to learn to play the piano when I get home. I can see myself playing it. All I have to do is draw a rose for Moddy on a poem she wrote.

Unbelievable! Yoli wrote a "kyte" saying that someone was flashing their tits at somebody else... so Blanca, Christina, Peanut and Marcella are all in the hole before we move. Yoli is responsible for several people going to the hole. I don't know what her problem is, but I don't understand she's a tattle-tale, anyway. Now those girls won't be able to get a job when we move, not for 6 months. I always thought that Yoli was very self-important; obviously I was in the ball park. We're already locked-up. Why rat on each other?

I finished a monkey envelope and gave it to Tink for her son. We'll be locked-down tomorrow afternoon until we move. We will carry our bedding with us when we leave here. I wrote to Clint and Niki and drew a corn cob on the envelope before gave up my colored pencils. The corn is a personal joke.

Now we are in D-Pod, Tink was rolled-out last night. It's all crazy now because we don't have our regular tables yet; it's like fish in a fish bowl. We all have to find the place where we fit. Mary and I went to the same table. We sat next to each other in A-Pod. Mary and I need this time together. They just announced that we need to get our boxes ready for inventory, so it looks like I'm done writing until we get to our destination.

Way later... Sunday, August 29th. I'm sitting on my new bunk out in the day room of F-Pod at FCC. It's freezing in here! I have a job already. Rolina and I are still tray porters. The volume of work has tripled! We were like a three ring circus, but it was our first time, and it's all different.

They don't use styrofoam cups or plastic "sporks" they use washable, heavy plastic glasses and fluorescent orange sporks that are much better. We have to collect all those cups, sporks and trays instead of throwing most of it away.

They had a medical emergency while we were working, so we never did finish the job. After dinner, we get to try it again. Rolina is in a different pod, so we meet in the middle after meals.

Last night the CO brought me an extra blanket. Ann, my sister-in-law, is in my pod. She made me some sock sleeves, because I was so cold and her room is warm. It took forever to get here. They took my sweatshirt when they strip-searched us. Nobody told me I had to pack it or lose it! They keep the temperature around here at 70 degrees or less.

I'm in the day room with 4 other girls: Veronica, Burrito, her lover, and their bad-ass dyke buddy, Mo Mo! They're pretty cool. The fourth girl is a Mexican illegal that doesn't speak English, so she's quiet. The other three were talking. Burrito said, "We don't like it here, but we belong here. There are at least 1000 fags here!" I thought that was pretty funny. They thought it was funny that I was laughing.

Only 15 more days until my sentencing. I know a few people are writing character letters for me. Johnny, Fred and Katie are each writing one for sure. I need to write to everyone and give them my new address, but I haven't got the envelopes. It might be a few days before we get money on the books, so the letters will have to wait. I think I'll do some coloring.

It's 6pm, Sunday. I just finished working the dinner shift. Wow, what a work out! Holy shit, we really earn our dollar a day around here! Assholes and elbows, I'm no longer cold in the day room. God has been good to me during this move. If they wouldn't have taken my sweatshirt when we were strip-searched, I would have been a goner on the bus and outside. It was at least 100 degrees outside and the bus had no air-conditioning, only hot air blowing. I was almost passing out and felt like throwing up. We were all chained up in leg irons and double chains around our waist. Roberta Brady emptied out her lunch bag so I could "Ralph" in it. She and I were in the back seat of the bus, and the hot air was blowing right on us. I didn't lose my cookies, but almost lost consciousness several times. Luckily, I'm an old soldier at not passing out all the way!

They kept us on the bus for over an hour, and we only went to the building next door. I'm so happy to be here with semi-cold showers and a one inch thick mattress with no pillow! I folded my dirty reds and put them under my sheet for a pillow. The food here is real good too. I don't have to throw my potatoes away anymore and the hamburger is mostly meat. Being in the day room, we have to use someone else's bathroom. Thank God for old friends from other places that allow you privacy when using their toilet.

They gave us our hygiene bag today with a toothbrush, toothpaste, toilet paper, shaver, a bar of soap and shampoo. I'm also happy they gave us a clean set of reds to carry with us in case it takes a while to get our property boxes. They didn't throw away my sweat pants that I had in the bag with my bedding. I don't know what time lock-down is, but I like being in the day room because the lights are on. It's better for drawing and writing. I have my writing pad and my art paper now. Life is good!

I'm having a little trouble thinking of something to draw. Maybe I'll work on the cross that Moddy wanted for her daughter's friend who died. She wants a large cross with smaller praying hands and a banner saying "In Loving Memory of Beth". Moddy's daughter had been in a terrible accident and her friend died.

She had to have brain surgery. I think that would be a good thing to work on. They locked everyone down early tonight because the medical people are here doing our intake process. They are asking questions like, "Have you ever had any diseases, and are you allergic to anything?" It only took me a moment because there is nothing wrong with me and I no longer have periods.

I'm going to go to sleep, even though I'm in the middle of all the commotion. I sure won't miss anything.

Good morning. I feel like I've been beaten with a shovel! There are five girls bumming coffee from me now. A lot of girls didn't get their property boxes yet.

They gave me a blue cup rack to put cups in before we take them out in the hall. It was my idea to use the rack. I don't know why they didn't think of it; maybe they like juggling cups! It's going pretty smoothly at work, but it's still a work out! I don't have the shoulder problem anymore and I'm able to sleep. I'm achy all over, now. I'm definitely healing, getting stronger every day.

Wow, Melody gave me a beautiful picture of a woman with roses all through her hair. I'm going to put it on an envelope. First I'm putting it on my art paper for myself. Exciting!

Sitting here on my bed, it's a perfect place to observe group behavior. Right now they are setting up for lunch out in the hall and the COs are in here changing people's living quarters.

Obviously, they have no immediate plans for me, so in the meantime, I will observe. The Unit Manager, Ms. Peace, wants me to do some mural work and painting for the beauty shop: scissors, blow dryer, etc. on the walls. I told her I did lettering, too. Burrito is the one who hooked me up there. While I was sitting here, I drew a pair of scissors. I didn't know if they were correct; it's been a long time since I've seen a pair. I may get to look at a pair when I'm doing the walls. The idea is to show her what they would look like, a scale drawing. On the wall, they will be about 3 feet long.

She was going to come and get me to start on it today, but it's been way busy around here. I still don't have a pillow and I'm sore as hell from freezing all night. God's got my back, so no use arguing with him.

Becca sat on my bunk and we talked for quite a while today. I enjoyed it. She wanted to know my story about why I'm in here. She was amazed at the whole thing.

They are talking about doing a mural out in the Rec. yard. They want my high-heel with the ball and chain on the checker board floor. The girls are trying to get it approved. That particular piece of art I had in my head for about 25 years before I ever put it on an envelope.

In my head, the ball and chain was an apple. Becca seems to believe that I should be rich beyond belief! She said I must be terrible with money!

The word is, we should all be in a cell and out of the day room by Thursday. Today is Tuesday, August 31st.

While I was lying here, I thought about how I was having a problem with keeping social contact, and was becoming reclusive. Since we moved, I've been right out here in the population all the time. I'm noticing I'm perfectly content. God did me a favor by letting me sit here doing my thing. I'm learning not to put so much on it!

The CO doing "special diets" rolled by me and said, "I'm feeling irritated today, so please excuse me." I told her it's perfectly OK to get irritated, so let it rip! She smiled and so did I.

They are going to be serving dinner in a few minutes, so time to put my stuff away for now. Oh yes, I have a pillow now. Shawnee brought it to me. Someone got rolled-up to go to prison and she snagged it for me.

I'd really like a cup of coffee, but the water tastes bad

and taints everything. When I get to order commissary, I'll get flavored creamer.

Man, I just took the coldest shower ever! At least it's way up there. We were all screaming and laughing because it was so cold! Mary and Shannon were at Bible study, so I was able to use their toilet without someone in the room or waiting outside the door.

Mary just came back. She had been out in the hall for a good hour with Patty, her old bunkie. Patty's husband died today. Oh God, she's so sad. What a great person, so happy-go-lucky, and she gets so excited about Jesus. I really love her, God please comfort my friend in her grief and help her to find peace, AMEN.

Mary left me her study Bible to use while we are in the same pod. She has another one she likes to use.

Shawnee is coloring her mind-bender designs with her head phones on, listening to her radio. That's all she's ever done since I've known her. Over at CCA, they gave her a random UA; she came up dirty for pot! They threw her in the hole and she lost her job. I hadn't seen her much until we moved. She's a white girl.

They just flashed the lights and everyone scattered to their rooms like cockroaches. Looks like it's a medical emergency instead of count. We lock down for everything.

We have two TVs in the day room, 20 feet apart. One of them is for English programs and the other is Spanish. The Spanish T.V. is always drowning out our English shows. Those girls turn it way up for that purpose. It's a constant T.V. war!

Good morning. I'm sitting in the middle of a flood! There's an inch of water all around my bunk! Someone put something over the smoke detector in cell 106, and it went off. Water is flowing out of the ceiling in the cell at an enormous rate! It's not stopping either. Melody, the one that gave me the picture, is the guilty party.

The water stopped now, and it's only two inches deep! Pony-0s are floating by, a cheese puff and a lot of hair globs! The girls are sweeping and mopping the water into the shower area drains, like synchronized mermaids! There has to be a link to the spoken word.

I think God is showing me something very important here. It's too coincidental; the things I have said and dreamed are happening. Some things, not right away, and other things, instantaneously! It's amazing how the girls worked together as a team automatically, without being told to do so. They have handled the situation beautifully; I am so impressed by the whole thing.

Thursday, September 2nd. I found my glasses after painting most of the beauty shop walls without them. There is so much happening. I'm having a tough time processing it all, and then Shannon goes "Writing will help you put it all together."

I met Shannon when we were locked-down in B-Pod for 30-40 days. She was one of the tray porters that came to collect the trays and trash. Later, when the lock-down was over, she trained me to be a tray porter, because she was really the math teacher. Shannon was also Tink and Shawnee's bunkie in A-Pod.

When Tink shipped out of CCA, she left an envelope with a girl to give to me. It was all of our art photos. She wanted me to show them to the warden so I could do a mural out in the Rec. yard. They already want me to do a

"Finding Nemo" theme in the Staff bathroom. I'll be taking photos of everything for the book. My life is getting more interesting, to say the least.

I finally have a room (top bunk) FG204. I'm starting to enjoy the top bunk. It's more private, and it's a good place to observe instead of being in the middle of the road.

Friday, 4pm, lock-down. We just came in from Rec. Finally, I wasn't working. I worked this morning painting in the beauty shop. I did a girl's face in flesh tone next to where the mirror will go. I'm going back to finish tonight so they can open it up next week. They already want me to do some lettering on the walls: numbers, rules, etc. Out in the yard there's a wall that's 25 feet by 15 feet tall, the one they want me to paint the mural on.

Tuesday, September 7th. I just got back from work as an "artist." I love that! I've been lettering the PREA by the phones in all the pods (Prison Rape Elimination Act of 2003), with the hot-line number. I have two more pods to do. I finished the Staff bathroom last night after dinner. "Ms. Peace hooked us up with a pile of cake and a half a tray of pudding. She said she would try to hook me up with a pair of black shoes so I don't have to wear these blue ones to court. I told her I feel like a cartoon character with the blue ones on.

The girls are "bonarooing" the pod, cleaning the crap out of it. There's going to be an audit soon, like tomorrow. Everything needs to be ship-shape or we will get locked-down. They are doing a great job, over and above. They are even cleaning the underside of the seats, and Scotch-briting the bases of the tables.

Only 6 more days until my sentencing. Wow, I'll be able to see Johnny, Nito and Ray. I won't be able to talk to them, only glance over and smile. I ordered a long sleeve thermal to wear to court and a new T-shirt. I can go either way. I have to see what the thermal looks like first; I know it will be cold in the holding cell. We should be getting our commissary on Thursday this week, two more days. I think I'll go to lunch and see what's up.

They finally fixed the air conditioning in our pod. Now it's more like 70 degrees instead of 65 degrees! I'm still sore all over from shaking for a week, and then I fell over a chair in the beauty shop, landing on my knee and left shoulder. Someday, I won't be in pain all the time.

We just got in from the yard, and its lock-down until dinner. I'm working on my tan for court. I want to look healthy for my sentencing. I can't think of anything to write about right now, so taking a nap seems like a good idea. It's about 100 degrees outside, and it drained my energy some.

I got called out to an attorney visit this morning. Gretta, my lawyer, stopped by to see me before court Monday. She had some inmates to see at CCA, so she visited me. I got to read my character letters for the Judge. My brother Mike, Darrell Hatfield, Fred Roberts, Suzie Dickey and Katie Milhalco wrote letters in my behalf. I thought my sons would write one, but Gretta didn't have them with her. She lost the letter I wrote to the judge when she saw me at CCA. Now I have to write another one and read it to him because I get a chance to say something on my own behalf. Gosh, I hate lying! I have to say that I was totally aware of my trunk being full of pot, when I was really on my way to do my laundry after delivering the 20 pounds from my back seat. What has this world come to? I don't belong in prison at all!

Anyway, enough of my pity-party. I have to be sincere in my statement to the judge and let him know what my future plans are. He needs to know how sorry I am and how embarrassed I have been for pulling such a stupid stunt! Really, so stupid as to haul 204 pounds of weed for no money! I need to get hold of Johnny to see if he has the letter I wrote to the judge somewhere. I thought I sent him my rough draft.

Saturday morning, September 11th. The nightmare I had last night was terrible. I dreamed of threatening to kill myself if they insisted that I do the class that I was unable to get to. If you don't attend, it's a violation of the probation, and you can be sent back to prison.

They like to set us up to fail because we make them money by staying in the system. In the dream, I went out and got a gun. I had been looking forward to living every day until last night. Their stupid words keep ringing through my head and I see their faces talking. The Devil is working hard on me right now. God please help me, only you can.

My bunkie told me that they don't always make you go to classes, just have you call for your color to UA (urinalysis) every day, and visit your probation officer once a month.

The more education I get in prison, the better chance I'll have. I don't want to sit through those classes hearing about drugs and alcohol for 2 hours a night, 3 nights a week, for three months. I don't even think about them now, classes would make sure they were on my mind! Plus, someone would have to take me there. My family would hate me! Now that I know that there is a chance for me to bipass that whole thing, I can forget about the gun. Thank God I'm not suicidal!

Sunday, September 12, 2010. They will be taking me after midnight tonight. My clothes are ready to go. I have my notes on what I will say to the judge. May God be with me. If God is my protector, who could harm me? AMEN.

September 14th. Yesterday was my sentencing. What a trip to hell and back! It all started the night before, at about 10pm. I had fallen asleep at around 7pm because I wanted to get some rest before they came to get me for court. They woke me up during 8pm count;we have to stand up.

I went back to sleep for about an hour when they came to my room and told me I had 20 to 25 minutes to get myself ready. They came back and got me and 4 other girls who were also going. They had us waiting against the wall out in the lobby area. Apparently, someone said we were out there too early, so we had to go back to our cells. I dozed off for about a half hour when they popped the door and hollered over the intercom for me to come back out.

They patted us down and we were escorted to R&D to get strip-searched and cuffed, leg irons too. Joanne, my friend in a wheel chair (the art teacher) was also there. She had court, but with a jury trial. She was acting as her own lawyer. They call her the "evil grandmother" because she can be really mean and nasty. I love her; she loves me too. Anyway, we got black boxes put on with our cuffs It's horrible! They really tear up your wrists and make your arms hurt from holding the same position. They use the boxes whenever they are transporting us

We 5 girls rode in the middle section of the van (two bench seats facing each other). It's all caged in. One guy rode in the back of the van by himself. Joanne had a van all her own because of the wheel chair. They also took 5 boxes of her stuff; she thought she was going home. We didn't get very far when we had to stop at CCA next door, right back where it all started.

We had to get out of the van and we were put in a holding cell, where we got a sack lunch of PBJ, cookies, corn chips and a tiny carton of orange drink. They uncuffed one hand, so we could use the toilet and eat our breakfast. All this took an hour or so, sitting on the cold cement floor. They black boxed us again and we got back in the van. A lot of guys were going to court from CCA, so they rode the big white corrections bus.

The ride to Tucson took about an hour and a half. When we got to the Marshal's (at the courthouse), we took an elevator up to the holding cells. They had 20 foot long metal benches on either side of the cell with a toilet at the end behind a 3 foot wall. They took off our black boxes and uncuffed our right hand again.

They stripped us out before we went to court. When it was my turn, they escorted me to the elevator and put me in a holding cell outside the courtroom. When it was time, the Marshals uncuffed me and took the chains off my waist. They left my leg irons on and walked me into the courtroom.

I sat at the table on the right and the judge was already

there. He was talking with the girls up at the front, the court recorders. My lawyer wasn't there yet; nobody was. After Gretta finally arrived, she asked me if I was prepared to say something to the judge. I told her what I wanted to say, and she said it was fine. The judge then called Gretta and me to step up to the podium.

Oh, I forgot to mention that Gretta told me Keith Barth called and talked to the judge's secretary, just before I came in to the courtroom, on my behalf. The judge said that he was going to give me 30 months until Keith Barth called, so 24 months was his new decision, with three years probation.

Gretta told him about my doing murals in the beauty shop and the staff bathroom, and that I was working the whole time I was locked-up. She also mentioned that I turned myself in on March 25th, which all looked good for me. The judge had several letters that my boys and friends wrote for me.

After the judgment was finished, I turned around and Fred was there with my three sons. Fred called out "Rhonda" and waved his hat. I waved at them all and my lawyer stopped me. They wouldn't even let me look at them. I only got a quick glance before the Marshals stood in front of me, so I couldn't see them! I called Johnny this morning and he said Nito skipped school to go. They went by the ranch and dragged Raymond out of bed, then they all flew to Tucson, going about 80 MPH to make it on time, only to see me for two minutes (the back of me). They got to watch them handcuff me and shuffle me out of there.

I was so bummed about that. I couldn't believe the way they stood in the way so we couldn't see each other at all!

They escorted me back to the holding cell with the other girls, where they gave us a sack lunch, bologna, cookies, corn chips and a totally frozen orange drink. Oh, I forgot to mention, the first sack lunch at CCA I had to share, because Rachel didn't get any PB or J in her bag. (We make our own sandwiches).

The whole experience up to this point was arduous! We were done with court at 10:30am, and had to wait until after 5pm to get a bus ride home. There was no noon bus that day. We all had our leg irons, and belly chains with one hand cuffed to them. If we wanted a drink, we were to get it from the sink.

Those metal benches are terrible; the back is too short to rest your head on. I only ate half of my lunch so I could roll the rest of it up in the bag to use on the back of the bench to rest my head. Every time someone moved, the chains would clang on the bench really loud because of the echo in the room. There were two cameras pointed at us at all times from two directions.

All my muscles were cramping up. I had restless leg syndrome going on, my shoulders were killing me because I couldn't lift my left arm, and I have problems without being cuffed. It was torture to put it lightly. I was thanking God for the strength to endure it.

When it was time to go, we had to be strip-searched again. Ms. Monay, from CCA, was the lady that searched us and put our cuffs back on before we traveled. I always really liked her at CCA and had the utmost respect for the woman. She had just been transferred there to the Marshals in Tucson, so she was just learning to do handcuffs, black boxes and leg irons.

She was already an expert at strip-searching as she has done many times at CCA. Needless to say, we were all cuffed incorrectly! My waist chain was too tight, so I was unable to move my hands at all, and the black box kept the cuffs from being able to swivel. They were cutting into my wrists and I couldn't move my left arm at all. That part was going on all day, not being able to move my arm.

The bus ride was still an hour and a half, then another half hour before they took our cuffs and chains off, discovering we all were cuffed incorrectly! I had tears running down my face when they finally got them off. I could not have been able to hold a pencil in my left hand.

I

It's now Wednesday. My hand is still very weak and my shoulders ache constantly. We arrived at FCC at 8pm (count time). We waited in a room (cage) with a cement floor and no benches for 2 more hours! Sitting on a cold cement floor for 2 hours after the day we had, I was getting a bad headache.

We were dehydrated from no water or any drinks other than the frozen orange drink, in a 23 hour period. I couldn't drink the water out of the disgusting sink at the Marshals, or any other sink in the holding cells! We finally got back to our pods at 9:15pm, I ran for the toilet upstairs. Everyone was waiting to hear what happened, but first things first.

I went to bed at 10pm after telling the girl the good news and how it all went. I was so thankful to be back on my bunk again, it's beyond explaining. The ecstasy of it! I slept like a rock! A bomb could have gone off and I wouldn't have woken up. I still feel achy all over and on the verge of a headache, but I'm recovering nicely.

I can't believe I left out the most important part of the story! While I was waiting in the holding cell outside the courtroom, my right hand was free. At the church service I went to the day before, they said Jesus will take you by the hand and lift you up. I closed my eyes and raised my right hand, as if to hold Jesus's hand. When I opened my eyes, there he was! He was facing me, and grabbed my hand. When I stood up, I was inside of him, and he was all around me, and about 12 feet tall, like a hologram. He was see-through.

The Marshals couldn't see him when they were taking off my cuffs and belly chain. Jesus and I walked into the courtroom together. When we walked through the door, he disappeared, and you know the rest. I drew a picture of my experience. Thank you, God. I will never be the same, and I will always love you. Thank you, thank you, and thank you from the bottom of my heart and with all my soul.

September 18th. We had commissary today. I got a writing pad, $5 in phone time and 3 photo-copy tickets to make copies of the picture I sketched of when Jesus took my hand. I already spent the phone time talking to my ex-husband Dale. Yesterday was his birthday. We had a nice talk about keeping the ranch for his mom and dad. They built that place for their kids and grandkids. Dale is determined to not let his greedy brothers sell it. I told him that love always wins.

I had a dream about the ranch, Dale, Ray and Dale's mom. I think the reason I never got the phone numbers on the "Ranch for Sale" sign before I went to jail is that it's not really for sale. Dale had put his heart and soul into that place and the brothers want to throw him off of it. Anyway, it was nice to hear Dale's voice. He's such a good guy, one of my life's choices that I don't regret. He is still very special to me.

I may only be at this detention center for another week or so, and then sent to either Phoenix Prison Camp or Wilmot. They try to keep you close enough where family can visit.

I think I will continue this in the morning. It was 106 degrees outside at Rec. today, and I'm a little tired... feels like I could sleep good tonight.

Sunday morning. I didn't sleep well at all. That song kept running through my head, "I wish I knew what I know now, when I was younger."

The sun comes through the little window in our cell in the morning, so I was able to do a card for Lynette's friend for her birthday. My glasses fell apart in about 8 pieces. The only way I can do fine lines is in the sunlight, otherwise the lines cross and double. I want God to heal me. I want to wake up one morning and have perfect vision. I need to stop saying, "I can't see without my glasses," and instead start saying that I can see without my glasses, over and over, all the time until it's true.

I'm taking a nap before lunch, thinking of it, anyway. Bryan keeps popping into my head. I often wonder what God's plan is for me, concerning Bryan. I loved him sooo much, and still do. His behavior, on the other hand, makes it impossible. I wish God would touch his heart, so maybe he won't die. What a horrible disability. It makes me sad. I know he loved me too, but where did it go?

Right now I'm sitting in the day room watching a show about ghosts, the paranormal. People used to be committed to mental institutions for seeing ghosts. Now it's cool.

What's funny is we are having bologna sandwiches for dinner.

Well, since I can't photo-copy anything, that means I can mail out Raymond's envelope with my book pages, artwork (Jesus), and the letters I've received.

Now it's 2:30pm and there's no Rec. today. Peace said something happened on the Rec. yard, so it's canceled. I don't know what to do with myself now, because the movie I just watched is starting over again. Someone just put it on SYFY, so I'm going to stay and watch it.

Ms. Peace just walked by and I asked how to spell her name. What's funny, she never asked why. I believe I asked so I could send her a copy of my book when I'm finished writing it. She really is something.

Now we are watching Superman. Not doing anything makes for a long day. I guess we might play cards, but Tina is sleeping.

The showers have been full ever since they canceled Rec. We still have 45 minutes until lock-down, so I may get my shower yet. Now we are watching "Law and Order." Good thing I don't care, the way they keep changing the channel every 15 minutes. The showers have stopped running, maybe this is my window of opportunity... got my shower, and it was nice. Peace was giving out account balances; I already know mine ($204.37). We are supposed to have gotten paid for the weeks we have already been here. I believe it's going on three weeks now.

I called the Public Defender's Office to see if I was in transit yet. The answer was no. I'll keep calling each day. They don't give you the exact time they will roll you up, for security reasons. I'm going to take a nap now.

It's almost lock-down, 8pm. I wrote a letter to Nito, thanking him for being there during my sentencing. I also asked him what he thought about Fred.

Tuesday, September 21st. I have a new job assignment this morning. It's titled "walls and windows." I went to the office to see what it entailed. Ms. Peace and Ms. More were in the hallway talking. I said, "Good morning ladies. I need to know what my job assignment means." Ms. Peace looked it up in the computer. She said it's only inside the pod where the trays and garbage are put, the windows in the door and looking out into the hall. It only took me 10 minutes. I have to do the windows as needed, and the girls are always touching the windows, all day long. It would be OK if I only clean them after each meal and then forget it. Then I need to get a CO to sign my time card every day.

Sitting back at our table, I watched probably 20 girls touching the windows right after I cleaned them. I think the only way that wouldn't happen is if they had my job!

One of my bunkies was cleaning our cell when they flashed the lights for lock-down. It only lasted ten minutes, so she was able to finish mopping. I'm going to just stay up in my bunk and take a nap. All I want to do is get to the federal prison; I hear they treat inmates better.

I got a real nice letter from Fred last night. I even had a dream about him for the first time. It was a good dream; we were hanging out, but closer than friends. The whole idea scares me. I feel stuck in the middle. I never had any closure from any of my previous relationships. The middle of what, I don't know. I don't want to make any decisions about anything concerning the subject.

Last night, there was a medical emergency. The girl wouldn't respond. They lifted her shoulder off the bed three times before she responded. They immediately locked us down. About 10 COs came rushing into the pod with their pepper spray out of the holster. They had formed a half circle, facing out, around the girl, like they had guns drawn. Who were they going to shoot with their huge, hair spray size cans of pepper spray? We were all locked-down, looking through the little windows in our doors. Two COs even cruised both tiers with their pepper spray drawn.

Somebody must have used the wrong code when reporting the medical emergency; they were ready for a riot! If that was the normal protocol, wow! It was the funniest thing I've seen yet! Like I said, who are they planning on spraying? They were the only ones in the day room.

April, the new girl, analyzed my handwriting. She said I was still in love with my ex-husband, Darren. I am disappointed with my father. I finish what I start, I think about things before I do them, I have definite future plans, I am open to a certain point, but I don't really trust people. My overall attitude is positive and confident even though I am really pissed off!

This morning while I was washing the wall by the garbage can, someone stole the two rags I had set by the sink. I hadn't left them there for even a minute. Those are my window rags. If it happens again, I'm going to shake down the girls myself. I definitely made it clear; stealing my rags is not going to fly with me.

Poor Ms. Peace. Every time she comes into the pod, girls follow her around. She tells them to stop following her, but they just keep doing it! She also told them not to ask her about their diets or their account balances; she's not an ATM machine.

These girls tend to crowd around anyone that comes into the pod that's a CO or a supervisor. If I didn't live here, I would never know about group mentality. It blows my mind. Most of the time, I'm amazed! I wonder if they have a clue to what they are doing. They just follow each other around, all acting pretty much the same, except for a few independent types, and maybe the most intelligent of the group. The stronger of the personalities are the group leaders. The soft spoken, shy, insecure ones are the followers. For some reason, I fall somewhere in the middle of the gray area of the whole mess.

Ever since I got sentenced, I have been calling the Public Defender's Office to see if I'm in transit. Every day now. Yesterday, the lady said I have already called, don't call again until next month. That's not fair; I could be in transit and not know it. Oh well, whatever makes them happy.

I have one large envelope to send home my journal when they roll me up. I hope they send me to Phoenix Camp in Black Canyon, outside Phoenix. The camp is for short timers. Nobody would try to escape; that's a 10 year sentence getting caught attempting to escape. They have a lot of educational programs available. I want to take advantage of whatever schooling is provided, not just drug and mental health programs. I am going to fill up my day in any positive way possible, plus get my teeth fixed.

Tina Marie Sinatra, my buddy, third cousin to Frank, went to court today. That means she had peanut butter and jelly for breakfast and bologna for lunch. Hopefully, there's a noon bus, so she could be back sooner. I pray she doesn't suffer like I did, with the black box and all.

Today is commissary. I ordered three photo tickets, a bag of potato chips, phone time and ten stamps. The stamps are for Julia Vasquez, to pay her back for the coffee she gave me.

Cassey just brought my laundry up that was done. I sure wish I knew how to get the wrinkles out of my "reds."

I just got back from Rec. It's overcast today for a change; the wind is blowing nicely. Patty and I talked for a good hour.

She just lost her husband. We were talking about how we never really die, energy does not stop, and it keeps going.

We lose our bodies because they wear out, or we destroy them, or whatever. She knows that Richard is still around her and is happy. He was in a wheelchair. Now she sees him on a beach in her mind, happy. She hears his voice in her head, helping her. I know my son is with me and I don't want to ever let him go, unless God wants me to. My heart still hurts when I think of him choosing death.

Joshua was so loving and wonderful; I will never stop loving him. I still blame myself for not being there for him. As well I should, because I wasn't; now it's too late. He took his own life in 1998, but it seems like only a year or so. I don't know how to leave the past behind. The past is what made my present, and my present is making the future. I don't ever want to forget. My memories are precious gems in my life; I won't let them cease to exist. For you, Joshua, I will carry on, and for Johnny, Raymond and Nito, and their children to follow.

Ms. Peace gave me an envelope of Tink's stuff. I think it should only cost about $5 to mail it to Johnny for her. I'll need to get a release of funds form to cover the postage.

I was standing by the window, when this little Mexican girl was swinging her arms around and hit me in the head. It was an accident, but it freaked her out. She and her friends were putting their hands all over me, apologizing, until I had to say "Stop touching me!" I just went and sat down at our table with my feet up. I don't know what to think or feel today. I'm sort of numb. Maybe it's my defense mechanism kicking in.

Cassey, Tina, Shannon and I have been playing cards every day now for about 3 weeks. We've had a lot of fun; we are all pretty silly. When Tina went to court, we had April sit in on the game, and then Jessica got in on it. Those two girls were one player, out for the kill! They managed to kill the fun. I began getting tired, and didn't feel like playing anymore. I don't mind losing a game at all, but they were way too happy about us losing every hand. I won't play anymore unless it's our regular group.

I really want to get out of here. It's feeling like the longest pajama party in the history of pajama parties. I'm tired of the whole scene. I'm not suffering, by any means. People are good to each other, for the most part, but I'm ready to leave them behind. A girl I'll call "Old Yeller," constantly yelling, got rolled-up three weeks after she was sentenced. I figure, going by that, my turn is soon.

I called Johnny yesterday. He said he's going to give me Lisa's car when I get out of prison. The windows don't work right, but I'm used to that. I sure do love him. I asked him to call my brother, Greg to make sure he was paying my rent. Last I knew he paid it through August. It's only right that he pays my rent because of all the money he lost of my kid's inheritance. It won't be nearly that amount, but the gesture is appropriate. Johnny said he'd handle it for me. He's such a wonderful son. I am so blessed to have such great kids. There are none that could compare. Now I need to focus on my suspended license.

I think I'll write a letter to Keith Barth, thanking him for his input to the judge in my case; what an honorable man. I have total respect and love for Keith. I would like to do a drawing for him, maybe the Blues Brothers. That reminds me that I haven't received my glasses yet from the Acts Ministry. I hope I get them before I leave. If not, I believe I can order them from commissary in prison. They haven't been on the list at either CCA or FCC.

We just got our commissary. Mine was a bag of sour cream and onion chips, three photo tickets and ten stamps. I gave the stamps to Julia for the Folgers she gave me last week. Lynette gave me a bag of BBQ corn chips for the birthday card I made for her friend. She gave me a hug, too. Julia was really happy about the stamps.

So many people don't do what they say. She only met me a couple weeks ago and now she knows I'm honorable. I was told once, that without your word, you are nothing. If your word is no good, you can't be trusted.

Cassey said, "Maybe this whole thing is one big nightmare you are having, so hurry and wake up, so I can go home!" It's time to take a nap until lunch.

The beauty shop is open now, and there's a pretty long list on the wall. I'm on the bottom as usual. These people make lists and post them without any authority. Each line above me has two people on it, like Shannon and Lisa, or Consuelo and Piñata. What's up with that? I want out of here!

I am going to totally enjoy Rec. today. I'm going to talk to Molly and see about getting the photo-shoot I need for my book. I'm also thinking that I should just let my hair grow awhile; screw that list!

I just filled out my commissary sheet for next week. All I ordered was 7 stamps and $3 phone time. The stamps are to mail the last of my stuff to Ray. The phone time is to let my boys know when I'm in transit to prison. Everything else I have left, Cassey can have, which is not much. There are a couple T-shirts, some socks, one soup, some hair gel and miscellaneous crap. I am so ready to go.

Casscy will miss me, and maybe some of the other girls. I'll miss them too, but that's part of this journey. They have all had an influence on me, one way or another. Now that Johnny told me about the car, I'm excited to finish my time and go home. Having a vehicle makes all the difference in whether I make it through probation or not. I can't stop thinking how wonderful my kids are. They are such a blessing to the world. There is no mistake that they are a gift from God, and that grandson of mine is the cutest little guy ever. I'm very excited to see him when I get out.

We just finished lunch. I folded all my whites, got my stuff together for a shower later.

Looks like there's no time for a shower. Good thing I'm not a smelly person.

Later, 7pm, the girls and I are playing Spades. A real stupid Will Ferrell and Ben Stiller movie is on with no sound; its Spanish T.V. day. Tina and Shannon just left for the library, so I thought I'd write a few lines before dinner. I got a shower, a hot one.

Molly is going to do a photo-shoot in the beauty shop after breakfast tomorrow, so I needed to get cleaned up. I loaned Tina my thermal to wear to court yesterday, and she sent it to the laundry today. When she got her bag back, you could tell that someone tried to untie it. They could have stolen my thermal. Cassey probably thinks I quit on her, but the girls aren't back from the library yet. I could go sit with her, but I like my solitude, not her.

Friday morning, almost 8am. We finished breakfast: oatmeal, spice cake, an egg, milk, coffee and juice. We seem to have oatmeal a lot. We were watching the news for a while, and now a SYFY movie. Cassey was saying, "Someone took the food schedule off the wall." I commented, "I like to be surprised." Right then the lights started flashing to lock-down. We're like Pavlov's dog, salivating at the sound of a bell! Anyway, I really need to get out of here; it feels like I'm going crazy.

Everyone wants to discuss stupid shit and then argue about it. I hate it! I hate it! I hate it! I hate it! God, please get me out of here! I don't want to do or say anything that I'll regret. Please give me the strength to keep my mouth shut! Everyone wants to be RIGHT! Only God has the "right" answer. We know nothing at all! When we think we know something, it's proof of our ignorance.

How did Jesus do it? He had such compassion, patience and love, in times of total turmoil. God, help me to be more like him. I want to go home and play with my grandson and my kids. I want to paint beautiful pictures and be thankful every day for fresh air, the freedom to walk down the street, have fires in my fire pit, clean my yard and water my trees.

Maybe when lock-down is over, things will be different. The door popped open just as I finished that sentence. I don't want to go out there right now. I'm feeling overwhelmed and ready to blow! I think I'll take a couple deep breaths, pull up my boot straps, go out there anyway and practice keeping my mouth shut. I want to watch the movie… here goes!

Things seem to be okay for now, I don't feel so insane. We started another game of Spades. They flashed the lights just as Shannon and I had a "wheels" hand. We have to play it out after lock-down.

Cassey is reading and my other bunkie is writing. The silence feels so good. I'm feeling relaxed without Cassey's input. After lock-down, they will be playing one of my favorite movies,"Avatar."

Shannon and I have to go to work today after Ms. Grayson comes on duty. They got some more boxes of rubber tiles for us to put in the shower areas. We have three more pods to do. That's enough work for two days. I am thankful for the distraction from my current dilemma. I would like to be more patient than I am.

Cassey just flushed the toilet twice to wake me up, unbelievable! Drama and more drama. I hope I get to work today.

Well, I didn't get to go to work yet. I didn't go to Mary's School of Christ. I went to Rec. instead, and I'm still pissed off! At Rec., Jessica was a disrespectful, smart ass little bitch! I'm thanking God that Tina grabbed my ankle, because I was going for her. I'm still praying to keep my mouth shut. I don't understand why I want to hurt her so bad. It wouldn't do any good; just get me thrown in the hole, or worse. Basically, she would win, if that's winning! Help me Lord; I need to get out of here. Maybe a nap will help my attitude.

Saturday, 8:30am. I was still sleeping during breakfast. Cassey woke me up as they were lining up. We had frosted flakes, pancakes (mine were blonde) and milk. It was terrible! I drank a cup of what they call coffee (chicory) and I don't feel so good right now.

Molly came in and did a photo-shoot in the beauty shop. We took three pictures of my work in there. I was in the pictures. Molly used her clip to pull my shirt back to show my waist a little; my clothes are so big.

The girls were lining up for church and they were only taking 20 at a time, so I got stuck in the Sally Port (holding area between exits). When I finally got to get in line, they said I couldn't have on a long sleeve shirt, so I had to go back and change it. I'm not going! I'm thinking about taking a shower instead. Cassey is asleep, and that's a blessing. Alone time, yes. I'm pretty achy this morning, so a hot shower is a good idea.

So much for that. The shower was freezing! Back in my cell, Cassey is awake. She was telling me how yellow butterflies mean death in a hospital. Yellow butterflies on a door meant the patient is terminal. She found one this morning in her window area. I told her to stop taking the magic out of it by explaining how it must have gotten there. I told her that God may have put it there, so quit rationalizing. Now she brought up babies, and when they are considered babies in the womb, concerning abortion. I made a comment that they are babies when the egg is fertilized, and she wanted to argue!

This woman brings up controversial issues, only to argue about them. I told her, "No argument from me!" People just keep talking and talking and talking!

I think I'll take a nap. The nap lasted all of ten minutes before Shannon knocked on the door. They wanted us to put some more rubber mats in the shower area of D-Pod. Ms. Grayson found 12 boxes of rubber tiles and it takes just short of 4 boxes to do a pod. She thinks there might be more stashed somewhere. We had to miss Rec. today because of working. I have a funny feeling right now, like Cassey is reading my journal. The silence in here is crazy. Well, if she is reading this, she may not be real happy. I haven't said too many wonderful things about her. That, however, is not my issue. Being sneaky is not cool. Like Mom said "Curiosity killed the cat!"

Sunday morning lock-down. It's not the usual 10:45am lock-down. It's another "been at the pajama party too long again" day. Someone fell in the shower area and actually blamed it on the people that clean the showers. How ridiculous is that? These people don't take any responsibility for their actions. No matter what it is, it's someone else's fault, like, "If it wasn't for so and so, this wouldn't have happened." What a total farce! We own all of our actions, no matter what it is.

I can't believe that the COs fall for that blame shit! Maybe everyone's mentality is below 100 IQ. I believe the condition of mankind is way off the chain, f#cked up! Only God can fix this mess.

Those who see the erroneous group thinking are somewhat helpless, like power in numbers. I really want to get out of here. I realize even the little town I live in is much the same, only not so concentrated. The citizens are more spread out and may be less dangerous. All I can do is maybe control the small area or "bubble" around me. Others keep wanting to invade my safe place. Even those who are struggling to walk with Christ are like I said, struggling. The ways of the world, mankind, are totally polluted with lies and deceit. People think they "know" stuff.

There is the same amount of molecules of matter in the universe as there was in the beginning of creation. They are continually rearranging. How could someone "know" anything? By the time you think you know something, it's already changing. I have a feeling we are in big trouble! Ha, ha, ha!

All day so far, I've listened to complaining, from everyone! They already forgot how bad it could be right now. They already forgot to be thankful for the bed they have to sleep on or the food we have to eat.

It's our turn to listen to English T.V. There's someone out there that loves us. Most of the COs are respectful and kind. We can call out on the telephone and get commissary. We are only in lock-down for a few hours a day, and at night. They do our laundry for us, we get to go outside for an hour and a half a day, we can go to church, the library, the beauty shop and we get paid $1 a day to work simple jobs. We get mail, we can send it and we play cards all the time. We have shower facilities we can use at our leisure.

There are two microwaves, we get two rolls of toilet paper, toothpaste, a toothbrush, a comb, deodorant, a shaver and shampoo every week. The food is good and they give us plenty of it. The COs are there to help us with whatever else we may need. They are willing to answer whatever questions we have, so why is everyone complaining?

I really don't want an answer to that question; it would be more justification and blame. I have already seen the answer as I have described. It's all bullshit. AMEN.

My son Joshua taught me that love is what makes life worth living. I will never forget it. The price was too high.

I went out to watch T.V. for about half an hour. The movie was "Million Dollar Baby" with Clint Eastwood. He trains a girl how to box and she becomes a champion. I don't know how it ended. They flashed the lights before it has over, plus Mary turned the channel to football. She seems to think she controls all the programming of the T.V. It was the same at CCA. Mary's the teacher of the "Purpose Driven Life" class and the "School of Christ. The real reason that I don't attend either class is because she is not very Christ-like.

My Bunkie, Cassey, is sick now. Nobody listened when I told them not to plan on getting sick because somebody sneezed. They had to keep talking about getting sick. They said I was "wrong," and they had no choice but to be sick, and are now blaming each other for getting a cold.

"I'm not sick!" I said out loud, "I'm not getting sick because someone has a cold!" Shannon said "Watch the whole pod get sick!" I told her it wasn't cool to say that! Now she is involving people that aren't even aware of what she has put out there. She doesn't want to believe me about the power of the spoken word! People don't want to be wrong or take responsibility for what comes out of their mouths! Blah, blah, blah.

Patty called me over to the bulletin board because they posted the jobs. All the jobs changed again. Now Lynette and I sweep and mop the pod at 7pm every day. Nothing like diversity. I sure couldn't get bored doing the same of thing around here. It changes all the time. I think I should take a nap before lunch. I want to be rested when I go out to the yard.

It's 7pm. We are locked down early; it must be an emergency. My bunkie is driving me nuts! Her argumentative, bossy and annoying behavior is making me so tired of this place. They just unlocked the door; we have 20 minutes before lock-down. I was playing cards and Cassey just asked me if I was coming back out to play. I said I didn't know. I thought she would give me some flack, but no. She'll probably want to read what I am writing. That makes me not want to play cards with her. I think I need to start hiding my book! God, please get me out of here.

Well, Cassey sent both Tina and Shannon up here to see if I was coming down to play cards. What a pushy bitch! We played one hand and both went over 500, so we all win.

Now the lights are flashing. I think it's because of the girls looking out the window at the guys in the hall. The guys that are here are doing serious time for their serious crimes. These girls keep flirting with them like it's a game. The COs keep telling them to stay away from the window when the guys are in the hall. They don't listen, so we all keep getting locked-down. This is the third time tonight.

I got my eyebrows done for the first time in my life. I don't have my Dad's furry eyebrows anymore, and I feel like a girl now. When I would look in the mirror, I would see my dad. His eyebrows are gross on me. Jessie did a good job on them, using a string. It hurts pretty badly, but I didn't flinch... hardly at all.

Molly said she got Ms. Peace to print the photos, so I should get them soon. I was hoping for tonight. These girls just can't behave! The door just opened for us again. Guess I'll check it out.

Next day. I didn't sleep too good last night. They keep turning the lights on for count. Going back to sleep can be difficult. I dreamed that Marlena looked up my friends in Mexico. She was my old bunkie. She saw the picture of me in Johnny Boy's bar and found out how many people know me there. She was all proud to be my bunkie because my friends there all love me. I really do miss them. Now I can never go back to Mexico because I can't get a passport. They will let you in, but not back out. I couldn't get a passport because of owing child support, and now I'm a felon. It was fun while it lasted.

Tina and Lisa got into it again today. Lisa called for a

CO. All three roommates had to go to the unit manager's office. The result was that they are all in different pods now. Tina moved to D-Pod (the worst), Lisa moved to B-Pod (the best) and Tracy stayed here in G-Pod. Things didn't work out exactly like Tina wanted them to. It looks like over-reacting is not a way to solve problems. The whole thing was about someone stealing. Lisa and Tracy are both thieves, so it didn't go well. Tina didn't believe me about Tracy being the thief, making it look like Lisa was doing it. Lisa was stealing, but not what Tina thought she was. What a mess. So consequently, we got to keep the original thief! Now we lost our Spades player, so we play Rummy now.

After lock-down, I'm going to call to see if I'm in transit yet. Please.... From what the girls are telling me, I'm going to a halfway house after I get out of prison. If I make it through that, I get to go home, under supervision for three more years. Technically, we do "all" the prison time, only not all of it is behind bars. Maybe because the prisons are so full.

I called the number to see if I was in transit. It was answered, but not accepted, probably an answering machine. We had a really big lunch today: spaghetti chicken patty sandwich, green beans, salad and chocolate pudding. Nobody is to take showers right now, because maintenance is here fixing toilets and sinks. Sitting in my cell, I can hear them talking in the cell below me, through the vents. In about an hour or so, we go to rec. I think I'll take a nap until then. When we were going down to lunch, I was praying to get happy. I'm having a tough time with that right now.

Well, I was sitting at our table when everyone started

yelling at me. "The Bubble Lady" wanted me to look up at the bubble. She was up there waving her arms like a crazy lady. She just wanted to say, "Howdy!" She made me laugh. Then we both waved our arms in the air, like crazy people! I love that woman. I met her in visitation when Gretta came to see me. She said, if it was up to her, she'd put all of us in her car and take us home with her. She definitely is an angel.

October 1st, 2010. I'm in transit to prison, no release dates yet! Gotta mail this in case I go today. Thank you God, for everything. Love, Me.

My crime won't be a crime after I serve my sentence. They will just carry on when pot is legalized, after torturing people over it! I guess that's the way people are, easily swayed.

We got locked-down today because of an incident in the Rec. yard. It was the men's Rec. so it was probably a fight. It could have been anything, really, or nothing at all.

I talked to the lady in the bubble about photo-copying my picture of when Jesus appeared to me, and she said I couldn't do it right now. They do photo-copies in the law library. Cassey, my bunkie, is going to take it to the librarian. I gave her the picture and 3 photo-copy tickets so she could do it for me, if she wants to.

Well, the problem must be resolved. They opened the door for us again. I think I'll go out and watch the show some more; it seems to be pretty cool. They decided to "mute" the Spanish T.V. on one day and "mute" the English on the other. There was no compromising otherwise. No matter what we were watching, the Mexicans would turn their volume up so loud we couldn't hear what we were watching. We'd be watching a movie and they would watch music shows, singing, dancing and hollering until we gave up on our movie.

Well, I guess they won't copy my picture. They only copy legal papers. They can't copy Jesus taking my hand. Wow! It looks like I can go ahead and mail it to Raymond.

They really ought to specify on the commissary list so people don't waste their money. I gave my copy tickets to Cassey in case she needed them to do some copy work in her legal search.

This SYFY movie is crazy! A scientist developed a locust that couldn't be killed with pesticides. He was fired and his research locusts were destroyed with a flame thrower. The guy torching them smuggled out a jar full of them. Go figure! Less than a few turned into a world catastrophe. That's just an example of one person's impact on the world. We all need God more than ever now.

We are having baked chicken on the bone. When I was going through my court experience, they were having BBQ chicken for lunch. I missed it. I've been craving it all week. Now I've only an hour more to wait.

I'm not sure this page will ever make it into my book. I'm supposed to get at least 3 stamps from Molly for the Halloween envelopes for her kids. I don't know if Peanut can give any stamps yet for her "Angel of Death" sporting a basketball.

It's October 4th and I am so ready to go. Cassey just came in the room and flopped down on the toilet; our knees are practically touching. I had to move. She does that to me all the time. I'm really tired of having her "kooter" in my face. She never stops talking either. She really spreads it when she wipes too, still talking. I am so sick of it. Talk about uncomfortable! I wish I could leave now.

They have the air blowing into our cell a lot colder, making it tough to hang out in here, and it's always cold in the day room. My neck is stiff along with the rest of my body, and my shoulder still hurts after all these months. I think the left one is out of the socket. I put a "kyte" in to see a doctor over a week ago and no response yet. It may have to wait until I get to prison before I get fixed.

I washed out my worn out sweats for April. They've been through a few girls before me, pretty thread bare. I'm giving my sweat shirt to Cassey, plus whatever is in my property box, a few pairs of socks and some other weird stuff.

I'm just waiting to go to the yard where it's warm. I'll see Molly and Peanut outside, too. When I'm out there it seems to be the only time I feel OK. I don't like being inside in the air-conditioning all the time. I only like it when we come in from outside. Peanut found out where Tink was. They shipped her to Texas. She was hoping to see her "girl," Cloey. Too bad. Tink is bi-sexual. There's almost nobody in here that isn't "gay for the stay!"

It's Tuesday morning. April and I got to watch "Supernatural" this morning because we traded T.V. time with the Mexicans.

I was just listening to Patty telling me how she thinks two "blonde" brains are smarter than 100 Mexican brains. I really get a kick out of Patty. She's Mexican. She's really into Christ and Christ is really into her. She reminds me of my friend "Scooby Doo." They both wear braces and have the same kind of Spanish mannerisms. I love both of them. Patty makes me smile all the time.

There's still an hour before lock-down. I'm bored. I want to go to prison now. Talk about a lesson in patience and tolerance, and a pile of other lessons. I am so ready to go.

Focusing on it probably makes it take longer, so if I can forget about it, then I can go. I do want to stay here for lunch; we're having BBQ chicken. I have been in transit since October 1st. It's now October 5th. Shawnee was in transit about a week before they rolled her up. I know I will go when God wants me to go, and that's all there is.

I've been thinking a lot about when I finally go home. I have to stay somewhere other than my trailer because it's not really livable the way it is. Maybe I'll write Johnny a letter and tell him that I have to move in with him if the ceiling in my bathroom doesn't get replaced. First I'll have to go to a halfway house when I get released. During that time, the counselors will inspect the place I will be living. They need to approve it, or they won't release me.

Since I already lived with Johnny, they may have me go back there, or I could live at Fred's for a while. It would be easier to work on my place from Fred's since it's down the street from my place. I don't know anything right now. Writing this stuff down is filling up the time that I could be wasting.

I told Shannon I would leave her my envelopes with these pages. In case I don't get stamps before I leave, she can mail them to Ray. I told her to collect for me, and keep the stuff along with my extra blanket.

It's Wednesday night, 10pm. I'm still waiting to go to work with Shannon. We're the midnight painting crew. Burrito and Pretty Princess are stripping the cement floors. Shannon and I are touching up the paint they scuff up with the buffer. We also re-painted the phone corral where you sit down.

Someone has started peeling the paint already this morning. I just painted them at 3am. No respect. I imagine it's the same little Mexican girls that are always pushing their way to the front of the line and jumping in front of me when I'm trying to heat up my biscuit. Tonight I guess we'll be painting in C-Pod. We'll be painting white tonight around fire escapes, and God only knows what else. Maybe they will tell me to roll-up before it's over. I've been sleeping all day and I still want to go back to sleep. It's best that I don't so I'm not an idiot at work.

Well, it's October 7th and I'm still here. Last night, Shannon and I went to work again at 10pm. We went to C-Pod and painted cell 105. Shannon, of course, did the rolling. She's not a painter. I know because I am. First of all, we have a 2 inch brush to cut in with and a bigger one that is all stiff. That's why she wants to roll. I'm without my glasses and I'm supposed to cut in with a crappy brush.

We had a blanket for a drop cloth, and she left it folded, put the bucket of paint and the pan on it, so the floor was totally exposed. We had no rag. Ms. Peace got us some towels, bless her heart, I love this woman; she works so hard and does a good job. She definitely earns her pay. Consequently, I had to keep wiping up Shannon's mess.

When I used the roller for a minute to do the short wall around the sink after cutting in, she barked at me, saying she will get confused if I roll too. I told her I would remind her not to do that wall again. No wonder she gets confused; she starts in the middle of the wall. Hey, for 12 cents an hour, I'm not going to sweat it. If we were doing a paying job, where my reputation was at stake, I would have to tell her to stop painting.

Anyway, it turned out OK for a prison paint job. We are only as good as our worst help, my dad used to say. We got back to our cells at 4am.

Thursday morning. I got up for breakfast at 6:30am and went back to bed until 9am. I slept until noon. I helped April do some Tarot cards, the drawings on them. I'm having trouble seeing without my glasses. The fluorescent light really messes with my vision. We're locked-down until dinner, so I'm going to snooze. Maybe they will have me roll-up tonight, please God. Peanut gave me two stamps, so I have the postage to send this letter home to Ray on my way out the door.

It's Friday, October 24th. I'm still here at FCC. I'm not giving up hope that they will call me out today to go to prison, Ever since October 1st, I have been hoping it was today.

Joshua, my deceased son, has been around this last week. He has been showing himself to April and her roommate. His reflection was in the window of her door. He keeps strolling by our cells too. One day, we were playing cards and some papers fell off the seat they were on. We both watched it happen and nobody touched them, and there was no wind.

The reason I believe it was Josh is because of the black dial phone on the television. That's how he lets me know it's him, one of the ways. April said that Joshua's presence answered something she was asking God about, so she told me to thank him. I'm sort of wondering if that's why I'm still here. It's not about me at all. Maybe he has work for Joshua to do, and he hangs around with me. We are a team, God, Josh and me.

I sure would like to move on. I'm in constant pain in my shoulders, and don't sleep well at all. I roll around about 15 times an hour. I sent another "kyte" in to medical; maybe they will answer me this time. I can't lift my arm above my shoulder, and have shooting pain all the way to my left hand. My right arm is also achy. I can't reach without having a shooting pain that almost drops me to my knees.

All I need is some 600 mg ibuprophen and a double mattress. Two inches of foam on a metal bunk is like sleeping on the floor. My hips keep going to sleep too. Every morning, I feel like I have been beaten with a shovel.

They finally got the temperature back up to 72 degrees from the 65 degrees it was in my cell. I had been shaking all day until "yard." When I was outside, it was the only time I quit shaking. I wish God would get me out of here today, unless I'm supposed to suffer toughing it out some more. It's all up to him. I can obviously handle it; most of the girls don't even know I'm suffering. I'll be happy for the least little bit of comfort. Well, the girls are waiting for me to play cards, so I'm going to go now.

I don't like to complain, but I feel I should document what is going on with me. The COs are good to me, and they all know me by name, for some reason. I guess I've made a good impression on the staff here. That's a good feeling. I'm thankful for them, and how they made me feel like myself. Signing off for now....

So much for playing cards; I've been replaced by two people. That's a sign that it's time for me to be moving on. I guess I'll rest, so they don't feel bad about taking my spot at the table. I don't really want to play cards today. I've been playing about every waking moment since we moved here, except when I get an occasional job. By getting a job, I mean painting the beauty shop, putting rubber mats together in the shower areas, painting a closet, a cell or all the billboards. For the most part, I get $7 a week to play cards.

Patty just came to my room, needing to talk to me. Her husband that died keeps talking to her. He told her that her son, Jerry, was in the U.S. She called her mother in Mexico, who tried to cover it up, but her sister told her the truth. I guess he's in Las Vegas. She talks to me because I believe her. Patty is not a liar and she loved her husband. His name is Richard, and he is guiding Patty through God. She prays to God and Richard comes to her in dreams. He writes things and calls her on the phone in them. He told her to pack her stuff because she is rolling out in 3 days, and this was a couple days ago. I told her she'd better start packing. I told her she ought to write a book about her life and all the messages from above and wherever, and to write about all the things she goes through, what she really thinks, people she meets etc. It helps to see where we are with ourselves.

I'm hoping the message to start packing was for me too, that the issue of waiting to roll-up is mine also. Patty has been sentenced for a long time.

Commissary came today. I didn't order anything. Cassey made me a cup of Folgers. We don't have any creamer or sugar, but it tastes good anyway. The so called coffee they serve here is terrible. It tastes like boiled gym socks with a hint of chicory. "Quick" gave me a 600mg ibuprophen, and Cassey gave me a 3.75mg Flexural, so this coffee ought to kick it in. Maybe I'll be able to sleep good during lock-down. Thank God for the drugs today. AMEN.

Becca just came to the door and brought me a pair of glasses from "Tina Marie Sinatra," third cousin of Frank. The power of them is so low that it changes nothing, really. I do totally appreciate the thought, though. She told Becca to tell me that she loves me and misses me since they moved her out of our pod. I love her, too.

I finally got my stamps from Molly. Tracy had them. She's a thief and she used one of them. There were only three to start with. She would have kept them all if Cassey hadn't mentioned them. Tracy said, "Oh, I'm glad you reminded me. I completely forgot." She's such a bad liar, and it's surprising to me because she's a Native. They are honorable, and she isn't. She's Navaho, and so was another girl that ripped me off. Yanaba is a Navaho. She's a thief, and a liar too. I hope there is no connection to the Navaho Nation. I'm glad I'm part Apache, just in case.

I'm feeling pretty good right now. My shoulders aren't

aching and I'm not cold now. Cassey gave me a pen to write with instead of my 1 inch pencil, but now she keeps talking so I may not get anything written, or any rest either.

It's October 18th. I'm still here freezing again and suffering with my shoulders. My right one seems to be healing, but my left is not much better. I just finished writing a kyte for the temperature to be fixed to some sort of comfort zone.

I don't understand why we have to suffer more than we already do. Maybe God wants me to thank him for suffering. Maybe I need to appreciate being able to feel pain and discomfort. Darrell, a quadriplegic, can't feel anything much, and wishes he could. Maybe they will roll me out this week and I can start over in a new place. Who knows, maybe this place is the best and I just don t know it yet.

I'm thankful that I'm right handed, so I can still work. Ms. Peace had me painting a metal door and their podium in the middle of the pods, out in the hall. I did a real nice job, no mess. Shannon asked to help me. I told her no. She's a sloppy painter and doesn't clean up after herself when she makes a mess. When she helps, I'm like her slave, or there are problems. She's just not a painter and I refuse to get into that discussion with her again. I'll just go on letting her think she's good at it. I'm so ready to go, it's not funny,

I called Nito on his birthday, October 15th, with 25 cents left on my phone time. That gives me 1 minute. He's 17 years old now, my baby. Anyway, he didn't answer, so I left a message on his answering machine so he knows I called. I'm going to save the 25 cents to call

Johnny when they roll me up. No sense in buying anything from commissary when I'm leaving soon. Every week that I stay here it's $7 more towards my radio and sweat pants. Winter is coming and I'm cold all the time. I'm still waiting for medical to call me. I told Ms. More that I can't stand it anymore. I roll over 20 times an hour, all night long, and I hurt all the time.

Good morning. Thank you, God, for allowing me to wake up and leave the night behind me. Thank you for my two blankets and my warm breath to keep me warm enough to make it until morning. Someday this will all be a memory, one that I will not forget. It's October 21st. Two girls rolled-up today, so there's hope for me. I have been in transit for 3 weeks tomorrow. I want to go to prison so I can buy a sweat suit. We can't take anything with us, so it would be stupid to buy one now. I also want to buy a radio and some magnifying glasses, so I can do artwork again. I'm pretty lost right now without being able to read or get warm.

Quick just sat down with Cassey and me. She compared getting along in here to a chicken coop. Like roosters scratch around and ruffle their feathers until everyone gets comfortable with each other, or not.

I've put in my 3rd kyte about the temperature. If I don't get some kind of relief, I'm going to file a grievance. The cells are supposed to be 72 degrees, not 65. Maybe I'm supposed to suffer the cold to prepare me for worse conditions. Maybe I should be more thankful for the crash course. Thank you.

I'm sure that I know absolutely nothing about anything.

I have been dreaming of home a lot, my trailer. I had an idea to use up all the bags of laundry that were in my trunk. Since the insulation in my bathroom ceiling needs to be removed, I need to replace it with something. What about washing all those clothes, cutting them into strips, fluffing them in a dryer and wrapping them in plastic to fit between the beams in the ceiling? Coating my roof is first on my list. I can't have a leaky roof with a new ceiling.

I'm flattered they gave me pads with my hygiene. I haven't had a period in 10 years. Ms. Peace asked me how I was doing, then she said she had something for me. She said she would bring it to me later. I wonder what it is.

The Mexicans just gave us 30 minutes of T.V. with sound because we let them have time on our day. We're watching "The Walking Dead." Now that it's close to Halloween, there are a lot of scary movies on the boob.

Well, Ms. Peace gave me a surprise; Shannon brought it to me. Funny how Cassey was saying that our pod wasn't clean; that's why we don't get soda or popcorn. Right then, Shannon walked by and gave me 2 popcorns and a root beer soda. Cassey is butt-hurt about it too. She didn't like it when I told her I didn't want to talk about it. Nothing is what it seems to be, so talking about how things are, and why they are, is stupid. We know nothing at all. Right now she is munching away on her BBQ chips like a mad woman!

News Flash: A 70 year old woman was brought in today. She was arrested for having a kilo of cocaine taped to her leg. Wow! She's probably going to spend the rest of her life locked-up. Granny is doing crime now.

Cassey is yelling at me about something she was mad about. Her cousin did a crime with Granny in the car, and she got 4 years probation. I asked if he ran and left her there, and she yelled at me, saying he was robbing a house and left her outside when the cops came. I didn't even want to talk to her today.

I'm tired of being set up so she can be nasty to me one minute, and fake being nice to me the next. I really want out of here! F#ck her and her crap! I try to be nice, but she's a bitch! She has to be right! What the f#ck is that? Now she's saying, in her sweet voice, "Oh, it's clearing up outside, so you girls can go outside and play." Cassey never goes out. F#ck her. I'm not falling for it anymore.

It's Friday, October 22nd. It's gotten even more eventful. Cassey got called out last night at 10:30pm, to go to court this morning. Her court is at 9am in Phoenix. She got her hair straightened, some new reds that fit her and a new T-shirt. I never saw her look so good. She went to sign her guilty plea.

Before lock-down last night, April went off on me. She was yelling that I complain more than anyone she ever met and I'm the reason she stays in her room. I told her to go f#ck herself. She told me to take my miserable self and go to my room. I told her I'm not miserable unless I'm in my cold ass cell with my achy body. It has nothing to do with her. She insisted that I was the reason for her misery, as she runs around reading a Bible 24-7. I told her I didn't mind if she wants it to be my fault. I'll claim it, if that is what needs to be done.

I have 3 pieces of paper left, and I am not buying another pad. My pencil is less than 1 inch long; I can barely sharpen it. This place has been filling up with girls lately and nobody is leaving. They have to make a prison run soon. I don't know why it takes so long, maybe a prison overcrowding issue. They arrested me; I didn't ask them to. Anyway, God has a plan for me, regardless of what I think.

Back to April blaming me for staying in her cell. She has been in her cell all day except for breakfast. Quick sat at our table since Cassey isn't here today. I was telling her about seeing Jesus when I went to court. When I described the experience, that's when April got up and went to her room, and has been there ever since.

She just came down and they flashed the lights to lock-down, so I guess she'll be in there until lunch. It's raining outside today, so I'll probably skip yard. Oh yeah, they finally fixed the temperature in the cells. I was able to sleep without freezing. I'm only a little bit achy in my arms now. What a difference it makes not to be tense all night. Well, I hope Cassey gets back on an early bus, and doesn't have to suffer the all-day affair. She stopped yelling at me and was decent last night. I guess she was nervous about court, and I was the whipping post. I sure wish they would tell me to "roll-up, Rhonda Brew."

I stayed in from Rec. today. I thought changing things up a bit would be good for me. Expecting a different result out of the same action is what I've been doing. The only thing I can count on is that each day counts as time served. On Monday, the 25th, I will have served 7 months of my 24 months. That leaves only 17 months. Hopefully I'll have enough prison time to get my teeth fixed. Also enough time to do a few programs and work to pay off my fine of 100 dollars. I want to leave prison with money in my hand to pay for my suspended license. If I can drive, it will eliminate problems with probation obligations. Actually, I only have to do 85% of 24 months, so on Monday I'll have 13 ½ months to do yet. That puts my release date around November of 2011. That means I'll be out of prison by Christmas of next year. I believe that will be my focus instead of rolling-out.

It's a let-down to look forward to something that's not happening. It feels much better now that I've figured that out. Well, the girls are back from recess, so I'm going to sign off and take a nap. Lock-down is in 5 minutes.

April is acting like she never said anything to me. I'm letting her off the hook by letting it go. "Constantine" is on tomorrow, one of my favorites. We traded T.V. time today, so we could watch it.

This is my last piece of lined paper. In fact, it's my last' piece of paper, period.

Well, its Saturday morning. Cassey is definitely back! She never stops talking. I'm doing my best not to really notice. That's not an easy skill to acquire. We're locked-down early so they should be popping the door soon, please. Usually it's for a medical emergency or they are moving prisoners, or who knows what. Mary gave me the order number for magnifying glasses, so I ordered a pair of them and two stamps. If I'm here next Wednesday, I should get them. I'm hoping my vision is getting better from not wearing glasses for so long.

I didn't go out to the yard today again. I think I'm getting depressed. I used to look forward to going outside. I know it has to do with April. She runs around with her Bible, manipulating people. I think she's evil. Anyway, I want nothing to do with her.

It's Sunday. Lock-down before lunch. For the last hour or so, I was drawing a picture of St. Jude for someone. She was so happy, and I did it without my glasses. I can't use that as an excuse any more. I did another buffed-out Einstein for Ms. Martinez. She loved that picture. We used it as a sign in the window, meaning someone is taking a crap. Well, I drew it in pencil for her, so she could frame it. The original picture is pretty tore up. The tattoo on his arm says $E=Mc^2$. I did both drawings without my glasses, so my eyesight is improving a lot. Shannon and Burrito want a sexy woman picture for their bachelor pad. I don't think that's high on my list right now. Nap time...

Monday morning. It's the 25th of October. Today it's 7 months that I've done. Also, it's been 4 weeks since I've been in transit. I drew an Einstein for some pills for my pain; she loves it. Now I have 3 IBUs so I can sleep. The girls were talking about shooting drugs at our table, so I came back to my room. Not a good subject for me. I'm thinking this is my week. I hope God does.

We just got locked-down and it's time for yard. Maybe there's no Rec. today; looks like it's going to rain. My aches went away now, so maybe I can take another nap. I didn't sleep at all last night, except about an hour. I dreamed I was dying and told April to jump off this cliff that was covered with cactus.

It's Tuesday. I'm still here. I can take the reading glasses I ordered with me, if they have them. The girls were telling me if I didn't get shipped out before Thanksgiving, I won't be going until after New Year's. There's no movement over the holidays. I love you, Raymond.

7.

We're Really Moving!

Finally! They rolled me up at about 2am. When the door opened, and the CO asked if I was Brew, I thought I was dreaming. When I realized what was going on, I told her I loved her! It was Quick, Tracy, Olivia and I. Oh, and Patty Padilla, too. They kept us in D-Pod until about 5am, and then loaded us on a bus, men first. There were only 5 of us women in the front of the bus. We were taken to Williams Airport, where we parked to wait for the DC-7 plane that hadn't arrived yet. They gave us sack lunches that we had to eat in 5 minutes, with shackles on.

After they picked up the trash from lunch, they called Tracy, Olivia and me to get off the bus. They took our shackles, belly chains and leg irons off and then loaded us into a van with nice padded seats and air-conditioning. We taxied over to where the prison plane had landed and waited for two more people to get off the plane. After they were in the van with us, we headed for Phoenix. Our destination was Phoenix Prison Camp.

I've been sort of in shock since I've been here. We got our new ID, filled out papers, got a TB test, a whole set of clothes, a fluffy pillow, a fluffy towel, a bag of hygiene stuff, a nice blanket, two sheets and 1 pillow case. They were so totally nice. There are no locked doors around here and no razor wire. There's not even a fence. There are no locked doors in our housing situation either. We have shower stalls and 4 toilet stalls, all with doors, on each level.

There's a T.V. room, water fountains, volleyball court, pool table, exercise equipment, foosball table, a track, picnic tables and beautiful landscaping. There's a cafeteria style lunchroom with great food, a beauty salon, where you can do your own hair, arts and crafts classes and everyone gets a job, eventually. They only pay 12 cents an hour except the first month; you get maintenance pay of $5.25 for the month.

We got a different color of clothes. We have a light green T-shirt, dark green pants and steel-toed boots, like the ones I have at home. I keep forgetting that I'm in prison.

I found a few friends here. Choppa, my favorite person, Kera, my first bunkie at CCA, Samantha, also a total favorite, Cat and Pricilla. Yoli is even here. They all arrived before me.

We can walk anywhere we want to, anytime, except we have to be standing by our bunk with our ID at 4pm. I'm in total heaven. God has blessed me way beyond anything I could have dreamed up. I feel like I'm on a college campus. They will be giving me a physical and checking my teeth on Thursday, so I'll be getting the IBUs I need for my shoulders and also my teeth fixed.

They have a nice library, so I checked out a Stephen King novel, "The Dead Zone." It's a pretty good story so far. The main character is John Smith, my dad's name. I think I'll go out and read some more before dinner. Oh yeah, the first night I was here, they had a jazz entertainer putting on a really good show. It got pretty wild; what a fun time! Not bad for my first night.

It's Monday. I slept good last night, I hustled an ibuprophen (400mg), so I could sleep. Actually, I got so relaxed that I didn't feel like sleeping. We have biscuits and gravy this morning with cereal. After breakfast, I checked in to see if I had a work assignment. About 7 of us had to weed behind the Hopi Unit. I held the bag. The guy, Mr. Jackson, likes my name, Brew. He just waved at me as he walked by the T.V. room window.

I was in the chow line with the art teacher and we talked about drawing classes. She said maybe I could teach her something. I told her we will learn from each other. Taya said she only started doing watercolors a few months ago. I told her she can teach me what she's learned so far. She told me she was a better teacher than she was an artist.

I also asked her for permission to copy a horse picture that she has. She told me sure; she copied it from a picture, too.

I just got the hook-up of the century! I get to paint the basketball court and re-paint the lines. Also I may be painting a mural or two. I've only been here since Thursday (4 days). I'm pretty happy.

Wow, I just got hooked up with pens, pencils, markers, glue, tape and a writing pad. The girls just gave the stuff to me. Earlier, Lydia saw me drawing outside and asked if I had a minute. She took me to meet the Rec. director, Ms. Hawthorne. That's when she said she wanted me to do the basketball court and such. This could be the break I need.

Samantha asked if I was going to play pool after mail-call yes, I said. Patty, Choppa, Samantha and I have been playing pool every night. It's good for my physical therapy for my shoulders and my arms. I'm getting better mobility and less pain. My physical is on Thursday, so I should get my IBUs, and that will be perfect. I don't know why, but this girl keeps bugging me, like I'm supposed to like her.

Tuesday morning, 7am. I just checked in with the officer to see about a work assignment. He said he'd call me if anything came up. My laundry is already turned in. I had to put my bras in a pillow case, but I left it in my locker, so I had to walk back to get it. It's like a college campus around here. When I was grabbing my pillow off the bunk, someone had put a little bag of laundry soap and some dryer sheets underneath it. I bet it was Rosebud; she's always putting surprises for me there. I knew Rosebud on the outs. We drank a beer together at my umbrella table the last and the first time I met her.

The cleaning girl just kicked me out of the T.V. room, so I'm thinking of going to the art room, because it's too windy out here. Another beautiful day; I can wander around anywhere, unless they page me or its 4pm count time. It doesn't feel like prison. The detention centers were more of a prison; this camp is like freedom.

I just got back from lunch and I am so full. They feed us so much. I'm putting on weight, so much that I am starting to get a little concerned. My butt and legs keep getting bigger, not to mention my mid-section.

On the way to check in to see if they had a job for me, I picked up my laundry that I dropped off this morning. The girl in there is phenomenal! She knew exactly where my bag was, and there were huge stacks of them. Amazing.

I got my hair cut today; Athena was the hairdresser's name. She said she had been doing hair for about 12 years or so. She did a nice job. She shaped it up and trimmed the ends a little.

I finished a drawing of five kids for Aaron to send to her mom. They are all her grand kids. She liked it. Looks like I won't have to do without too much around here, with all the drawings I'm doing. I don't really charge people; they tend to gift me.

I have a top bunk right now in the hallway, but the girl that had the bunk below me went home today and her bunk is empty. I'm going to Open House at 3pm and see if I can get her bunk. It's 1:30 pm right now, so maybe I'll start another drawing. I've done a total of three drawings since I've been here. Later... make that four drawings. I did a picture of a little boy named Carlos. Child Protection took him away from his parents. I did it for Paula.

I went to Open House, and their answer to my request was that I needed a doctor to recommend it, and I need to talk to a counselor on Sunday before 8am.

After a 3 hour nap, I finally got rid of a headache. So far, aspirin and ibuprophen seem to be easy to come by, so I know I'll make it through.

We're watching "Sons of Anarchy" in the T.V. room. This girl "Duly" asked me what my name was. I told her Rhonda, but they call me Brew. She was told to look me up to see if I would like to paint some back-drops for the holidays. I told her I'd love to. She has some that need to be re-done and probably some new ones to make. Duly said she'd get with me this weekend.

While watching T.V., I finished another picture for

Aaron. It doesn't take me long at all to do a portrait. I don't think it even took me an hour; I'm getting real good at it. I still have another picture of a little boy, but I guess I'll do it tomorrow. It's almost 9pm and we'll be going to bed soon...goodnight.

Wednesday morning, 6am. I just got back from turning in my "greens" (laundry) after breakfast, which was at 5:30am. The girls around here are pretty cool so far. Anyway, I'm enjoying my day and the sun hasn't even come up yet. There are about 20 minutes before I can check in, so I'm starting another portrait of a young boy for Michele. She gave me a nice pair of shorts yesterday. The day before, she's the one that gave me a bunch of pens, pencils and plain white paper. She also gave me some aspirin for my headache yesterday. Michele said she was leaving in a week, so I need to do her drawing right away. I'm not going to charge her anything since she has given me plenty from the goodness of her heart.

It's nice here in the T.V. room in the morning watching the news. Morning is my best time.

Well, I checked in and now I'm back in the T.V. room drawing.

Lunch was really good today. We had hamburgers and fries, with salad. Awesome. Check-in time is noon, so I went down there after lunch. The guy in the window said he liked my name; I told him that I did too. There wasn't anything that he needed so I'm back watching a show about cocaine.

I got hold of a commissary list so I could decide what I wanted (for two drawings). My choice is a long sleeve thermal. It's starting to get cold now, so I think that would be a good thing to have. I get cold so easily. I think I might go read my book in the sun for a while; it's so beautiful out here. I'm on page 125 of the "Dead Zone." Looks like I'd better go in the unit where it's cooler. It must be 95 degrees out here.

Later... 7pm. I left early from a special deal, with 3 ex-inmates talking about re-entering the community. It was pretty good, but kind of an overkill.

I ordered some stamps, envelopes and hair gel, I think. I kept changing my mind. Whatever I asked for will be something I can use. I'm pretty bored right now; maybe going to bed would be a good idea. I have to be at the dental office by 7:30 am. They are checking to see if I need dental work, which I have plenty of. Oh joy, oh joy, yippee, yahoo! Now that I'm thinking about it, I'm going to bed.

Thursday morning, November 4th, 6:45am. I'm going to have to start eating between meals, with all the apples and sweet rolls I get from the breakfast tray. I can't let it go bad if I'm going to take it. When I was lying in my bunk last night, I could feel how my legs and butt are getting bigger. Obviously, I'm getting concerned. Right now I'd better go brush my teeth. My dental appointment is in half an hour. The time has arrived when I get to see the dentist. How long I've been waiting!

This is great watching the news; they're discussing legalizing marijuana. They just found another tunnel between the Mexico and California border. They found 30 tons of pot. I'm sure they will sell it back to us retail when it's legal, or use it to bust people until then. Thanks to all of us pot smugglers, they will have a good supply to start with when it's legalized. Somehow, it all seems so crooked. The cops and other authorities are all such crooks. If I were a Mexican, they probably would have taken the pot and told me to run. They did that sh#t over and over again before they stopped me. The Mexicans that they let go have no proof of what happened to the pot. So they are killed, or worse, by the big bosses.

I just got back from the dental/medical exam. I need to go to "pill-call" tonight and get ibuprophen for the pain in my shoulders. I also need to go to "sick-call" and sign up to get my teeth cleaned and maybe pull my broken one. They were real nice over there; the dentist liked hearing my story. I really do like this place.

Right now I'm sitting on a park type bench in front of my unit, enjoying the sunshine and the beautiful landscape. The doctor was going to set me up with an appointment to see an optometrist for my vision. I think I'll read my book until time for lunch.

Next day...Friday, November 5th. I did the dumbest thing today, first thing. I mailed an 8 page letter, including visiting forms and a map to Johnny, but forgot to put his address sticker on it. I already put it in the mail box. They said I could retrieve it at Open House. Also I mailed a "cop out" (kyte) request form to get my teeth cleaned.

The kitchen manager, Mr. Kimball, also signed a "cop out" asking for me to work in the kitchen. He told me to give it to my counselor, who won't be back until Sunday. It looks like I'm going to work in the kitchen. I'm going to be cleaning the bathroom stalls in our unit, starting in the morning at 8am. There are only 4 of them, but I have to clean the tile walls from ceiling to floor, and polish all the chrome, besides cleaning the toilet. I'm sure I will be doing more than that, because I'm a good worker, happy to do my part.

The girl who's giving me the thermal is going to leave it somewhere so I can get it myself. Its big trouble to get caught buying or selling anything. Well, I guess it's back to my book until check-in time.

Later... we're watching "The Day the Earth Stood Still." I missed the end because I went to "short line" (early dinner). I acquired another photo drawing order in my wandering around. Now we are watching funny videos.

Monday...I'm the first one in the T.V. Room. Joyce Meyers is on. Awesome. She's preaching about blessing others, and not taking advantage of them. Woe to him who builds his house on self-righteousness.

Speak of the Devil. She just walked out of the T. V. room. This one girl just rubs me the wrong way. She constantly asks me questions that she knows the answer to, like "Oh, is that where you are sitting?" Come on. Joyce tells me to have mercy, especially for those who don't deserve it. AMEN. God, help me with that, please.

I already scrubbed the walls in the toilet stalls. Come to find out, we were only supposed to wipe them down. That was blatant. The inmate in charge took advantage of us, using her authority. I have her number now. I have another girl across from me yelling about people showing no respect, that she is sleeping and has a headache. I think she's going to have to get over it. There's no way to keep 75 girls quiet in their own unit; its 10am. I'm sorry about her luck, but her life could be way worse. She could be where I just was!

Looks like Tina Marie Sinatra and Angela from FCC are here. I saw Tina last night when I was in the bleachers watching a volleyball game. She came walking back there and saw me. She came running, "Rhonda!" I got the big hug and the "I miss you," and all that. I'm happy she made it here, or when anyone makes it here. It's the nicest place.

I'm sitting outside in my shorts, T-shirt and boots. No stress. My book that I'm reading is sitting here. I have 3 photos that I can start drawings of, so I'm all kinds of happy. Two of the drawings I'm not charging for. One girl is indigent, and I just want to do it for her.

I finished another one for someone else, Cheryl, an old woman. I drew a picture of her daughter. She came to visit her today, and she had to go back out to her car and find something acceptable to wear in the visiting room. Her daughter was wearing shorts. She found a pair of her son's pants, but they were too big for her. When she was getting something out of the vending machine, her pants fell down to her knees. The visit was cut short because her daughter was too embarrassed to stay. I think she'll be back tomorrow, only dressed properly.

Cheryl doesn't have any money, so I can't charge her for the picture. I was happy to do it for her. Now I'm going to start another one. I have about 4 hours before I go to bed.

I almost got in trouble this afternoon. I went to short line to eat. I was supposed to go to the visiting room to set up chairs at 3pm on Saturday and Sunday. I had completely forgotten. The lady didn't write me up, but she said be careful tomorrow. Don't be late; you'll get special duty!

Sunday, November 7th, 7am. Paula, Cheryl and I are watching the news. The first issue was how registered sex offenders are becoming homeless because nobody will rent to them.

Lisa walks in here with no bra under her T-shirt, walks over to Paula, grabs her sleeve and says, "Oh, are these the long sleeve thermals?" She is very....

I just ran out of ink, so I won't finish what I was going to say. I need to watch my mouth or things will keep continuing to happen. I will curse myself if I judge people. They will keep doing the same behavior if I support it by saying and thinking that's the way they are. The written word is also powerful, maybe even more so. I don't know, but I will try to remember not to write what I don't want to happen.

I think I'll go comb my hair and go to breakfast. The girls are lining up right now. Oh, they're going in. Bye. Coffee!

I got all the walls in the stalls wiped down before anybody could say, "Hey!" Nobody is going to fool me today, not like yesterday, anyway. I just gave Lisa her drawing; she loves it. In the picture, she's hugging her little boy and they have their cheeks smooched together. It's a great picture.

After I read awhile, I'll start the second one for Lisa, of her and her guy. I know she appreciates them so I am more than happy to do them for her.

I just met a girl who works with UNICOR, which does work for outside companies. Her name is Veronica. Another girl was doing her hair at the umbrella table outside. She's going to have a visit from her family and her grand kids. We talked a long time. She knows Patagonia pretty well. She's very interesting and very talented. She also crochets Bugs Bunnies and other characters, along with blankets and whatever else you can dream up. Very nice work.

I played cards today with Donna, Jolissa and Debbie. Jolissa was on some antibiotic and they didn't tell her to stay out of the sun. She burned and blistered. It was terrible. Donna weighs 300 pounds and the girls make fun of her when she works out or walks, so she quit doing it. Debbie is a real nice old girl.

I wish my husband, Darren, would come home to me when I get out. That would make doing the right thing so worth it. I would never even ask why he never came home. I still love him with all my heart and soul. God, please hear me. It's been a lot of years now; I don't know if he even thinks about me. He may be married to someone else, for all I know. Wishful thinking on my part. I'm going to get back to my artwork and reading my book.

Monday, November 8th, 10am. I went down to the Rec. director's office. She wasn't there yet. Lydia saw me and asked if I had been approached yet about the Christmas backdrops. She's the one that threw my name in the hat for that job. She said she was going to look for some photos that show me what they had before, which really doesn't help me out too much.

Ms. Hawthorne called me down to her Rec. office and gave me a pile of sheets and a bucket of paint, and also two brushes and a work bucket. We rigged up a clothesline behind the exercise equipment, out in the dirt area. I hung the sheets over the line to paint them that way. I didn't have to worry about a drop cloth. My back hurts a little, but I'll be fine in the morning. I have to double coat them, so I'm halfway there. Actually, I'm over half way. She gave me 7 sheets, so I have my work cut out for me. It takes an hour to do one.

The girls are gathering by the lunch room getting ready for mail-call. Hopefully, I'll get the letter back that I mailed to Johnny.

The meatloaf tonight was real good. I ate my whole tray of food; I usually have something left on the tray.

Wow. Michele gave me some candy that she and Samantha made. Really good!

They called mail-call and she had Johnny's letter, so I went and got a label from my locker and mailed it again.

It's starting to get a good chill in the air the closer it gets to Thanksgiving. I thought it was going to rain, but it changed its mind. The sunsets are so beautiful here, too. There's a lot of cactus with the sun going down behind them. With all the colors, it's awesome. I'm ready for bed; my boots are off.

Tuesday morning, 6:15am. We already ate breakfast and I fixed a photo drawing where I made the girl look too old. My laundry is loaded up already, so I can drop it off on my way to check in. This morning I'm going to tell the dude in the window that I have a job and I'm not available to do the orderly job now.

I got my toe nail clippers, pen and two manila envelopes, so now I have someplace to keep my book. I must have sent Johnny pages 1-4 of the book, because I can't find them. I need to tell him to give them to Ray or send them back to me. Those are the first days of prison, and what it was like to roll-up. At 6:30am, I'll be able to go to the laundry room and check-in.

Long day. Wednesday, November 11th, 2010. Today was orientation for all A&O (new girls). It started at 7am and lasted until 2pm. I turned in my greens on my way there. Now it's after 5pm and I'm just folding them. They brought in the head of each department in this place. I signed up for computer classes and just got the word that I have a job in the kitchen that probably won't start until Monday.

A Native girl across from my bunk asked if I could do her a favor for their Pow-Wow in two weeks. Little favor? She wants a painting of an Indian Princess in a lightning storm, in black and white, on a full sized bed sheet. It's probably the greatest thing

I've taken on in my entire career! I told her I'd use one of the sheets I coated for the back-drops for the photo department. She could trade her sheet for a coated one. I'll coat it later when I need it.

Anyway, I'm pretty busy. I like it. Starting Monday, I'll be making 12 cents an hour.

Yesterday, it made me laugh when I was painting 3 sheets in the wind. That saying has a whole new meaning now.

Thursday, Veterans Day. I didn't realize we could sleep in this morning. I got up at 5:25am. Tilly was in the bathroom when I walked by. She told me I couldn't walk around in my socks because of scorpions. They could give me a "shot" for that. I think it's time to read my handbook before I wind up in Durango for something stupid, like not wearing my flip flops.

One lady, Dianne, went to jail for 30 days for wearing pink underwear back from a furlough with her husband. Joe Arapaio's jail is nothing nice. Like the lieutenant here said, "Your very worst day here is better than your best day there!"

I imagine they will be calling me anytime to go to work in the kitchen. I need to get with Ms. Hawthorne and arrange to use the room next to her office to do the artwork on the back-drops. That room is not being used right now, so I can use the floor. I'm going to schedule the drops between working hours and days off. Now is the time to finish preparing my canvases. I sound like an artist.

I just had a moment of reflection. When my son, Josh, left home he stopped me in the little hallway of our trailer and said "Mom, I'm gonna leave now. It's time to paint my canvas." He gave me a big hug and told me he loved me. I can still feel him hugging me when I close my eyes.

He went on to skateboard to Washington state from Tucson to be with his girlfriend. He met her after he graduated and went to visit his dad in Seattle. She had eaten a bunch of pills to kill herself and went into a coma. Josh heard that she wasn't going to come out of it, so he went back to his apartment that he shared with two other guys. He went into his roommate's closet and got his grandfather's 12 gauge shotgun. After writing lyrics to explain his pain, he went into the bathroom, put the gun in his mouth and blew his head off. They had to take the door off the hinges to get it open.

I got a phone call Saturday morning, May 16th, 1998, at 10:30am. It was Joshua's dad, Larry Hooley. He said "Rhonda, I didn't know Josh was up here!" I said, "Oh, you've seen him? I thought he might be dead or something!" He said, "Oh my God, Rhonda, he is!" All I could do was yell at him. I kept saying, "No, no, no, no!"

I don't know how I recovered. Well, that's not true. I do know every minute of every hour of every day until today. It's a long way from there to here. Now Joshua is always with me. Some days it's like no time has passed.

The sun is coming up now and it's beautiful outside. The trees are blowing in the wind, so it might not be a good idea to paint sheets. When the wind stops, it should be nice and warm, so I'll wait until then. That will give me enough time to locate everyone to arrange the room to work in, and acquire a brush and paint. It's a holiday, so I may have to get another CO to help me. There are 15 more minutes before they call for mainline (breakfast) so I'm going to read my book. I haven't read it in a day or so. The only thing I've accomplished so far is to catch up in my book, "The Dead Zone."

Veronica and Rosebud were arguing over the T.V. selection. Veronica said, "I'm gonna kick your ass." And Rose said, "It's going to take a while, 'cause I'm all ass! So better go and pack a lunch!" Ha, ha, ha.

So much for getting it together to paint the back-drops. We can't get the brushes until tomorrow. I also found out that Ms. Hawthorne doesn't come in until Saturday, so I'm on hold until then. I think I'll work on the Indian Princess today. I was going to use a projector, but that would be too easy! I already drew her face on paper so I could transfer it onto the drop.

Friday, 2:30 pm, and I'm watching the silliest movie, "I love you, Beth Ann." I've been coloring my scale drawings for the Christmas backdrops all day. I have a magic marker to start the Indian Princess. I don't know why but I seem to think I need to always be doing something. I'm not comfortable doing nothing at all.

It was the hardest thing I ever had to do, being locked up with two girls for 35 days with a toilet in the middle of the cell. It was hell on earth. Not to mention the sack lunches until I was so constipated that I wanted to die! Then having a hard time crapping in front of someone. That was truly "hard time." Being a good person has paid off. They would not have brought me to this camp if I was trouble, or broke the rules of confinement. Very few get to do their time at a camp.

Saturday morning already! I've only been up for 10 minutes and one girl turned up the T.V. because I made some noise getting a chair. Making a big deal out of it was a little much. I'm not even going to know her name, because I don't want to. Then Olivia came in with her dust mop and we all had to leave the room. We were watching a movie! She could have done that at another time. Good thing I heated up my coffee when I did.

Those two girls go down in the archives of stupid bitches! I have better things to do with my time. I'm glad they exposed themselves, before they tricked me into doing anything for them. I have a line of people that need my help now. I didn't realize how much an artist is needed. I know how it is in my town, but it never occurred to me until I was in prison.

Finally I'm in a room instead of the hallway. It's sort of a room, three and a half walls with a desk and a light. I like my bunkie too, a Native. Her name is Joyce. She always wears a bandana, so I asked her what was up with that. She said only Natives can wear bandanas. She said we can wear hats but we have to buy them. I think I'm gonna buy a white one. That would solve my bad hair problem.

I was talking to Monique about 1977, when I was part of an experiment performed by Howard Tooke, head of biofeedback in Phoenix, and his buddy, John Worthington, who studied religion for 15 years or so. "Programming and Meta-programming of the Human Bio-computer" was the so-called Bible. The experiments involved a sensory deprivation tank and other mind control devices and exercises. Their goal, one of them, was manifesting reality consciously by eliminating erroneous thinking.

That's all I'm going to say about the subject at this time. Monique's friend looked the book up on the Net and found that it was written by John C. Lilly. This morning at breakfast she said he sent her 8 more pages on the subject, and it all stems from Timothy Leary. I told her I wasn't surprised. I spent a whole summer tripping on acid so I didn't have to sleep in my car behind a gas station in Detroit. I'd stay up all night selling drugs at an arcade and sleep on people's couches during the day! Anyway, we are going to read the stuff later when we get the time together.

Hopefully I get to paint my Indian Princess today. Ms. Hawthorne should be in about 10am. Later today, Lydia needs to talk to me about doing some artwork for somebody on the outs. They want 3 photo drawings at $20 each. They want to put the money on my books.

Lydia also wants me to do a drawing of her whole family for a Christmas gift.

Sunday morning, 8:30am. I just finished a photo picture for Lisa. It's of her and her boyfriend. I'll surprise her later today. I saw Monique in the breakfast crowd; she said we could go over that stuff after we eat.

Last night I made a list of things I'll need from commissary when I get my money. The balance comes to $94, which includes a radio with a clock, beanie hat, thermal top and bottom and a sweat suit. That will leave me about $115. I have $209 coming from FCC. I checked the computer for my balance, and it's still 0.

They really take their time on transferring money. I don't know how long I've been here. Long enough to write 35 pages for my book. It looks like I can't do much until count at 10am, in 20 minutes.

My head feels like it's swimming with no direction. Maybe that's why I constantly need to be doing something. I have a hard time doing nothing. Ever since I talked to Monique about my experience in 1977, I've been in a little bit of a spin.

It's a beautiful day, so I'm sitting out in the sun. That way, I can see when Ms. Hawthorne gets to her office. She needs to open up the room that I'm doing the drops in. Also, Monique can sit with me and go over the information she has collected so far. This is the first time in thirty-five years that anyone has been interested enough in my story to actually research it. Maybe it's worth my time this time.

Lydia may come by and talk to me too. I'm sitting where everyone can see me. I think reading my book would be enjoyable right now.

It's 1pm, and I have a whole shit-load of stuff to do. I got another order on the outs, another order from Hopi Unit. Ruth and her husband, who looks like Danny Glover. I'm not sure, but that one may be free. I picked up a "cop-out" to request the beading class.

The whole thing about aging is pissing me off. I hate it. I don't want to have paper thin skin and wrinkles on my face. My forearms really show it all. Being 55 and feeling like I should only be 30 is not fun. My hair is totally gray. I'm thinking of dying it blonde. Maybe I'll feel better about myself; I'm not going gracefully. My joints are all stiff. My whole body hurts, especially if I'm in one position for a long time. I think it was partially to do with being locked up for over 30 days when I first turned myself in. My muscles started seizing up. We never got to go outside. Now I have to keep moving it or losing it.

Well, I finished one of the 6 pictures that were ordered from the outs. I'm running out of drawing paper so I better stock up tonight if I can.

Good morning again. Its 6am and I've already been called to the Case Manager's office. She couldn't find a form that I turned in last week.

November 15th, 8am. Time seems to be flying. Maybe my money will get here today since its Monday, a work day.

The weather is rapidly changing in temperature. The sun is out, beautiful. The entire commissary I buy will have to do with staying warm this winter. And let's not forget my radio. I could really use some tennis shoes, too. I'd like to walk the track, but these boots aren't made for walking. Ha, ha, ha.

The paperwork is done for my kitchen job. I start in the morning at 5:15am. I don't even have to shop commissary, being a kitchen worker. They take our store order by noon on shopping day and shop for us. It doesn't get better than that. So I guess I might start another drawing today and finish the Indian Princess in the sky for the Pow-Wow. Later... I have finished two of the six pictures now. I'm gonna like my work schedule of 2 days on, 2 days off.

Sitting here on a bench in the morning sun is really wonderful. It's perfect weather. The birds are chirping and the breeze is slightly blowing. I haven't written in a while. A lot has happened since the last time.

It's Friday, November 19th, and it's my second day off since I started in the dish room. They have been cooking for an early Thanksgiving dinner at the trading center. We did enough pans to fill a 747 three times! Those first two days of work really kicked my ass!

My shoulders feel better because of the physical therapy at work. I have regained almost total movement in my shoulders. No longer do I wake up at night in tears. The doctor prescribed me 800 mg IBUs, 2 times a day, for a month. He obviously knows what he's doing. I hear a lot of crap about what an idiot he is, but that's how these people (women) are, so critical of everything and every one. I am so thankful I appreciate most everything, all the time. God has blessed me in abundance.

I almost finished one of the back drops that I designed for photo-shoots, a giant rose with a bud. I'll finish today. I also finished Grandma holding the baby and I have one more of the mother kissing the baby. And two more of just the baby. Each of them is a different picture.

My bunkie is going home in a week. I'm real happy for her.

Two days ago, I was called out to "camp team," which is when they tell me what they expect, my release date and how much halfway house time they plan to give me. My release date is December 18th, 2011. They are going to give me 2 to 3 months half-way house time in Tucson and I'll be released to my son, Johnny.

The address they have for him is my trailer address. When they asked me if that was correct, I said, "Yes." I'm not sure why. Maybe I was nervous, or didn't want any complications at the time. I have to write to Johnny to find out what to do, or not to do. Sure hope I get a letter from somebody soon.

I polished my toenails and my fingernails the other day and I feel more like a girl. I just got word there is another batch of girls coming in today, so maybe there will be someone I know. It's so beautiful out here; it's hard to believe this is prison!

This girl gave me a puzzle book last night. I enjoy that kind of thing. There are about 15 different puzzles in it. Pretty soon it will be lunch time, so I'm going to lay down my pen and lay out my next drawing.

Saturday morning. Unbelievable! Nobody told me I didn't have to be at work until 7am on Saturday! I woke up because the girls were moving around, and the showers were going. I went to the bathroom and checked the time. I was late for work! It was 5:15 am and that's the time I'm supposed to be there! If my bunkies hadn't stopped me, I would have run down to the cafeteria an hour and a half early. I wondered why Choppa hadn't woke me up yet.

I found a white hat in the garbage yesterday. It's pretty tore up, but it will do. Now I can feel all right. I've been hating my hair. The girl cut it like "Spock." I hate bangs and my hair wants to all go to the front. The hand dryer doesn't do the job of blowing it back. A hat was my only solution. Now I'm up and ready to go. 7 pm was my bedtime last night, so I've had plenty of sleep.

I still save two more pictures of the baby to do, and a group picture of Grandma, Grandpa and the parents with the baby. Almost done with that project. Everyone else that wants me to draw for them. I tell them it will be a week before I can start anything else.

In the meantime, I've personalized a couple of cups with permanent marker, one for Samantha and one for Olivia. One says "Sam" and the other says "Livie." I'm pretty happy these days, doing what I enjoy. I know when I'm leaving here. And I have a hat to solve my bad hair problem.

It's pretty bad when I leave my hair net on because it looks better than my hair!

Pink Panther is on the T.V. right now. That's about my speed today. I need to get that group picture finished so I can go on to something else.

It's raining on this lovely Sunday afternoon. Choppa, my boss, told me to go home and come back at 2:30pm. This morning started at 7am. We power-washed the floor and all the equipment; the kitchen is clean.

I just sat down and Gloria asked me if I had started the picture of her mother-in-law. These girls must think I'm magic, or something. She only gave me the photo two days ago and I told her it would be a few days before I started it.

It stopped raining. I have two more hours before work, so it looks like I'm watching a Christmas movie with the girls.

Tuesday morning, 7am, November 22nd. My bunkie is a bitch! I spilled some coffee crystals on my locker and I thought I wiped it all up, but apparently not! I can't see very well with the lights off. When I came back from looking for the back-drops, she was up and ready to confront me. Actually, she threatened me. She told me I had coffee all over the f#cking place! She said she was going to be nice about it this time, but next time, she won't be so nice.

I just told Rosebud about it. She told me to talk to my counselor, and let them know she is trying to intimidate me. I guess that means going to Open House at 3pm in order to do that.

I'm at the library filling out a "cop-out" about my situation. I looked up my horoscope and it jives, like always. After the floor dries in my unit, I'd better get rid of everything from the kitchen in case they shake me down.

It's 8 am and I forgot to look at the "call-out" list today. I'd better go do that first, before I clean my locker. If you're on the list, you must be where the list says, on time! Good news, I'm not on the list today. I got my locker and property box cleaned out, ready for a shake-down. I am so pissed off right now, but you would never know it. I have learned to appear calm and indifferent. I am so not! God knows my heart, and he's my guide, so it's all okay. I believe that reading my book right now, would be a good idea.

It's 2pm and I'm in my own room, or another room, with a girl named Deborah. Before I went and asked to be moved, I got her permission to be her bunkie. She told me she was good with it.

I went to meet with Mr. Hindenburg. I told him about Joyce and how she was threatening me this morning. I told him I already had another room to move to. He put the new room number in the computer, and told me to go move. What a good guy. He could have blown me off, but chose to help me instead. He retired right after helping me and I never saw him again.

I like it a lot better. There's a flowering little tree outside the window, with blinds instead of a sheet. Let the sun shine in!

A girl just came in the T.V. room and gave me a sweatshirt. Now I don't have to wear my 6X coat everywhere. Well, I'd better go check on my laundry and the back-drops before dinner. Maybe I'll set it up for this weekend and Friday to paint. I work tomorrow and Thursday, which is Thanksgiving. Oh, the girl who gave me the sweat shirt came back in the T.V. room and I said "I don't even know your name." Her name is April.

Three days later... I just got off of work and it's almost 5pm, Sunday night. Exactly one month ago, I landed here. We are watching "The Mummy." Anyway, I almost had a confrontation with a co-worker today but I walked away! It took me an hour to cool off!

This girl likes to piss people off and she chose me this week. She'll be gone in 6 days, 5 now. I'm not even going to say her name. She can join the ranks of the faceless ones.

This morning it rained and I said to my boss, Mr. Evans, "Isn't it a beautiful day?" He said, "Yeah, if you're a duck!" Ha, ha. I sure needed those two days off; I could hardly move. I sent Johnny another letter, hoping for a response. I'm feeling a little forgotten.

Friday I started my watercolor class; we made Christmas cards. On Saturday morning, we practiced some more. The night before, I dreamed about this one card all night. It was a wooden door with a wreath on it.

I wasn't even back at my unit for 5 minutes when April talked me out of that one. Now I have to make another one for me, next Friday. I also started a drawing class on Saturday evenings. Every class lasts 12 weeks. I'm also on the list for computer class December 13th.

The sky is red and purple as the sun is going down. So beautiful. Supposedly, it's not going to rain tomorrow. Red sky at night, sailor's delight.

My book "Roadwork" by Stephen King is finished and I'm almost halfway through another book, "Fear Nothing," by Dean Koontz. They say he's a lot like Stephen King, and so far I like the one I chose to read. I had to choose from about 25 books by him.

This morning I had to be at work about 7am because it was Sunday. Tomorrow it's back to 5am. I'm thinking about a shower and an IBU. Here I go....

Monday, 3:30pm. It's 15 minutes before count. I got off from work only until count clears. We have to go back and do the final dishes for mainline. Mr. Evans rushed us out of there so fast that I left my coat and my book in the kitchen coat room. My book has been really good all the way through.

The dishwasher seems not to be working properly because people don't know what they are doing. I knew what the problem was, but Claudia, the girl who hates me because I'm white, went running to get Choppa. Claudia accused me of breaking it when I wasn't anywhere near it. I was washing pans. I wish I could "dot" her eye. She even knocked my biscuit on the floor and said nothing. She only looked at me and walked away. She was laughing when I was getting spaghetti on my face, banging the trays in the garbage can.

Apparently, she gets off on other people's blunders. It's my day off tomorrow. I have to throw my hat in the laundry because I got tomato sauce on it, too. Well, back to work for an hour and then I'm done until Thursday.

The spaghetti was good but the toasted hamburger buns could have used a little more garlic. Still, they were good, too. I'm all happy now, waiting for mail-call. I hope I get a letter from somebody. After that I'm getting in the shower.

Tonight is early bedtime, because I work in the morning. Choppa will wake me up at 4:45am, so I have enough time to get ready. The dishwasher is fixed, so no more wall scrubbing and power washing everything for something to do. We worked our asses off at work Saturday and Sunday! Thanksgiving is going to be busy too. I'm sure tomorrow and Thursday we'll be rocking out.

My new bunkie seems to be pretty cool, quiet and nice. I feel retarded because she works in the laundry and I didn't put it together that she was my bunkie, for some reason. She even gave me my laundry without asking my name or how many bags I had. When I got back to my room yesterday, I asked her where she worked. I must be in dreamland or something.

Thanksgiving and no letters from home. It was a year ago, November 19th, when I got busted and spent Thanksgiving at Johnny's trailer, playing catch the football with the boys. Nito was showing me some moves and we had a really great time. I imagine they are all together somewhere.

I think after work, I'll write to Suzie and Johnny. They are the only two on my contact list, so far. I need to get Keith Barth's address from Suzie. I need to make sure I was cleared of my charges of forgery and theft.

John Haviland Sr., Nito's dad, went to the cops and said I stole my son's Christmas money. I had my dad send the boy's Christmas checks to my address instead of to my son's. The year before, John kept Nito's money for months, depositing the check into his own account. Ray and Johnny's dad did the same thing. I told my dad to send the checks to me so they will get their money. I signed my kids' names on the checks and cashed them at the Market. I gave the cash to my kids with their Christmas presents, but in the meantime, I went to jail for 6 days.

The judge laughed and said she wasn't going to charge me with anything since the checks were from my father's account. My boys had to wait until I got out of jail to get their money and gifts, thanks to John Haviland, Sr. What a jack-ass!

We already made 300 sack lunches, so everyone gets one after they finish eating Thanksgiving dinner. I go back to work in an hour, but this is the last shift of the day. Friday and Saturday are my days off. I have so much food in my locker, it's stupid. I clean everything out of my locker and then they give me piles more from the kitchen. I could never eat that much food. They gave me a sack lunch already, and I ate breakfast. Now they're giving me another sack lunch after turkey dinner.

Later...they ran out of sack lunches, and I told them I didn't need one. They already loaded me up with 4 pieces of pie, one sack lunch, a soda, 2 sweet rolls and a banana. I just heard someone say, "Are we ever going to stop eating?"

No. Everyone gets fat in prison, at least bigger than when they checked in. I'm already 15 pounds heavier than I have been in 20 years. I haven't weighed myself lately, but I started getting a pretty good roll around my waist area. I stopped going for breakfast, eating only lunch and dinner. On the days I work, I eat breakfast, but only one or two things with coffee. I don't let them fill up my tray anymore. Thank God I still have some IBUs; I can hardly move.

I took one and lay down for a couple of hours, until count. I woke up to, "They're coming! They're here!" I jumped out of bed and grabbed my hat, first thing. Rosebud was laughing because my hat was more important than my ID. We're supposed to be standing with our ID in hand when they walk by, or we could get a shot. I whipped out my ID just in time.

I'm feeling a little heavy hearted today, missing my kids. I love them so much, and little Josh. I don't really feel like writing right now, but we are waiting to be counted. We can't leave our cubical until the count is clear.

It's Thursday night, and I work early in the morning. After count, I'm getting in the shower while I can. That's if there's not a line already. Tomorrow night I have my watercolor class and Saturday is my drawing class. I just found out that my computer class is 5 days a week for twelve weeks, from noon to 3pm. Choppa says to come back to work after the class. Class comes first.

They just came through and took our names. They usually only count us but the lights went out earlier, a couple times. They had to make sure we were all there.

No mail again today. I did get a paper saying my immediate family was OK for visiting: Johnny, Nito, Raymond and Mike.

The shower line is really long right now, so maybe there will be no chance tonight. I'll just get my hair wet in the sink; I was wearing a hat all day.

I've been slipping a lot lately. I just now folded my clothes that were washed on Wednesday and put my socks together from Tuesday. I'm feeling pretty boring. I'm not sure what my problem is.

No longer do I feel jazzed about writing this book, or anything else. I'm pretty sure it's because of not getting any letters from home. Things are becoming normal and ordinary, instead of interesting and temporary. I don't even fold my laundry until days after it's been washed. I believe I even mentioned that already.

I haven't gone out back and played pool in a long time. I barely finished the Christmas back-drop for photos, and I only made one. Tonight is my watercolor class and I'm hoping it will get me inspired again, like I was. My drawing class is tomorrow night. I did draw something on my own that I've wanted to capture for a long time. The picture is of a saguaro cactus, next to an old, red, fire hydrant here at the prison camp. It's a beautiful cactus, but it was the fire hydrant that inspired me to draw it!

A real good movie just came on, "The Sorcerer's Apprentice," with Nicholas Cage. I've been wanting to see it for some time, since I saw the previews at CCA. In about 45 minutes I have to return to work in the kitchen. This movie is too good; I have to watch it again.

Monday morning, early. I just got back from work. I don't have to go back until short-line. Right now, I'm watching the news. The satellite keeps popping in and out. My two days off were nice. I got to work on my drawing class homework all day yesterday. I have been drawing all my life, but the class has helped me to get better and I'm finding it easier. Amazing! I'll be a better artist when this nightmare is over.

I missed one of my brother's birthdays, but I have always missed all of them. I had no address for him, anyway. Johnny was supposed to send me Greg and Jeff's addresses. So far, he hasn't done much of anything that I asked him to. He has his own agenda.

There's a girl in here, Jessica, who was at FCC with Ann, my sister-in-law. I don't know what she is now, since Kurt is with someone else now.

I sent Christmas cards that I made in watercolor class to Fred, Johnny and Lisa, little Josh, Raymond, Nito, Grandma Jean, Suzie and Alan and Keith Barth. I feel bad that I sent nothing for Bryan. He's written me one letter since I've turned myself in. I told him that I was giving up on him, moving on. Obviously, it's bullshit because I still feel bad. I wonder all the time what he's doing.

I sometimes wish I had a boyfriend to write to. I really wish my husband, Darren, would come home. I'll never stop loving him.

FCC still has not sent me my money. It's exactly one month on November 28th that I've been here. Maybe this week! I imagine they want their books straight for the New Year. If I don't get it by this week, I'm going to write a "cop out" to Ms. Gonzales. I really don't want to talk to her; she is such a bitch! She enjoys making people cry.

I got a Christmas card at mail-call! My first mail since FCC! It was from Clare, Grandma Jean's daughter. At first I was afraid to open the letter. Grandma Jean hasn't been in good health. I believe she's somewhere close to 80. I was so relieved it was a Christmas card! Clare is having trouble painting signs; she just doesn't get it. She wants to partner up when I get out.

I am real sore right now from work, so I'm going to stop writing for now. My arms are sore, but they're getting stronger. I still get pretty beat up when I rock and roll and kick some ass at work!

Tuesday morning, 9 am. I already worked my first shift, turned in my laundry, drew a Coat of Arms and another drawing for April, and I still have 20 minutes before I go to work again.

Oh yeah, I went to medical at 7 am and turned down a flu shot. I seem to get a lot done in a small amount of time these days. I also read another 10 pages or so in my book. I think I'll read a couple more before I go.

Work is done. I picked up my laundry and got a letter at mail call. Suzie had written a letter and it got returned to her because I was transferred to prison. I got two letters in one. That's two letters now since FCC, and they still have not transferred the money. If I don't have it, I certainly can't spend it. Suzie tells me that Bryan is still there with her and Alan. I didn't include a card for him. I didn't know if he was still on the planet. I'm going to write to him and see what happens.

Good morning. It's Wednesday, December 8th. I thought I'd use the blue pen to save the black one for artwork. I turned in my "greens" and now I'm going to stay here in the T.V. room until they kick me out for cleaning. I had to bum coffee this morning from my bunkie. I'll be getting my own later today, with creamer, for April's artwork. Also, I'll be getting stamps for drawing Jody's parents. I already did a picture of her brother and she loved it.

I'll be putting a kid's name on a hat today, for $5 commissary. I could get into big trouble, charging for my work, so we keep it on the "down low." I just found a whole stack of magazines in the recycle bin. I'm going to go through them for material to draw for my art class.

Well, its noon and I finished the parent picture for Jody. Right now, there's a girl in the T.V. room that I can't stand. Her name is Lisa. She's one of the two girls we waited for at the airport on the way here. She thought she would sit right next to me. What's wrong with her? I really don't want to know, but she's not right. Lisa likes to ask stupid or personal questions for no reason at all. She also enjoys ordering people around. I think she's a total whack job! I don't like her vibes at all. I'm always catching her staring at me. Maybe she's an alien, the lizard kind. I need a break from drawing, so I'll read my book.

This morning is a little different around here. Yesterday there was a "town hall" meeting in front of the cafeteria. We all gathered to listen to the new rules being enforced. Now we can't take anything in the T. V. room with us. No books, food or drinks.

We can no longer take anything out of the cafeteria, or in, not even salsa or soy sauce. They always gave us fruit and a pack of cookies that we could eat later, but now it's a shot. Looks like they will be throwing away a lot of food instead of letting us eat it. I guess a few girls were stealing onions and what not out of the kitchen, so we all suffer for it. The guilty parties were very fat.

Starting February 7th, we have to do a stand up count at 10 pm, mandatory. Some of us, like me, get up for work at 4:30am.

I'm going to be spending a lot of time in my room doing artwork and reading my book outside, weather permitting. I can't wear my hat in the kitchen anymore, either. It was my total solution for very bad hair in the morning. The "Pet Detective" has nothing on me.

The FCC still has not sent my money. They certainly are in no hurry; it's been about 40 days now.

Yesterday, while I was standing in line for chow, they opened the warehouse door right next to us. They were giving out issues of clothing. I walked over and said "I don't have a cop-out, but I need new boots. I work in the kitchen." They told me to come in and they gave me a brand new pair. I didn't know they were padded inside.

My feet are so happy right now.

I stripped my bed and got everything in the laundry this morning. I think I'll write Suzie a letter today. I sent something to everyone just last week, Christmas cards and letters.

Friday afternoon. I got a letter from my brother, Mike, and a letter from Fred. Mike said he never heard from Miriam again. He's still waiting to be financially blessed. Also he said his car broke down; it's ready for the crusher. Now he's walking all over town. Good thing it's a small town.

Fred said that he was real sorry for his last letter. He said he couldn't be around me because of drugs and alcohol. He didn't realize I was no longer in that scene. I told him not to worry so much. He said living with me would be like living with a panther. It may kill him, but he'd rather die than live without me. I told him I was his friend and I know how he feels about things. I don't want to be that close anyway. It creeps me out. I told him, "One day at a time."

Monday, December 13th, 2010. It appears I am 20 minutes early for my computer class, so it's a good time to recap the last couple of days. I got a letter from Johnny. I hadn't cried in a long time, but I did after reading his letter. He's doing well with his life financially. He's care-taking at a ranch in Sonoita. He has free rent and utilities, plus $2,400 a month wages. He's still doing his mechanic business on the side, part time. Lisa told him if I have to live with them after prison for a while, she's going to leave my son and take my grandson to Phoenix. Sounds like emotional black mail! We already had it set up that I would be released to my son. What kind of a person does that? I'm pretty upset. I'm going to have to talk to someone here to change the plan, if it's possible. Enough of that subject for now.

Yesterday, Rosebud and I were walking down the sidewalk when my boot stuck on a crack and I went down. I fell forward and put out my right hand, which landed on the cement. I tucked my head and did a complete front flip in the air, landing on my feet. Then I fell back. I was totally not injured, not even the hand I used to vault from. My knee seems a little sore this morning, but that's it.

There are still 10 minutes before class starts. I'm really excited.

Next day,Tuesday, December 14th. I'm writing until 4pm count, then I go back to work for mainline dishes. I went to class after the breakfast dishes. When I got to class, I was soaking wet. It was my turn to spray the trays. The class was "turbo typing." We have to get good at typing, first of all, before we can really go on.

This morning after my first shift, I drew Mickey and Minnie Mouse on a three foot board. They were dancing. I also drew a fireplace on another cardboard for Christmas decorations, which might be all I can do for the moment. I'm not really into Christmas this year, for some reason. I have one more shift for the day and my work is done.

I was just talking to Melody; she was at CCA and FCC with me. Hers was the room that flooded that time. She was also the one that helped to save the day. She corralled the water, directing it with sheets and blankets.

Too funny. She also ordered a lot of envelopes from me, so I'll give her a "fleet" price.

Next day. I'm in computer class, so I'll write later. After class I tried to see Ms. Gonzales about my money, but I had to get to work. They were slammed!

Today is my day off, except for my computer class. Maybe Ms. Beccerra can let me go early so I can catch Open House. That's the only time I can talk to someone about my situation. I can't wear my sweat shirt when I go because I have a zero balance; I don't need her asking where I got it. She'd probably make me throw it away. We can't share. It's against the rules.

Of course I have things I'm not supposed to have. I've been here long enough that it looks like I could have bought everything. There are too many girls to know who don't have money. They will know after I see her.

Here it's my day off and I could have slept in. For some reason, I woke up early enough to make it to main-line at 5:30am.

Priscilla is leaving today. In fact, she may be gone. I told her I'd always keep the white hat she gave me, also the Reebok shower shoes. Priscilla Hernandez has a kind and gentle soul. She said she'd be looking for my book.

Rosebud is probably my best friend here. Her cubical is right across from mine. My bunkie, Deborah, was in the same halfway house with her-- The Haven in Tucson.

Thursday, December 16th, 2010. It looks like I'm the first one here at my class. I'm 15 minutes early and it's raining. At lunch, I saw Ms. Gonzales in the cafeteria. I mentioned to her that I wanted to talk to her about my money. She told me to write a cop-out, mail it to her and she would handle it.

I got two letters today at mail call and a Christmas card from my brother Jeff and his wife, Dani. They had a baby boy, Colt. He's only about 2 months old, born 10-1-2010. They sent pictures in the card of the baby, Dani, Jeff and the baby, and Jeff on his Harley with the baby. I think I will send them a picture of my nephew, drawn in pencil.

Friday morning, December 17th. I'm almost on the countdown. Tomorrow it will be exactly a year to my release date. I got some disturbing news from Suzie. It looks like Bryan is dying. His kidneys shut down and he's having blood pressure problems and heart problems, too. I'm sending him a card that I painted of Christmas candles. I put this poem in the card:

STAY WITH ME, GOD. THE NIGHT IS DARK, THE NIGHT IS COLD: MY LITTLE SPARK OF COURAGE DIES. THE NIGHT IS LONG. BE WITH ME, GOD, AND MAKE ME STRONG.

Love,

Rhonda

I found one more address label with his name on it. I can't mail my brother's card yet because the printer is out of labels. Now I need to get my homework done for computer class and also my drawing class. I don't need my drawing done until Saturday night. I have watercolor class tonight.

Everybody has been way too nice to me because they all need me. They need stuff done for Christmas decorations. I missed my watercolor class. Choppa told Taya I had a headache. Actually, I was so tired that I couldn't keep my eyes open. I made it to my drawing class on Saturday after work. If I miss more than one class, I can be thrown out, so I can't miss any more watercolor classes. I love that class. I drew a picture of "Colt," my nephew, and a picture of Jeff and Dani to send with a letter. It's in a big envelope, waiting for $1.05 worth of stamps.

This is Monday, December 20, 2010. I got a letter from my buddy, Terry Otto. She's living in Missouri now as a fire fighter. I love her a lot. She writes an awesome letter, too. She lives on Peaceful Valley Road. I bet it is, too.

I finished another book by Dean Koontz, "The Vision." I like his writing. He always has several twists to the stories he tells, almost like Stephen King but not as scary.

I also got a letter from my other brother, Greg, in Florida. Actually, it was only a Christmas card. It looks like they made it cute. It's from the whole family.

I'm so glad I took typing in the 8th grade (40 years ago). It's really helping me in my computer class now. I'm typing about 15 wpm with about 92% accuracy.

It's December 24th, Christmas Eve day. They applied the money to my account. I even got my maintenance pay of $5.25. I'm going shopping on Tuesday. I'm going to buy a book of stamps, a medium claw clip for my hair, a Sony M35 digital radio, medium size sweat pants and two thermal shirts! All that comes to $71.75. My balance will be $149.25. That's all I can spend because I have a $100 fine I need to pay before it's all said and done. I have a payment plan, but I want to keep the entire balance in my account. No worries.

I don't work today or tomorrow and no computer class until Monday. At work yesterday Cathy called me into her office and asked if I wanted to change jobs. I told her, "No problem. I like diversity." She said, "You're not going to ask me what job?" I said, "I figure it has something to do with the kitchen."

Veggie prep was the position, but I was to keep it under my hat. Someone was leaving and the position needed filling. I was so happy, her first choice. About a half hour later I was reminded of my computer class from noon to 3pm. I told Cathy I couldn't quit my class. I was at the point of no return. Looks like I'm destined to be a great dish washer.

It's one of the most beautiful days ever. I'm wearing only a sweatshirt. The sun is shining, and its Christmas Eve day. Rosebud had me sign up for the "over 45" Yahtzee tournament. I wanted to do the softball throw but I don't want to throw my shoulder out again. Doing dishes here at the Prison Camp has been the best physical therapy for my shoulders. Now I need to get some tennis shoes so I can walk the track; my knees are weak. They gct locked up when I sit too long. It's hard to walk at first when I just get up from sitting. I figure I need to exercise my lower body. Maybe the weight I've put on has something to do with my difficulty.

They gave us a nice Christmas bag yesterday. It was full of all kinds of chips, cookies, candies and other snacks. It ought to last me a while since I've only eaten two mints out of my bag so far. I'm not a junk food freak like most of the girls are. I get too full from what they feed us at meals. There are a lot of fat women here. They just keep getting fatter and fatter. I had to cut back on my eating because I'm heavy enough.

I would sure like a surprise visit from my kids. I'd love to see my grandson. Well, I'm going to read my book on that note. Merry Christmas, everyone.

Sunday, December 26th. No surprise visit. I'm also working today. I feel like drawing for a while. I have a photo that Monique wants me to draw for her. I like to do a portrait and a regular picture every week for my drawing class. Perspective drawing is the subject this week. I drew a barn with a windmill.

There is so much food in my locker and my property box. It's silly. I don't know how these girls eat so much food. They ate all of theirs!

I need to write my boys and let them know they can visit me anytime. They don't need approval; they're family.

"Scar Face" is on right now. I've seen it a lot of times. Watching it would seem like wasting my time. I keep thinking about Bryan since Suzie wrote me of his condition. I wonder if he's still alive. Maybe he'll write, if he's not dead. Men can be such assholes and for some reason, it's all excusable.

I'm in the Yahtzee competition with Rosebud in an hour. Rosebud won first, Lydia got second and she'd never played before. The prize was a box of chocolate turtles. Always food. We eat a lot of sugar around here. They do, anyway. I still haven't touched my Christmas bag or my bag of cookies. I feel full thinking about it.

It's Monday morning, 7am. I woke up pissed off! I

woke up several times in the early morning hours. I go to bed really early when I work at 5am. The girls never shut up until well after 10pm. Last night they were really loud and laughing. When all was finally quiet, someone started singing, off key!

By the time it was all quiet I was totally awake. I tossed and turned the rest of the night, half sleeping until time to go to work. These girls act like this is a pajama party, from sun up to sundown and beyond. I'll be so glad when this is over.

I have computer class today. In the last class we were learning to create files and folders. Now I have to figure out how to find them again, after I put them somewhere. We are doing a "lab" every class (written instructions), several pages long. I'm sort of behind. I'm still working on one when she gives us another one. I hope I get the new one pretty soon. I'm going to read my book for a while before I go back to work.

Next day, Tuesday, December 28th, my day off. All I've done is finish reading my book, "The Watchers" by Dean Koontz. I checked out another one by him, "Forever Odd." I think it's time for lunch so I'd better get going. Oh, I started another photo-drawing, too. Outta here.

Vanessa sent me a Christmas card and asked me to write. I just wrote her a letter explaining my situation with Johnny and my release, also about the ceiling in my bathroom. I asked her to find me some help. I'm mailing the letter now, after I get her address on the computer.

Good morning, it's December 30th, and it's been raining for two days. The news says it's going to snow. They already had two feet in Flagstaff and are expecting about a foot in the higher elevations of the Phoenix area. It's probably snowing in Patagonia.

I'm the 8 am girl in the dish room today so I go back in an hour. They are baking chicken. There will be about 25 baking pans to scrub. Choppa said she'd come back to help me.

I'm going to write to everyone about my problems and maybe they will become solutions. We will see if I'm really missed or not. I don't think I want to know. I really do already know how it is.

I also hope Bryan hasn't died on me. I miss him alive, so if he dies, I will always and forever miss him. God, don't let him die. Please do a miracle and save him from himself. AMEN. God, you know my heart. You know it's always breaking. I'm going to read a little before I go to work again.

This is New Year's Eve day and I woke up two hours early for work. I'm in a MOOD. I'm really bummed out about my kids not writing to me. In fact, I'm going to write Johnny and tell him so.

New Year's afternoon, January 1st, 2011. They just did count. I've been watching movies all day. Rosebud got a visit from her sister and brother-in-law. They brought one of her daughters that she hadn't seen in 15 years. She's trippin'.

I can't seem to get the issue I have with Johnny's girlfriend off my mind. She doesn't want me around. I'm thinking it's because she lied to her parents and friends about me. She made me out to be a monster. Having me around would prove that none of it is true. Her lies would be exposed for what they are and she would look like a fool. Her only recourse is to threaten to leave my son, if he lets me live with them. I'm having a hard time believing this is all happening this way. I'm waiting for a letter from Johnny before I write to Lisa directly.

Well, it's Monday, January 3rd. I just got back from mail call. Nothing for me, maybe tomorrow. I'm not giving up. Like Raymond told me "I'm not giving up, if you don't give up." I love that kid, I sure miss him. Ray is pretty to me; they all are. They all have a different "special" to me. It's tough for me sometimes because I lose sight of where I am in the world. I get confused about what is important for me to be spending my life doing, or thinking or what. Maybe it doesn't matter at all, unless it matters to me. My heart is so broken and my life looks like one big mess. That doesn't mean I'm not happy. I'm pretty used to the condition of things.

I'm doing a lot better in my computer class. I'm starting to grasp the concepts much better. My typing is improving, too.

I'm drawing a picture of Mount Rushmore for my drawing class.

Good morning, it's January 4th, 2011, and I just got out of the shower. It's 7am and I already did my first shift at the dish room. I'm thinking about how good it feels to be clean again. Using the hand dryer on my hair is my new solution to "flat to my head" hair and my bangs don't look like the Beatles! Finally my bad haircut is growing out. I'm totally gray and white now but I think dying my hair would look like shit. The roots grow out and it looks like shit. Actually, I've had girls come up and want to touch my hair because it looks so soft.

8.

Feeling Old

Seeing myself in the mirror still freaks me out; the wrinkles blow my mind. There are a lot of girls with a lot more wrinkles, and much deeper. I'm talking about girls ten years younger than me. I feel like I'm only thirty something, in my mind. I refuse to be 55. On that note, I'm going to start a drawing for Jody. There are two more hours before I go back to work. I may also have a few minutes to read my book, "False Memory" by Dean Koontz. I just finished "Forever Odd."

January 5th, early. It's my day off but I'm up early to get my laundry down to the girls by 7am. I don't do my own. These girls do their own with five washers and 8 dryers, and 300 women. It doesn't compute. I had to do my own one time, and I'll never do it again! It took all day!

I don't give a shit about wrinkles in my clothes. After folding them in a stack, they aren't that bad. The soap alone is more than a person makes in a month. Someone had to put money on the books for the girls to do their own laundry. Not very honorable, if you ask me. There are about 10 out of 60 girls that are continuously ironing their self-washed clothes, while making rude comments to those of us that don't. I guess that's how they attempt to maintain their self importance. Good luck to them. This is prison and we're all the same, like it or not. Anyone can easily be sent to Durango for having a banana in their pocket, or a Sweet-N-Low in their locker. If it's not on the commissary list, you aren't supposed to have it. Also, if they want to take it to the moon, you need receipts for everything you have. It's against the rules to accept anything from anyone. No sharing! If we get caught, we could get a shot. They will decide the punishment. You don't want to get a shot. So far, I haven't gotten any.

I don't do anything or hang out with anyone, except Rosebud. I'm so happy I've got my radio. I love music. It brings on the memories, those precious gems of time.

I keep seeing Raymond sitting on the couch in his diapers, all mad at everyone. His brothers picked on him pretty bad. I had to tell Johnny to be nicer to his brothers, before they start planning his demise! Now the boys are all very close. I love them so much and I totally miss their brother Joshua. When I go to my grave, I pray that my soul is back with him again. I feel like he's still with me now. Maybe when I pass on, he'll come with me.

I've been feeling pretty alone lately, but I'm confused if it's erroneous or not. I believe it is. How could I be lonely, when Josh is with me? I think it's because I wish I could hug him again.

The Phoenix station that I listen to, 97.9 KUPD, has a hilarious morning show. Girls keep looking at me when I walk by because I keep laughing. I'm using ear phones, so they can't hear what I'm listening to. I used to listen to the same station when I lived in Phoenix back in the 70's and 80's. Rock and Roll is off the chain. I love , too! Actually, I like almost all music, but the hard stuff is my favorite! THE BIG REDRADIO, "morning sickness," is the show I'm listening to.

December, I mean January something, 2011. I'm losing it! I was waiting for 6pm so I could go to my watercolor class. I found out it was yesterday. That means I missed my drawing class at 5pm today. This whole thing bums me out. I look forward to my classes. Ever since the holidays and canceled classes, I've been getting mixed up! I feel like crying; my life has gotten so mixed up. I'm so unsure of where I belong anymore.

Life seems so short. I see how much I took for granted. I ran out of time for the things that I love. Now I'm on my own after being part of something and I don't know what's going on; I'm lost. Where did I go? I'm going to go to sleep and hope God saves me from myself. AMEN,

Well, so much for sleep. I woke up in the middle of the night. I had to write a letter to Lisa, asking her why she made me out to be a monster. I also asked her a lot of other things about her behavior. I'm going down to mail it right now. God only knows what will happen now, but it's already screwed up anyway. The letter is to the point, explaining the chain of events leading up to the present day. I hope I can have a happy family situation someday. She's the mother of my grandson.

Monday, January 10, 2011. I have another 10 minutes before I go to computer class so I thought I'd write a couple lines. I talked to my art teacher, Taya, and she said Saturday morning I can make up the water coloring I'm behind on. Also, I can draw a picture for the drawing class I missed. That makes me feel better. I was in the chow line with Rolina. I always really liked her since we were partners doing the trays and trash.

This is January 13th. I haven't written in a couple of days and its count soon. I'll try to remember the highlights. In Computer class, we were making up an event with a cool heading (Word Art), date, time, etc. Mine is: Local Art Show and Sale, Location: by the gazebo in Patagonia Park. Date: 12-12-2012, Time: 9am to 7pm, Featuring: Local artist's work for sale. Everyone is welcome. There will be refreshments and everything is for sale at reasonable prices.

Rhonda Brew will be there to sign her new book, "Laundry Day".

New artists are welcome. Please make arrangements before 12-01-2012. Hope to see you there!

For Information, call Rhonda Brew @ (520) 604-6204.

I figured by making the flier maybe it will actually come true. At the end of my class, we all have to do a presentation of some sort. I'm making up something I want to really happen.

I got a letter from my brother last week asking for information on how to send me money, Western Union. I got a letter from Suzie Dickey yesterday; she told me that Darrell Hatfield died in his sleep, December 21st, 2010. Mike was taking care of Darrell, but he never mentioned that he died in his letter. Suzie also told me that Bryan lived. It wasn't his kidneys. His sugar was so out of whack that they air-lifted him to Sierra Vista. They sent him back to Suzie's after five days in the hospital.

Alan, her son, goes in for surgery on his shoulder, if

his heart can handle it. She said her bronchitis keeps hanging in there, but she's hoping the antibiotic will kick its ass! Suzie also said they are supposed to start building Grandma Jean's house in about a week. She's been waiting about a year since her house burned down. She's hoping for them to finish it by Memorial Day.

I'm expecting a letter from Fred pretty soon, if he hasn't forgotten me. A Christmas card was the last thing I sent him. I also sent that letter to Lisa and I'm expecting a response because of the content of the letter. I wish we could just all get along. Well, I guess I'll go and re-mail a letter to my friend, Terry Otto, the fire woman. I'm so proud of her.

It's 8pm and "The Witches of Eastwick" just got over. I love that movie with Jack Nicholson, Cher, Michelle Pfeiffer and I forgot the other girl.

Anyway, when I get back to my room, my bunkie, Deborah, said we got our room searched today. Nothing looks like it's missing, so everything must be OK. The officer just walked by and said nothing to me. I guess we are good to go.

That's weird; I had two pens run out of ink at the same time. I guess its pencils until next week when I can buy a pen. Commissary was yesterday and all I bought was a note pad.

Most of these girls buy piles and piles of stuff, every week. Most of it is food. They feed us way too much already. There are some pretty big girls in here, and it's a shame, too. Eating in prison is a pastime. I've noticed that women don't get very many letters from home. Women just seem to get forgotten. Out of sight, out of mind. Now the men get a lot of mail because women keep reminding them they are missed and loved. It's not the same for women. So I'm thinking, the "fat" problem may have something to do with that. They reinforce each other on the subject.

I never throw food away off my tray, if I can help it. I look for somebody that wants what I don't want. There's always a taker. I used to bring back food to my cell to eat later. They no longer let us take food from the cafeteria or the kitchen. They call it contraband. We get "shots" if they search our rooms and find it. When they searched while I was out, they must not have found anything to shoot me for.

The only thing that bothers me, really, is that they keep changing the rules on us. They canceled my computer class yesterday so I watched T.V., "The Witches of Eastwick," and read my book. I'm going to finish my "False Memories." I have to finish it before I start my new book, "Conversations with God," by Donald Walsh.

Monday, Martin Luther King Day, January 17th, 2011. Yesterday was a BITCH! They left me alone at work without telling me anything. I collected 200 trays and cups from the inmates after eating. I can't believe I didn't panic. They came back a while later from the kitchen, where they were helping to make tostadas. They are always talking Spanish. Even though they all speak English, they only speak English when they are talking directly to me, which is hardly ever. I'm just glad that I have today and tomorrow off. I can do some drawings and read some of my book.

I still haven't gotten any response from the letters I

wrote last week. My counselor, Ms. Stern, is letting me wait for a 12 hour drug class until my computer class is over. That is very cool of her. I told her it was important to me to successfully complete the computer course. I will be able to do a better job writing my book when I get out. I really do appreciate people that really do care about things, instead of just wielding their power around. On the street they have no power, but we are forced to be here for them to exploit, if they so desire.

I respect those who find no need to do that, when they could if they wanted to. Bless them all. AMEN.

People keep telling me I don't have to make my bed today, but I make it for me, to keep my mind organized. That was my problem at home. Everything was in such disarray that my brain was too.

Well, I guess that's backwards. My place was a mess because my brain was a disaster area. I didn't give it a chance, either. I still have dreams about cleaning my place up; it still has to be done. There are two truckloads of laundry still bagged up in my tub.

People say I'm a hoarder, but people have left all their stuff for me to deal with over the last 18 years. I didn't go out and collect it. Some of it, I did, but I need help to get the crap out of my life! I can't handle my problem with only a bicycle!

Later today, I'm going to write to Suzie about checking into my suspended license, give her something to do. I love her so much. She's always grumbling about doing stuff but it's only because she doesn't feel well a lot. Maybe I can take her mind from it for a minute or two.

It's been sort of a long day. I was working on a

drawing, but Deborah has been using the desk all day. We almost got into it earlier. The washers are broken down in the laundry room, so they haven't been able to do our laundry for about a week now. My dirty socks were stinking up my locker, so I had to wash them in the trash can and hang them on the towel rack.

Deborah is so worried about getting in trouble! I told her that it's a holiday and it's OK. She said I should go down to the laundry and get in line for a dryer. I told her I wasn't waiting for a bunch of bitches to use a dryer.

After I sat in the T.V. room, chilling out, I came back, loaded up my wet stuff in a laundry bag and marched down to the laundry for the sake of getting along. When I got there, 30 girls were laughing at me for thinking I could use a dryer! I went back and hung them back up. I knew I was doing the only option in the first place but I'm still a little pissed off that I fell for her stupid attitude! She works in the laundry. Her stuff is clean.

I have one more day off, except for computer class, so maybe I can get my drawing a little farther along. I think I'll read my book while there is still daylight. I'm sitting in my top bunk using the light coming in the window.

Thursday, January 20th, 7am. It's my Friday. The washers are fixed in the laundry room so no more problems with stinky clothes.

I'm excited about my computer class and my presentation. I keep having dreams about being in a cyber world, where we can't move unless we know how everything works. In my dreams, I can only do about 50 per cent of what I need to, so I'm stuck in cyberspace. I'm working with others to move around, using our knowledge of the program to progress. Pretty wild.

We have been slammed at work. I usually stay in the morning after breakfast on the first day. The second day, I go in when everyone else does. Today is chicken day. That means over 20 trays of oven baked chicken, and a lot of grease!

I was just at the laundry with my whites. Rolina is working there. She was my partner doing trays and trash at CCA and later at FCC until I was made the "artist." She continued to do the trays and cups until she got here to camp. She got here only last week. I'm so glad she's out of there. I told the girls at the laundry they were lucky to have her.

I thought we were going to get her in the dish room. We only have four people and we need six. Anyway, good for her. Rosebud just woke up and asked me if I went to the laundry yet. She's getting used to me dropping off her laundry for her. She's too late today.

Last night when I took off my wet boots and soggy socks my big toe on my right foot was bright red! I'm sure it's infected. When I cut my toenails the other day, I cut that one a little too close. I pulled out a sliver of nail that was sticking out the side. It bled a little, but I didn't think too much about it. Now I have to keep an eye on it. I took my boots off since I don't go back until later this morning.

My brother wrote me a letter in response to my asking for help with my bathroom ceiling. He said that he took Robert Woods over there to look at it. They decided it wasn't worth fixing! That is not acceptable! I wrote him back and told him to please do what I ask or nothing at all. I also wrote to Robert Woods, explaining my situation and asked for help. We will see. Talk about lazy.

This is the first page of my new pad, the only thing I bought. I'm not buying anything that I don't absolutely need. I'd rather have the money when I get out than use it now. I bought that radio, and that's the only thing besides sweats and shoes. I can wear the sweats and the shoes when I get out of here. I gave my clothes away, donated them to the cause.

I have finished another Dean Koontz novel, "The Good Guy." I really like his stuff. I think I will finish "Conversations with God" before I check out any more books. If I don't get a letter from Fred today, I'm going to write to see if he's OK. There's an hour before I go to work, so it's a good time to make a rough draft of my presentation.

Wow, I'm off work for two days! I know my toe looks bad from infection but I don't want to take my boot off until after mail-call. The tennis shoes are a tight fit, so I better just stay with the boots.

Claudia got me some salt out of the kitchen while I was watching for the boss. I'm going to soak my foot in my garbage can and I need the salt to draw the infection out.

Claudia was wondering if she and Choppa would be in the book. I told her that they've been in the book since CCA. Then Choppa left and we didn't know where she was until the Camp. Claudia got shipped out before me, so we thought she went to Dublin.

We all work together on the same crew and Choppa is the boss. Lynette, from CCA and FCC, just got here this week. Tilly, Melody, Tracy, Olivia, and Samantha were all from CCA and FCC, with me. Oh, let's not forget Tina, Patty and Rosebud, the girls! I guess Shannon is still at FCC and Tink is in Texas. Shawnee is in Sea-Tac Prison. Rolina and Lena just got here from FCC.

There's a new officer at the message center, so mail-call is late. I think I'll start limping that way.

I am sooo... enjoying this moment. I have one foot in my garbage can with hot water and salt. I'm wearing my sweats and rocking out to the "Big Red Radio." I love this station. They get down with the hard rock.

My toe was totally bright red when I started soaking it. Now it's only pink.

I lost a tooth at work today, the one I needed pulled out. Looks like I don't need that done now. I'm going to have it checked out on Thursday when the dentist is here.

Next day...Deborah is cleaning the room all around me. My poor toe hurts and I don't want to jam it on my property box, moving it around to mop. I worked on my drawing for a while and read a little in my "Conversations with God." I think I'll write to Fred and see if he's OK. I haven't heard from him since Christmas.

I'm waiting in the Education Department for my computer class. I'm a little early. I already mailed Fred a letter, asking what happened to him.

It's Wednesday, January 26th, 6pm. I'm showered and ready to go to bed, read, draw, write or all of the above. I'm listening to the "Big Red Radio." A lot has happened, if only I could remember. I shouldn't let days go by before I write it down. I miss a lot that way. I don't really miss a lot, but you do.

Anyway, my computer teacher quit. They weren't

paying her like they should. They got into it so she quit. I still get my certificate but I don't get to give my presentation. I'm not sure that I'll even get a copy of it.

We only had a couple weeks to go but now I'm not afraid to turn on the computer. The teacher said I was doing a good job. I think I learned enough to figure things out when I get home. I'll be able to type my own book. Ms. Beccera was a good teacher. She had the patience of Job. I made her a card and the girls signed it. She'll have to buy my book to know about her card, since she never came back.

Uncle Mike wrote me another letter saying that I shouldn't worry about my trailer until he gets some money. I wrote him back and told him I'm not worried. I only need my bathroom ceiling torn out and hauled away. I asked him what that had to do with money. He's lazy.

I got a letter from Terry Otto, my firefighter friend. She reminded me that when God takes something away, he replaces it with something better every time. I guess she's getting a lot of snow there right now. She's vegging out on the couch, playing board games and such. Like she said, it's not like Arizona.

I got two books from the library, "Cell" by Stephen King, and "The Taking" by Dean Koontz.

I've been getting the letters I've written to Johnny back in the mail, The PO Box in Patagonia is closed. I don't know what's going on. I'm sure I'll find out eventually.

Suzie wrote me a letter. Alan and Bryan are driving her crazy. All Bryan does is watch T.V., movies and documentaries. She said that Fred is fine and has been helping some lady. I expect a letter from him soon.

I need to write my brother, Greg. For now, I'm going to start one of my new books before I go to bed. I get up early for work tomorrow.

A couple days later... Wednesday. I'm frozen! I just got back from standing in a lunch line for over half an hour. It's about 50 degrees with 20 mph winds. I'm still shaking. Today is commissary day, so I'll get a couple photo tickets and a couple manila envelopes. I want to mail Greg the drawing of his daughter, Sophie, my niece.

I have to get stamps and batteries, too. I finished the book I was reading, "The Taken."

When I walked into the T.V. room the girls were talking about the end of humanity, and how the president is the guy in the "Blue Turban," the anti-Christ. They just destroyed a museum in Egypt with all the artifacts and stuff from King Tut.

Looks like I'm going to sick call for my teeth in the morning. I imagine that I will get mail today. I have given my last two stamps to Rosebud. I'll have more later.

There was this really great looking guy in the kitchen yesterday. He brought his tray into the dish room and set it in front of me. He was only 6 inches from my face and I went into a trance! I couldn't concentrate the rest of my shift.

The other day, Mr. Swift was talking to these girls about "Lunch Lady Land," with Adam Sandler and Chris Farley. He said it had to be the funniest shit he had ever seen.

We were having Sloppy Joes for lunch. Swifty was singing "slop, slop, Sloppy Joe" and I chimed in "hoagies and grinders, hoagies and grinders." We both sang "navy beans, navy beans!"

Everyone was laughing. I kept laughing on and off all day after that. It's definitely the funniest shit I have ever seen. Adam Sandler is playing his guitar, singing, while Chris Farley is dancing around him in a hair net and orthopedic shoes, dressed as a lunch lady!

I think I'm going to change it up a little and read a Stephen King novel, "The Cell," as in cell phone. I'm still reading "Conversations with God," but that book I'll read over and over.

Well, I made it to the dentist this morning, 6am. He wrote down what was wrong with me and then said, "Good Bye." They are going to call me when they want me to come in.

I'm eating Christmas cookies dunked in chocolate coffee! I haven't eaten breakfast so my teeth weren't full of crap for the dentist. I'm pretty hungry.

Later, when it warms up, I'm going to block out the word "happy" on the Valentine's Day photo drop. It doesn't fit in the picture. I work tomorrow, so I'd better get it done today.

I read half of a novel and then went to the art room, after retrieving the photo drop. While I was blocking out "happy," the girl from the visiting room came in. She asked me for some art work to display. Taya gave her my high heel picture and a couple more. Finally, my work made it to the display case. It's almost time for lunch, so I'm going to read until then.

I got mail from Raymond! He told me that I don't need to be freaking out any more because I can move in with them. They have an extra room that's full of boxes.

He said he'd clean it up for me. I cried for some time after reading the letter. I am so relieved! I no longer have to sweat where I am going to live when I get out of the halfway house. Ray is so wonderful. I couldn't ask for greater sons than I already have. They are all really very special.

Today is watercolor day and tomorrow is my drawing class. We are supposed to do a drawing of a person. The subject is the human figure. I have one more chance not to miss the drawing class.

Monday, February 7th, 2011. Yesterday was Super Bowl Sunday. They shut down the kitchen and gave us sack lunches. I still have mine. I ate the PBJ, but I'm throwing away the burrito.

My pen just started writing. I'm glad I didn't throw it away. There's plenty of ink, it just wasn't ready to come out yet. I finished the two novels yesterday, "The Cell" and "Taken." I love that SYFY stuff.

Anyway, now I'm reading "Duma Key," by Stephen King. It's about a rich guy that got screwed up in an accident. He moved to the Florida Keys, where he sketches. He lost an arm and his head is messed up, but he is rehabilitating in a house off the Gulf of Mexico. His urges to draw are what keep my interest the most. I can totally relate.

For the last couple days, my bunkie "Lynette" has been hanging around with the blinds closed. It's too dark to do much except maybe read my book under the fluorescent light. I don't feel like writing. Well, this morning, she went to work and I opened the blinds to let the outside in. The sun is coming up.

At mail call today I imagine that I will get a couple of

letters, maybe from Fred, or someone. It feels like it.

Wow, I've written 101 pages since I've been here at the Phoenix Federal Camp. Hopefully, my writing isn't too boring. That's what prison is like. Today would be a good day to write the DMV about my suspended license.

Tuesday, 6:30 am, February 8th. I finally remembered to take my whites to the laundry before 7am. The last couple of weeks I spaced it out, like my drawing class. I finally made it on Saturday. I'm still missing a couple of classes.

Drawing extra pictures makes it up. No problem there, I feel like drawing all the time. Next week we are doing the human figures. I sent off my letters to DMV and Superior court.

Lisa Spivey wrote me a letter. She apologized for all the crap she did to me. Johnny left her.

All those times she left Johnny high and dry. Now she's the one to be left behind. I know it's got to be tough for her now, having to find a job and pay bills. She had it made before. Johnny did every thing for her. Maybe she'll appreciate it now that it's gone. I asked her for some pictures of my grandson so I could do a couple drawings.

I hope to hear from Fred soon. I need to tell him that I'm moving in with Raymond and Dale in Rio Rico. I totally appreciate Fred's offer, but it's best I stay with family. I miss Ray and the other boys, even Dale. I'm hoping to help him fix his place for something to do. I could write my book while I'm there. I'm going to continue until the "Laundry" book is done. This could turn out to be quite a long book, describing a very long day.

Well, I'm going into the T.V, room, if they aren't mopping, and look through the magazines in the recycle bin. I need a good picture to draw for my human figure.

That's out of the question. They threw them all away. I'm sure Taya will have some stuff to choose from. I still have until Saturday to find something. My headache is subsiding so I'm going to read for a little while. If I lie down, I might be late for work, second shift. I go back to work at 9:30am.

Next day... this is my Friday. Yesterday was my Monday. I love my radio morning show. Those guys are hilarious! I've got a couple more hours before I go back to work. My book is getting really good. This guy paints things, and then they happen. There's power in art. My bunkie saved me from being late for work. I'm usually up in time but now and then, I walk the fence.

There was no mail for me yesterday, maybe today. I'm pretty calm these days since Ray told me I could stay with them. I hope Johnny is okay. I imagine Johnny got tired of Lisa leaving him, more times than one can count. So he left her. My grandson has Johnny's last name. Johnny was a good provider. I imagine he could get custody of Josh, if it went that far. I miss that little boy. Maybe he'll play the piano and be an artist? Genius?

I think I'll get back to my novel. There's only an hour before I go back to work. Only two more rounds and I'm off for two days. Something I haven't done in a while, sit out here at the cement table with no umbrella. It is an umbrella table. I seem to be possessed with the book I'm reading. I'm thinking about drawing and painting things the way I'd like them to happen. Maybe I could paint Lisa, Johnny and Josh back together again.

Right now, all the girls are shopping. We got paid today. They paid me a whopping $35 this month. They must have given me a bonus. Still, I'm not going to shop. I have three stamps left and I don't need anything. These girls are spending money in massive amounts on food, sodas and candy. That's a lot of money coming in from family, and whomever. One container of ice cream is $3 and you have to eat it right away, all of it. I'd rather have the money when I get out and not stress my family out trying to support a fat ass.

I still have half of my Christmas bag. The half that's missing, I mostly split with Rosebud.

It's so beautiful out here right now. Too bad I have to go back to the kitchen pretty soon. After work, I'll go to mail call and then the laundry to pick up my greens. That's about the end of my day. I usually play some solitaire in my upper bunk and listen to my radio before I go to sleep. Showers are in the morning, unless I get lucky to get in line early after mail. I'd better get ready for work.

Ta da! Done! I'm in my sweats and have my slippers on. I'm going to read awhile, maybe see if the girls are watching a movie. I feel like going to bed early, maybe listen to my radio. I can't get the "paint my way there" theory out of my head. I used to always say, "I'm gonna paint my way there." Now this has a new meaning, literally.

Thursday morning, February 10th, 2011. I woke up still thinking about Edgar, the artist in "Duma Key." He's drawing a ship in the sunset, off the coast of Florida.

That's where Dale's dad lived, in Florida, where Dale was born. His dad, Lloyd Feldmann, was in the Navy when Pearl Harbor happened. He was a navigator on an ammunition ship. Dale and his brothers were put in a boarding home because Mildred, their mom, had TB and was in a sanitarium. Dale was only about 18 months old then. He was four when they came back for them. Dale couldn't even talk. They had him in a basement, in the dark, on a leash.

When Lloyd came and got the boys, he took them to see their mom. It was the first memory he has of her, looking out a window, a couple stories up at the sanitarium. Dale was the youngest. He remembered her waving at him.

Dale is Johnny and Raymond's dad. That's where I'll be staying when I get out of the halfway house. They are giving me my own room. I don't mean to repeat myself. I plan on doing my artwork, writing my book and looking for a job, first thing. I need to get my license reinstated. Anyway, I'm going to make some coffee and get back to my book. Time seems to be flying in here. Soon I'll be home.

I've been reading for a couple of hours or so. It's still early and I'm cold. I'd like to lie down, but I may not wake up for lunch. I already missed breakfast. Maybe I'll check out the T. V. room after I get my boots on. We can get a shot for not having our boots on between 8am to 4pm, when we are out of our rooms. I wish I could sleep for a couple days.

Unbelievable. After I wrote the previous line, my name was called over the intercom: "Rhonda Brew, come to medical, last call." I ran down there and found out that

I was on the call out sheet for 10am. It was on the back page and I missed it.

They pulled my tooth and gave me papers to say I was to take a week off from work. Wow! The papers say that I can go to work if I want to. How cool is that? The only thing is, the dish crew is short on people, and I'm torn.

Sunday, February 13th, 2011. I'm at work. The DAP program wants me to paint a mural in their library. I'd better put my sketches away and get busy.

Well, pretty much I have it figured out how I'm gonna do the artwork. I saw Taya at lunch. She said she would help me paint on the library project. It ought to be fun, doing it together. I have two photo drawings and the library artwork to finish in the next couple of days.

Good morning, it's Valentine's Day. It never was a good day for me. The song I'm listening to is, "I feel Like A Monster. I feel it in my skin. I'm a Monster."

This is also Arizona's 99th birthday. They are reflecting on Arizona's past, like the "Lone Ranger" and "Carlotta Sales," a used car commercial. Anyway, I guess I better pop a couple aspirin. After having to use my glasses all day, I don't need a headache. The aspirin will climinate the possibility.

Enough of sitting inside, trying to see under the fluorescent lights. What a beautiful day. There's only about an hour before chow, so there's time to start another photo-drawing. The table is still cold in the shade. The cement takes awhile to warm up. I don't need any glasses out here. Being in the sun is best, but it's already too hot with my thermal on under my T-shirt.

It's difficult for me to understand the crushes these

girls have on each other. It's depressing to me. Unnatural might be a better word, because I'm not really depressed. I'm disappointed and amazed. The idea of being in love with a woman is senseless, to me.

I sat visiting with Joe. She's a cook, a great person. She prefers women. I told her if they gave me a "zing," I'd probably go there, too. Anyway, the conversation was about cooking and art. She told me that she goes in the art room everyday to see what I've painted. She told me that my artwork does something to her. My latest was a gallon jug full of tomato juice with two glasses filled with ice and juice. It was all sitting on an old rusted round chair, next to a barn wood wall. She said when she saw it she could imagine grabbing one of those glasses and having a refreshing drink.

Joe was surprised when I told her it was colored pencil. She thought it was paint. I finished the photo-drawing and that's all I have to do for now. I'd like to watch T.V. if they are watching a movie.

I love my radio! I'm sure by taking good care of it she will see many years with me.

Rosebud sat down on the bench to see what I was drawing. Carrie came by and said I should do caricatures of people while they are standing there. I told her that would take practice. She said "How much practice do you need?"

Tuesday, February 15th. I don't even recognize myself anymore. I look in the mirror, and it seems like it's somebody else I'm looking at. Now it seems that I have acquired bad breath. I brush my teeth every hour or so. How embarrassing.

I finished drawing Lady Gaga, "the bubble girl." It

turned out awesome with colored pencils. I'd like to hang it up in the art room. Right now, it's on my bulletin board. I'm sitting here wishing I could do some watercolor. It will have to wait.

Fred will be getting my letter by the end of the week. He was hoping I'd move in, but I'm not. I want to be with Raymond and Dale for a while. It might be better to be out of town at first, not so easy to fall back into bad habits. I'm a little nervous about everything, anyway.

Well, I just got done with eating and we figured out that I have an abscess on my left side. It's swelling up pretty good. I better let Choppa know what's up. She's sleeping, so after count.

Thursday morning. I just got back from sick call. I signed the book and they sent us away. We had to wait for quite some time in the waiting room. Two girls in there were acting like little children. They do that a lot around here, like role playing. One's the mom, one's the child, one's the Grandma and on and on. It's pathetic! I'm really having some trouble understanding it.

I know in DAP, (drug program), they have big sisters assigned to them. The drug program isn't about drugs at all. They are turning the girls into robots. If they don't agree with their stupid shit, they get thrown out. Most of them allow themselves to be brainwashed in order to get time off their sentence. However, after they get released early, they have a no tolerance type of probation. 75% of them are back here before six months. They barely make it through halfway house time. It doesn't have to have anything to do with drugs.

Prison is merely an industry and I hope, by the grace

of God, I make it out of the system. Quite a racket they have going there. The general public doesn't have a clue. Prison is someone's pay check. If you can't prove your innocence, see ya.

I'd say that 20 to 30 per cent of the girls in here are actually innocent of their crimes. They use conspiracy whenever they have no evidence or can't prove any crime against you. Conspiracy is their loophole to convict innocent people and they know it. Well, that's enough of that subject, before I bum myself out again.

This prison camp is owned by federal judges. How convenient is that? They make money convicting people. Like I said, no more of that subject.

I'm on page 118 of my book now, since I've been at the camp. Later... I was thinking about Fred. He'll probably think I'm not moving in with him because of something he said. This is my last chance to know Raymond before he leaves home. I'm not going to miss that.

Only a half hour left before I go back to work. I finished another great pencil drawing of a baby in a hand. The hand was the size of an adult hand. Very cool. I got another book from the library, "Winter Moon" by Dean Koontz. Can't seem to get enough.

Next day, Friday, February 18th. I just got back from medical for my infected toe. They gave me five days off work. Dr. Blanca prescribed ibuprophen and a foot soak, with antibiotics. I go back in five days to have him assess the situation.

Boo hoo. I can draw and read all I want. Choppa is sleeping right now, so I can't give her the good news. That's what they get for letting me work my ass off, while they play around constantly. God is watching out for me.

Tonight is my watercolor class and I need to come up with ideas.

Monday evening. I haven't written in a while. My focus has been on my artwork. The subject in watercolor class was clouds. I just happen to have a picture in mind from the book my bunkie is reading. It turned out good.

Saturday morning. I painted two women's faces. I've been anxious to do them for a while. They came out awesome. I'm starting to get the water coloring thing and I like it a lot. For my drawing class homework, Taya gave me a piece of colored paper (charcoal paper). I chose khaki green to do a portrait on, using white and black colored pencils. The green paper was the medium tone.

The picture turned out fabulous. I love this colored pencil thing! It was my first time with colored paper. I finished the picture in only a couple of hours. Today I drew another portrait of a girl. She had a rose on her eye. Her eyeball was in the center of the rose. That one was colored pencil. We have our last class on Friday and there's going to be a test. I need to study because I don't remember a lot of stuff. I just do it.

I finished my Dean Koontz book, "Winter Moon," last night and I finished "Conversations with God" today. I can't believe how much I've accomplished. I'm thirsty for doing another art project all the time. I have to keep a book going all the time, too.

My five days off is up so I must go to sick call. My toe needs more time to heal. I also need to get my whites together for the laundry.

Now we have the 10pm stand-up count every night. It's kind of inconvenient but the guards do it a little early sometimes, which is nice of them. They are pretty cool around here.

Tuesday morning, February 22nd. I made it to sick call and got my laundry in. The doctor gave me an extension on my pass until Saturday, February 26th. I'll go back and then he can decide what to do from there. I was soaking it too often, and I wasn't keeping it covered. I told him I didn't have any band-aids or gauze, so he gave me a pocket full.

I stopped by the library and got two more books, "Key to Midnight" and "Dragon Tears," also by Dean Koontz. The first one had a pair of eyes that look just like the ones I drew, the girl with the rose over her eye. I figured this is the book I'm supposed to be reading. The second one has an eye with a dragon in it, windows to the soul. Dr. Blanca told me not to be running around all over the place. He's too funny. I don't run, hardly ever.

Now I have to find something to draw, I have to. I can feel it. I'm having a little bit of trouble deciding what to draw. As I'm writing this, now I know.

Next day... it's early and I've already delivered the scale drawings for the library in the DAP unit. Now I don't have to deal with Karen, an inmate. She acts like she's the one to get the credit for finding me and getting me to agree to do the job. By taking the proposal to Mr. Roth directly it nullified any credit she may be taking. I can already see it finished. Very cool.

A funny thing, ever since the 21st of February, my page number has coincided with the date. On the 21st, I was on page 121, on the 22nd, I was on 122. It's the handwritten manuscript I'm referring to.

Still, I've gotten no mail since I sent Fred a letter saying I was moving in with Raymond and his dad. This is my last chance before my little boy goes on to do his own life, without parents around. I love him sooo much. He's really a cool kid. He'll be 21 this year. Johnny will be 24 and Nito will be 18! Wow, they grew up fast.

I'd better take my antibiotics and Ibuprophen while I still have something in my stomach. I'm still walking around with one tennis shoe and one shower shoe. My guess is that I'll go back to work on Monday. They miss me when I'm gone.

Nothing at mail call for me today. Tomorrow is Thursday, and I thought today was, so I guess that gives me an extra day this week. That's wonderful. It feels like I'm on vacation. I keep hearing how great the drawings are for the library. Most likely, they will approve the job. I told Taya maybe we could start painting in a week or so. She has a furlough from March 11th through the 14th.

Thursday morning, 5am. This is unusual for me to be awake this early. My bed is made and my teeth are brushed, waiting for the morning wake-up call and breakfast announcement. My dream was about being dead, or appearing dead, for some reason. It was like a practice of being dead. The creepy part is that it wasn't creepy! That's all I can remember, except Dale was in it, and maybe Bryan, along with a few other friends and a couple I didn't really know. We were in shelves, with no doors and just our heads were visible.

I did it. The cop-out for the creative writing class is in the mailbox. Done deal. I was impressed with the creative writing presentation yesterday evening. At breakfast this morning Linda was sitting at the table next to me. I was finished eating, but I moved over to her table.

I was really impressed with her story about being a chaperone for a group of teenagers visiting the "Holocaust Museum" in Washington DC. She really took me there. We were all in tears. After getting back to my unit, I found a cop-out in my locker. I filled it out. I'm requesting the privilege to take the creative writing class by learning to write more creatively.

So far, my rough draft is about 500 to 550 pages. That's a lot of re-writing to do. I need to acquire some skills in order for my book to be a success. People will enjoy reading it and recommend it to others.

I enjoy my morning radio show, "The Brady Report." They had a story about dealing with sadness by dancing. Also someone's mother was a 90-year-old prostitute. She'd had 1300 clients. Also, a guy disguised as a mummy robbed a convenience store with an ax in Herminez.

I'm taking a little break from reading, folding my laundry that's been in the bag since yesterday. The pants are totally wrinkled, but I fold them by the creases and hope they'll look better when I have to wear them. Lynette, my bunkie, has all of her clothes pressed on hangers at the end of the bed. Mine are stacked in a locker, haphazard but folded.

I find no reason to press my clothes, working in the dish room. I get soaked, head to toe, with crap all over me by the end of the day. My boots are really wet!

My bunkie works in the commissary warehouse and

drives around on a golf cart or forklift. I often wonder if I would make an effort to press my clothes if I had a different job, or if I would care one way or another. If I was meeting people from the outside, I believe I would care how I looked. If I had a visit, I would totally care.

Since I don't get visits, or haven't yet, looking pressed with my hair done is not an issue. I do have two dress shirts on hangers for visits, just in case. Other than that, I just don't feel it's necessary. I was thinking about pressing the shirts, only because I never did.

After that cute guy in the dish room, it's good to know that someone can thrill me, just by standing close. That means there's hope that I would find someone on the outside that can thrill me.

Today I start my drug education class. It's only 12 hours. Choppa is in my class. With an hour and a half before I go back to work, I might as well read my book. The characters are adrift on an ice-berg that's loaded with explosives.

Choppa and I left work early to go to our class, only to find a note on the door saying, "DE class will be Wednesday and Friday this week." At least we're off work for 2 hours.

I suppose I could get back to my story. That gorgeous guy wasn't there when I went back to work.

Wednesday after work. I'm at drug education. We are taking a 10 minute break right now, so I brushed my teeth. I could taste onions.

Thursday, March 3rd, my day off. I took my whites to the laundry and dropped it off. I read half of a novel, wrote a letter to Lisa and got her a visiting form. Lisa wrote me a letter thanking me for writing her back. She told me she didn't realize Johnny was so unhappy. I told her that he was unhappy for quite some time now. I also mentioned how upset he was when he'd come home and she was gone again, and again.

Also, he could do nothing right as far as Lisa was concerned. No matter what he did, she wasn't happy. I also told her that Johnny doesn't deal with depression very well. He's too happy naturally.

Johnny always hung out with his guy friends, so I don't believe there was anyone else. Anyway, things have a way of working out.

Friday morning, very interesting. Over coffee, Yolanda, the new crew member and I had a very interesting conversation. She used to do the paperwork for UNICOR at another camp. What a scam! Everything is privately owned.

The company that the inmates work for makes about 300%' profit! They show expenditures like $20,000 for furniture, $30,000 for blueprints and a $100,000 for a cement slab! Every expense is through another supposedly government owned business, really privately owned. They wash the money back and forth like a circle. The Keefe Co. is the source of our entire commissary, with huge mark-ups on their products they sell to the inmates.

The prison camps are privately owned by judges, the Bush's etc. They make approximately $40,000 a year for each inmate! Prison is not about reform and rehabilitation. It's an industry. Finally, I have confirmation that I was correct, from someone that did paperwork for them.

Once we are out, we aren't wanted by the public to work, or to represent their companies. Doing crime no matter how small, during desperate times, puts us right back in the system. They use whatever record we have acquired to lengthen our time to serve, even if the debt is already paid. Each item on our record counts as points against us. Twenty years from now, you get in trouble. They pile all that you have ever done before they sentence you. It's not personal; it's a business. $40,000 a year for them for every year you serve. It's probably a lot more by now.

Slave labor and governmental money laundering! The government would lose a lot of money by making pot legal, or anything else for that matter. The general public is totally not paying attention! 300% profit is huge for one company to be making. Enough of this depressing subject. I'm going to draw a picture of a little boy in a doggy suit, so cute.

Monday morning, March something or other. My bunkie says it's the 7th. I'm waiting for the dentist to possibly show up, and getting into a disagreement with the retards on the bench, waiting for pill-call. Martita, the one that sings to Mexican music with her headphones on, is making us all crazy! She may not be retarded, but she sure is practiced in fooling the general public that she is.

She kept telling me he doesn't come in until Thursday, so I asked the officer if the dentist was coming in. The officer didn't know. Martita is yelling at me for asking the officer after she told me he wouldn't be in today. I yelled back, "At orientation, they told us not to rely on inmate information." I swear, what is wrong with these people? Now I'm the bad guy, and it's my issue!

My crown fell out on Saturday while I was eating pie. Fortunately, you can't see the hole in my mouth when I smile. Apparently, the dentist isn't coming in today. My mouth doesn't hurt, so I should be good for a while. After lunch, our dish crew has to go to work; it's our day off. Mr. Swift decided to power wash the kitchen before he went on vacation. Sometime this morning, I need to get in the shower. Everything depends on the girls cleaning the bathroom. Someone just jumped in ahead of me, so it's time to read my book.

Tuesday, March 8th, 2011. Today is my DE class, and also a work day. The head of the kitchen just took another good worker from our dish crew. Now Yolanda is a line server. As soon as the girls get trained on the dish crew, the kitchen moves them to other positions. This morning there were four of us.

We are supposed to get two new girls today. There are about 300 girls here. Choppa and I will be having to leave at noon for our class, so I don't know how Flaka and Claudia are going to handle it. We'll have to come back right after class to help. I'm going back in a half hour early this morning, in case they get swamped.

Yesterday I wrote a letter to Suzie Dickey. I haven't heard from her in quite a while, so I pray she's OK out there in the real world. Watch, I'll get a letter from her before she gets mine, like usual.

Days later...March 11th. I went to the dentist today, and found out they couldn't glue my crown back in. I have to go back so they can extract two teeth. At mail-call, I got a letter from Suzie. The news wasn't good, as I expected. They ended up telling Bryan that he had to leave because of his drug abuse problem. He got upset and ate all his meds, trying to kill himself. She called the EMTs, and they air-lifted Bryan out. Suzie called his mother and she can't deal with it either! Hopefully he lives, and gets the help he needs, both mentally and addiction wise.

She said my brother stopped by for a minute. The church gave him a truck and money for repairs. He still lives at Darrell's.

I guess Ocael got picked up for the third time, and Camo Dave had been living with him. Dave had gone to Oregon to stay with his mom when she was sick. She may have died if he's back in town. I think I'll write Suzie another letter tonight, or after work in the morning. She's the faithful one when it comes to making sure I don't feel forgotten. My kids take it for granted that I'm OK, even if they never write to me. They know I love them, and I know they love me. I totally understand. They have GFs (girl friends) and Johnny is a busy guy.

Monday, March 14th. It seems like a lot has gone on with me until I sit here to write about it all. For one thing, the person in the mirror is not me. The person looking out of my eyes is me, but I don't recognize the reflection in the mirror. It seems so unfair somehow.

Johnny still hasn't written to me, so I sent his birthday present to Raymond's address. I drew a sexy girl who looked a lot like Marilyn Monroe in a push-up bra. I did it on gray charcoal paper with the black and white colored pencils, another masterpiece. It's definitely worth framing. After finishing the picture, I read an entire paperback, and am thinking of starting another one. Bryan is still on my mind since his suicide attempt. I still don't know if he lived or not.

My dreams have been focused on cleaning and fixing up my trailer, with the help of my boys. Several dump runs would be a good place to start. I have a few sign jobs that are waiting for me when I get home, so I shouldn't have too much trouble getting the money to pay for my suspended license. One step at a time.

It is getting so difficult to tolerate the behavior of a few of the lesbians in here. Not an ounce of class. Today I found out they gave a blind girl a job in the yard! No way. She is so vulnerable to getting hurt. She was raking today. There are cactus and rocks everywhere. I have a hard time believing what I'm seeing.

Taking a break right now will maybe help me to remember what I so needed to write about. Maybe Rosebud is in the T.V. room. Those girls have been watching "House Hunters" every day now; nobody here is looking to buy a house! They have been watching it faithfully. These people are crazy. I want to go home.

Tuesday morning, March something. A strange thing happened today. My bunkie didn't blast the light in my face this morning to put on her makeup. When girls ask me what I'm doing in the chow hall on my day off, I usually say "My bunkie turned the light on and woke me up." The news must have gotten back to Lynette.

I slept until 7am this morning. It's a beautiful day and I opened the blinds all the way. My bunkie likes a dungeon and I like the sunshine. It's easier on my eyes. I don't know how that girl reads in the dark. My brain seems to be somewhat scrambled this morning. I keep thinking about only having 6 more months to stay here, and I don't have a clue what to do with myself. There is so much to do when I get out of here; it's hard to sit on my hands. I'm reading a new book, "Servants of Twilight," by Dean Koontz, of course.

Yesterday I mailed off Johnny's B-day gift. I hope he likes it. It's the best one I've done yet.

Going outside is probably a good idea, instead of being cooped up in this cubical. It's better for me to read in sunlight, anyway,

Thursday morning, 6:45am, March 17th. My bunkie is still not talking to me. In fact, she was hoping I'd be late for work. She didn't wake me up this morning. I woke up on my own, like I always do. One time since she was my bunkie, I was late for work. To me, she has joined the ranks with all the rest of the mindless people. Through information dot "con," I learned why she was sent back to prison.

While she was in a halfway house for four months, she tested dirty for alcohol. Her story was that the restaurant served her bourbon chicken without her knowledge. How stupid can you get? What a crock!

I really don't care if she ever talks to me. A girl came into our room and kissed her good night. It scared the crap out of her. For a minute, she thought it was me! I have an angel to draw before my next shift, so I'll be back.

Friday, March 18th. I curled my hair last night. This morning I look like Dolly Parton, without the boobs. It's really big hair. I haven't gone outside yet, so I'm in for some shit from 300 girls.

I finished another masterpiece of a man and a woman. Slowly I'm getting men into my artwork. The next one is going to be of a woman singing into a microphone, and she'll have hair like I have today.

Being my day off, reading the end of my book and starting another one is in my plans.

At work, Choppa told me that the immigration people are sending her husband back to El Salvador, after 13 years of living here. Choppa has a "furlough" for three days to see him and their kids. It might be the last time they see each other. Choppa feels so bad that she got busted and wound up in here. Now her whole family is dissolving before her eyes. She gets out about the same time I do. Now her dreams of uniting her family again are crushed.

Days later...Sunday morning. My eyes are crossing from reading this book . Earlier I said my curled hair looked like Dolly. By the end of the day, it looked like Vicki Lawrence on "Mama's Family." Missy and I couldn't quit laughing for about 10 minutes. It settled down after a while; my hair, that is. Everyone said they liked it but they were lying. They told me to get a picture taken and send it to Fred.

Speaking of Fred, I think he's mad at me for my decision to move in with Ray and Dale, instead of him. My children come first, no matter what.

My artwork is steadily getting better. I just drew a picture of Johnny Depp on blue paper. Awesome. I want to draw something right now but my bunkie is ironing her clothes in our room. The ironing board takes up the entire floor space. Today is my day to stay at work in the afternoon by myself. There's only about a half hour to do whatever I want, so I hope Lynette is finished with her wardrobe soon.

Tuesday, March 22nd, 2011. Johnny's B-day was yesterday, his 24th. Sure wish I knew what was going on with him these days. Hopefully, these two aspirins take away this headache. I have to test for my DE class tomorrow.

There are massive guns going off right now in the back of the camp. There's a rifle range for the cops back behind the track. They also do training, hiking up the hill and back down with packs on. I wouldn't want to hike it! Johnny had to do something similar for the fire department.

Choppa wants to sit next to me during the test. She believes I will pass it, even if I don't study. Apparently, Choppa thinks I'm intelligent or something. Now that my headache has subsided, I'll start reading the drug book. Taking a list of statistical facts from each page is my plan.

There's still no word from home, and it's really pretty sad. I know how my oldest son Joshua felt when I never wrote to him.

Wednesday. I've been everywhere today and haven't accomplished anything. The laundromat wasn't open for another hour when I showed up, so I brought it all back and went to breakfast before they called "mainline," and two girls took "cuts" in front of me.

The girl in front of me let them in. Those were the same ones that took cuts in front of me yesterday. They act like they are talking to each other, like nobody is going to notice. Lousy acting for sure.

After breakfast I took my laundry back and went to the library to weigh an envelope full of artwork. I'm sending it home. Anyway, I got to the library early and all three of them were there, the ones that took cuts. Their eyes got real big when I came in the door. I didn't think I needed to tell them about their rudeness. They already know. Later I went back and weighed my envelope for Raymond, and two of the girls were there again.

Believe it or not, I cleaned the room. It took all of 15 minutes. I even dusted the blinds. This is the third time I've cleaned the room since I've been locked-up. My bunkies usually do it because I'm always working or busy with something.

Today is my DE test. We have to get at least 70% to pass the class. Having the day off on the day of the test is good. Now I'm going to take a shower if they are done cleaning. I bet I run into these girls in line again today.

Sunday, March 27th; it's only 9:30am. This place trips me out. Friday, the "parenting" class was having a special "get together" at the end of their class. The children and the parents that these girls hadn't seen in years were attending. Some of them had flown across the country after saving and borrowing money to get here. One girl, "Bree," had a baby when she first was incarcerated, five years ago. She hadn't seen her little girl since birth. Another girl had 13 children that were all on their way here.

Another girl, Tina Sinatra, had a special needs daughter. Her parents drove 12 hours to get here. There were several other similar stories. Twenty minutes before the big deal, they canceled the whole thing and were not allowing any visitation for at least a week. They said there was an outbreak of chicken pox at the FCI (the men's prison) next door. The officers rotate from there to here all the time, so we are under quarantine.

There was a lot of anger and tears around here the last few days. Myself, I'm just doing my artwork and reading books. I'm washing dishes, watching time fly by and dreaming about going home. Being back with my family is my focus. For the first time I'm glad nobody visited me.

My bunkie is running around complaining how she can't sleep in on weekends, when she works "so hard" all week. She was telling her lesbian buddy how she is so respectful, that she doesn't even know how to slam a locker. While she was talking crap, she was slamming her property box closed and shoving it loudly under her bed, while I was taking a nap.

I'm so not giving a crap about much. Everyone is so full of shit! This isn't a prison. It's a camp for preschoolers! Actually I'm blessed to be here, instead of an angry prison. However, this permanent pajama party is a personal hell for me. I never liked pajama parties when I was young, and they were only overnight.

My memories still haunt me. Joe is always there and my other boys, too. I love them so much and I have wasted so much time on stupid shit. It's hard not to hate myself.

Looking in the mirror kicks my ass! Where did it go? Why did I f#ck up everything I ever had going? I'm afraid of myself and my future, at the same time. I have the chance that I desperately need to change things around. I don't want my life to be so damn difficult anymore.

It's Tuesday morning and there's a mandatory meeting for the kitchen workers. That gives me a couple of hours.

Choppa goes on her furlough Friday, so we'll be short in the dish room this weekend.

The "Dappers" (DAP drug program) talked me into helping them paint roses on four skirts made out of sheets. There are 12 roses on each skirt. I haven't gotten a letter from anyone lately. It's very depressing to know that I am so forgotten.

These girls have been playing softball lately. It's fun watching the games. Rosebud has taken it upon herself to be the cheerleader of the "Baby Dolls." She talked me into wearing pigtails. Everyone though it was real cute. A good chance to get some sun.

Wednesday night, March 30th. I got three letters today, one from Suzie, Fred, and Raymond. Right now I'm going to answer them back.

Saturday, between breakfast and lunch. Choppa went on her furlough yesterday. Her family was waiting for her in the parking lot, Mom, Dad and four kids (one set of twins). They arrived at 7am and weren't able to leave until 10am. Choppa hadn't arranged for her meds, thinking they would already have done that for her. They don't do anything they don't have to.

I wrote to Ray. He said he was a mess. I sent him my book from my drug education class. I told him that the information can't hurt. Anyway, he just now told his dad that I was coming to live with them for a couple of months until my trailer is livable. That ought to inspire Dale to help me fix it up. Before anything, I need to coat the roof.

Fred said he thought I made a good decision to stay with Raymond, and he had been too tired and too busy to write. He has been helping an old lady across the street from Suzie, who has brain cancer. He's the only one that doesn't charge her money. The nurse she has isn't strong enough to lift her.

Lisa Spivey wrote to me and sent back the visiting form. She said she wanted to visit me on Easter. That would be so great. We are working out our problems, and she's bringing my grandson to see me. He's almost three years old now. She sent me Johnny's address too. Wait until I send him a letter. I have a lot to say to him.

Monday morning. The wind about knocked me down on the way to breakfast. It's already the 4th, and Choppa is back from her furlough. She tested "clean," of course. Her daughter started crying about a mile outside of Phoenix and didn't stop until they dropped Choppa off at the prison. I suppose she'll never see her husband again.

They are telling him to go back to El Salvador or he will be deported. Then he'll never be able to come back. He has been living in the U.S. for 17 years, working the whole time. They've been married for 13 years. It breaks my heart how our system doesn't work.

I'm going to attempt writing Johnny a nice letter. I'm a little pissed at him for never writing to me. I know I won't be mad when he explains why he hasn't written. I need to keep that in mind.

Friday, 6:40pm. I'm changing things up a little. My bunkie, Lynette, pushed the bunks to the other side of the room; only a foot, but now we have our pillows at the other end of the bed. Now I'm looking at my bulletin board when I'm in my top bunk instead of hers. I can look at my latest artwork while lying here.

I did a pencil drawing of a man kissing a woman on

the neck. I wanted to brush up on my pencil portraits because I want to do a good job on a picture of Lydia and her husband. They have been together for 37 years, and have 6 kids. He's a huge dude. Lydia got him to quit the gang shit years ago. They are still so in love.

I usually don't climb into my bunk this early, but like I said, I'm changing it up.

Johnny's letter is on its way. I hope he answers it. I've also been reading Stephen King's "Bag of Bones," instead of Dean Koontz. There's another author that I'm going to try out, Daniel Kallas, who wrote "Blood Lies." Well, I'm going to listen to music for a while.

Tuesday, after breakfast shift, I dropped off my whites at the laundry with 5 minutes to spare. I noticed it was April 4th already. I woke up with the same headache I had in my dream all night. I think I'm dehydrated. Before taking off for the kitchen, I took a 600 mg ibuprophen, and I'm pretty good now.

I thought Choppa was going to make me stay this morning, because its chicken day. I know how to make the trays easier to clean, with boiling water. Since I showed them how to do it, they let me do it all the last few times. Flaka had to stay because she took off, thinking someone else would do the work if she wasn't around. Choppa called her back and made her stay. I might have volunteered if that had not happened. I need to take a nap so my headache doesn't come back.

Thursday morning, April 7th, 6am. Wow, I have a lot to do. I haven't even started the project the "Dappers" talked me into, roses on their skirts.

Rolina got a photo from her uncle. He wants a drawing of himself in full dress, with his helmet and gun.

He wants to blow it up when she sends the drawing to him. This one is money on my books. Rolina has a brother that wants a drawing too, but she hasn't received a photo yet. Right now I'm in the middle of drawing Lydia and her husband. I think that's where I'll start.

"Bag of Bones" was an excellent book by Stephen King. Finally, I finished it. Cookie found me another book by Dean Koontz, "Odd Hours," so I'll be reading that one next. My brother, "Uncle Mike," wrote me a letter saying he's doing OK. He wanted to send me money, but he's not doing that well. He's hoping this is the month to win the sweepstakes. Mike told me he would help me with the plumbing in the bathroom when I get home. He sent a stamped, self-addressed envelope. God love him.

I'd better get busy if I'm going to take advantage of my day off. I was thinking that it's time to start sending Raymond my book. Actually, it's more of a journal. Sending him my latest artwork will clear off my bulletin board, and time will move faster. Like having my board change all the time. It keeps things moving, plus I will have to fill it up again, too. The envelope is ready; now I need to weigh it at the library.

Later… 6pm. Plenty of stuff has been accomplished for a day off at a women's prison camp. The roses are on the skirts now, the outlines, anyway. I have three more to do and then I have to paint them. I figure transferring the pattern on one garment a day, I'll get done in plenty of time. Also, I finished Lydia's drawing.

The package I sent to Raymond weighed 14 ounces. It cost me 8–44 cent stamps. I returned my Stephen King book to the library and I'm halfway through "Odd

Hours" by Dean Koontz. Tomorrow, I think I'll write my brother Mike a letter. He could use a little love in the mail, too.

I started the drawing of Rolina's uncle in his army get-up and his rifle. She told me to take my time, but I'm almost finished with it. I'll finish it tomorrow. Some things just come easy for me and some don't.

The sewer backed up today and the kitchen flooded. I'm glad I didn't work today. Japan had another earthquake today, but under the ocean. The T.V. is broken, or not working, so there's no way to see how the world is doing. Rosebud was telling me that her boss was talking about the government shutting down today. I don't really know what that means. Maybe they'll let us go. Ha, ha. I can't imagine the government shutting down. I imagine going to bed early would be a good idea. The sun isn't even down yet. I don't hang out with anyone, so I'll read my book for another half hour before I get in my bunk for a couple games of solitaire. It helps me to sleep. They'll be waking us up at 9:30pm for stand-up count to make sure we are all alive.

Friday morning, April 8th, 2011. Rosebud is so happy she could scream. She's been dragging me around the camp. First to the computer room to check our accounts, and then to the library to read the newspaper. The government is shutting down, for real. I guess that's why we get paid again early.

Rosebud got moved up a grade. Plus, she got a bonus this month. She's so happy; she's glowing. Rosebud was telling me that her boss, a government worker (cop), told her when he got his job with the prison, he signed papers saying he could never STRIKE or he would immediately be fired. The same goes for other government workers. So it looks like they will be working for free until things get settled, if they do. In that case, we'll all be working for nothing. I never heard of a government shutting down, but it looks like I'm here to experience it.

Yesterday, while I was in line for lunch, this lady that used to be at CCA with me, said when I get out my business is going to go high. She said she could read those kinds of things in people. She is sure my success will be great; I could see no doubt in her eyes. It made me feel good to hear that. I'm going to believe her. She does.

I took a shower this morning after missing breakfast. I slept through it, so all I had was two cups of coffee. Now I'm real hungry. I was attacked by Lori (the hairdresser) and Alice to do something for them. I told them I didn't charge anything, but I was lying. Rolina can fill them in.

It's time for me to start a new picture for myself, since I sent everything home to Ray.

It's Friday. I already got my picture on the way. It's a redhead lying on gold satin. I got it sketched. I'll begin the color process later. It's movie night after mail-call and I have those stupid skirts to do. I don't want to get behind.

Later… I did it! I put the roses on skirt 2 when I didn't want to. Now I'm on schedule. Everyone wants my artwork, all of a sudden.

It's my day off again, April 10th or 11th. I wonder what I'm going to take up my time with first. I picked a drawing I wanted to do but I'm not ready for that yet. Tina Sinatra gave me a picture of a panther and wants me to turn it into a tiger. She wanted it to be tearing a hole in the sun. I don't think I can visualize that well enough to draw it. Her son wanted her to draw it but she doesn't draw well. Being Frank Sinatra's cousin, you'd think she could sing well, too. Not!

These people run around thinking up these ideas, in hopes that I can make them come true. Or bail them out. To be honest, I'm into my own thing for a change, and I only want to draw what I want to draw.

Mary Ramirez, a nice older lady from the kitchen, asked me if I would draw her grandchild for her bulletin board. I did it between breakfast and lunch. She loved it. I told her 7 stamps, but she gave me 10. I gave Tina her panther back.

Betty Stiverson gave me a prayer book with a really good picture on it that she wants me to draw for her. I told her a book of stamps. I need the stamps to mail this journal and all my artwork to Raymond. This journal helps me to not be so confused.

I bet I get some mail today. I also I want to write a nice letter to my brother. I don't really care anymore, because nobody wants to help me. Advertising in the Post Office might get a reply. I'm starting to get excited because I'm not going to be here as long as I figured. I can feel it.

Margaret, the Native next door to me, is leaving right now. I did a picture for her in colored pencils of buffalo in the clouds. I didn't charge her because it was a nice challenge for me. Later she gave me about 20 colored pencils. She said she didn't really use them and she was leaving. She's going to Tucson, about 60 miles from her home.

9.

New Pad, New Day! New Life?

This is the first page of a new pad. Maybe I'll be out of here soon.

Rosebud is having a hard time with her anger. She's pissed off all the time these days. For one, they gave her time for a load of pot. They didn't catch the other guy who ran, so they charged her with his load, too. Also, the girls in here will not shut up! They yell, run, horseplay, sing and are totally loud all the time. They are like a bunch of stupid little girls. Saying anything to them causes them to be louder and more rude on purpose.

Rosebud is a target for them and I live directly across from her, so I get it all. She put in a cop-out yesterday about it and she made me go with her to mail it so she wasn't alone. I'm not concerned one way or another. I'll be her token friend. I'm her friend anyway, even if she is mad all the time. I don't blame her, but it doesn't do any good. It only makes things worse. She's actually manifesting it and doesn't know it. It's always someone else's fault, and she is totally focused on the problem all the time. So there you have it, the spoken word and then the written one (cop-out). In other words, that's the way it will stay for her, no matter who's in here with her. She has decided to always be disappointed and pissed off and bummed out. To tell her about what she's doing only makes me an enemy, too. I've tried. My decision is to leave it alone. Otherwise, I take on her problems, which are all-consuming.

An hour later.... It's so out of perspective, but I drew it anyway. I never liked copying another artist. The picture was jail-house art.

I'm a little hungry, so I opened a bag of pretzels from my Christmas bag. They aren't too bad. There's still an hour before lunch, so I think I'll read until then.

Betty gave me 10 stamps for the drawing, two more than I asked for, just in time. She's leaving today, somewhere. She didn't know about it until just before I saw her. Things only seem coincidental. Oh, and Choppa's husband didn't show up for court, so I guess he's on the lamb.

My bunkie is complaining about the dust from my colored pencils. They leave a residue on the floor. Now I'm sweeping every time I draw a picture. Today in the lunch line, because I'm white, I got the smallest piece of fish in the whole pan. The Mexican girl next to me got the biggest. When I said "Hey!" the server just smiled at me. She'd better hope she never needs my services. Maybe it's time to work on my own drawing.

Tuesday morning, April 12th. I don't really care for my bunkie anymore. She came back from her job yesterday, and right away she went crazy over a black mark on her blanket, implying that I did it. She was already giving me crap about my pencils. Who knows who's been in our room? I've been outside all day. Her friends are all the time coming in our room, which is against the rules.

I finished my picture of a young guy, Justin Bieber,

singing. I did it all in blues with a black background. It turned out pretty cool. I don't feel like doing anything right now. Maybe I'll lie back down for a while and listen to my radio station, 97.9 FM.

April 12th, Wednesday morning. Unbelievable! Kiesha was complaining about doing the morning shift by herself. She said she always had to do the morning shift. This is only her second week of working and we all take turns covering between shifts. This black girl always complains. Don't they know it makes them a target? Her complaining only got her the shift for sure. The mentality is amazing.

I volunteered for chicken day tomorrow. That's the hardest shift of all. Better I do it than someone else that doesn't know what they are doing. I finished another picture yesterday; it turned out OK. I'm sending Ray as many as I can do, so I can sell them when I get out. I hope Raymond is alright. I sure miss him.

Good morning world! Fat butts are in my way, constantly! They walk side-by-side on the walkway so no one can pass. They stop in front of me without notice. Wherever I need to go, I must wait for fat butts to get out of my way. Talk about a learning lesson in patience! When these girls are talking, it's impossible to get by unless they make an opening for you. They keep talking about working out and walking, but they eat all the cookies, donuts, and in-between-meal snacks. They ignore that fact when discussing their diets! I want out of here.

Then there's Ray-Ray, a young girl who's really loopy. Every night, she runs around, sitting on people's beds, giving them hugs and kisses good night. Thank God, I'm on the top bunk! Last night she was sitting on my bunkie's bunk saying "I love you Lynette, you're so beautiful. I love you, I love you." Yuk! If she ever got caught doing that, she'd be sent to Durango Jail (hell). They could send me too, for allowing it to happen. No touching, hugging etc. These girls act, as I said many times before, like they are at a pajama party. This is a prison camp.

Well, enough of the ranting and raving. Raymond wrote me a letter. He thinks I love Johnny more than him. I feel so sad about that. He wrote a scary letter. He's pissed off and wants to run away. I need to get out of here so I can be there for him. He seems to be the only one that cares about anything. God needs to help me on this one. AMEN, please.

I finished a little Mickey and Mini project for my bunkie's friend, but I still can't stop thinking about Raymond. I already lost one son to this f#cked up world. It's a screwed up society, and nothing is easy anymore. I'm afraid for all the kids in the world. Maybe reading my new book will help. "In the Dark of the Night," by John Saul. I have to try another author because I read all the books by Dean Koontz and Stephen King that they have in the library. Later, I'll write Fred a nice letter.

It's the weekend again. I hurt my back at work on Thursday, but it wasn't full blown. I can walk. I thought it would go away after a hot shower and Ibuprophen, but it didn't. After sitting in a chair reading a book, I tried to get up and got stuck.

Rosebud told me to get my little shoes on and go to medical, which I did. I was given four pills and told to come back on Monday, if I'm not better. So far this morning I feel pretty good, but Choppa knows if my back stays tweaked I won't be at work. I'll have to show up, to show them I'm injured. Hopefully I'll be OK. I don't like to be laid up when the crew needs me.

I'm going back to bed after I start another book. I was thinking of listing all the books I've read since I've been locked-up.

An interesting morning. I gave Taya a letter that I wrote to her last night. I told her to keep it between us. Yesterday, I was painting in the art room. Patty Faye and Justine were there the whole time I was there. Some of Taya's paints came up missing and she was really mad at me. Those girls used the fact that I opened the paint locker to blame it on me, for not locking it. In the letter, I explained what went on. Taya is my friend and those girls are assholes! Anyway, I finished the costumes for the DAP girls. They were very happy, yeah! They're going to look real cute out there dancing around.

Rayna Yatzee (Ray-Ray) is on the dish crew again. Oh boy. She hasn't messed with me yet, but the day will come. I guess I'm projecting negativity. I think I'll read a while before I start another picture.

Later. I finished a photo picture for Mary Romero. It's of her daughter and grandchild, cheek to cheek. Like Taya tells me, "You're prolific!" I had to look it up.

Taya came by and we went out to the picnic table and talked for almost an hour. We are the friends I thought we were. I admire her way. It's a breath of fresh air to talk with someone intelligent. She said she was ratted out; the Feds never caught her with the goods. She used to run loads of pot across the country in a trailer full of

Mexican pottery. The weed was in a special compartment. She gets out about the same time I do.

My other friend, Patty Montoya, got back from her "Rit." She went to court the first week she was gone, but they kept her in the Durango Jail for an extra three weeks before getting back here. She lost fifteen pounds. They feed them mush! The dogs eat way better. That is Joe Arpaio's claim to fame. "Torture the inmates, and they won't come back." Patty said the guards treated them all like shit, and talked to them like they were scum. The general public has no idea what's going on, not that it would matter. Nobody does anything, anyway.

This is April 20th, 2011. I have the morning shift, so I need to get back to work in about 15 minutes. This time, I'm going to bring my book, "Suffer the Children" by John Saul.

Later. Friday evening and no work for two days. I finished another drawing for me, or maybe for Ray for his birthday. It's a bare-breasted girl with her hair hanging back, propped up on her elbows, a knock-out! I did her in pencil. I think I'll watch the movie tonight; it starts in a few minutes.

We have a whole new batch of girls in our unit the last couple days. The girls that started DAP moved to the next building, and the girls who have graduated are waiting to go to the halfway house. The new arrivals moved into our unit. Well, I'd better go and get my place before it's gone.

Easter Sunday. I'm ready for a visit from Lisa and little Josh. I did the test run on curling my hair, so I decided to wear it straight and tease it a little. I'm wearing my dress greens for the first time since I've been here. Also, there are two photo tickets in my pocket.

I don't know what happened, but I got so sick yesterday. It started with a headache and then I decided to throw up. I had to throw up four times through the night for my head to quit throbbing. The fourth time, about 1am, it felt like my stomach was going to come up, too. My eyes were exploding.

This morning, at about 6am, I got up and took a hot shower. The shower felt great. I blow dried my hair, teased it, sprayed it and brushed it a little. There we go, a couple aspirin and Rosebud and I are off to breakfast. She said my eyes were totally bloodshot.

Visiting started at 8am and they just did 10am count. Visiting ends at 3 pm, so there's still a good chance that I will get a visit. God willing, AMEN.

Well, it's almost 1 pm, and they haven't called me to go to the visiting room. I'd like to lie down, but I don't want to mess up my hair, and my clothes are pressed. My headache has started to come back, so I took a couple more aspirins. I'm going out to read in the sun, so the fluorescent lights don't give me a bigger headache. Rosebud said she would call me if they say my name over the intercom. We can't hear it outside.

At 1:30 pm, Rosebud stuck her head out the front door and told me they called my name. I almost had a panic attack! I went down to visiting and I was so excited I just whipped the door open without knocking. A girl was on the toilet but she said to go ahead. The inmate bathroom is between us and the visiting room, probably for strip-searching. When I got in there, I had to sign the book.

When I saw Johnny, Lisa and little Josh standing there, I was shaking so bad that I could hardly write my name. I walked over and hugged Lisa first and then Johnny. We were all freaked out and happy. Little Josh didn't remember me. His little mouth was blue around his lips, because he had a snow cone before he got there. He was so cool.

It feels like I'm going home soon. What a good feeling. I'm pretty fed up with the girls, but that's what prison is all about. I got into it with Ray-Ray. Her frequent visits to my room to see my bunkie has gotten out of hand.

I had to listen to her talking about masturbating in the shower and reenacting it for Lynette. She is always touching me and I finally snapped. I told her I was sick of her lewd, disgusting behavior and I absolutely don't want to hear about her TWAT anymore! She laughed at me. For some reason, she's not laughing now. Anyway, I think the direct approach was the correct one. We could all go to Durango for her bullshit. My bunkie should never have let her continue, but I think she likes being told how beautiful she is, and how Ray-Ray wanted to lick her.

It's my day off today, and I finished another book. My plan is to finish another photo picture before I go back to work again.

Later... I finished it and delivered it to Lori, the hairdresser. I told her I wanted a book of stamps, and that next week will be fine. Now it's time to start another book, "Perfect Nightmare" by John Saul. I still have all day because it's only just after lunch. Cookin' with gas today!

I need to write Raymond a letter to go with the pictures I have to send home. Also, Uncle Mike, Lisa and Nito. A lot of letters. Tonight will be a good time for that.

Next day... Thursday. I guess today is a better day to write letters, since I didn't do them yesterday. I'm up in time for breakfast, even though I don't work today. I have one more picture to draw that I have committed myself to. It's of five feathers, like five members of a family. She's going home in four weeks, so I need to get it done. They should be calling "mainline" pretty soon. That's why I got up so early, for the coffee and donuts. I'll come back after that, and either go back to bed, read or draw. Usually I don't go back to bed; I don't want to waste my day off.

Looks like my bunkie and Ray-Ray are an item. Ray comes and kisses Lynette good night and is always telling her how sexy she is. My bunkie seems to like it. Anyway, Ray has cooled her jets around me. She doesn't shove her sexuality in my face anymore; not yet, anyway.

"T", a black lesbian, got sent to Durango for being in another girl's room, her girlfriend's. My bunkie better be careful. Ms. Gonzales is out to catch people. It's her nature. Looks like Rosebud is about ready to go to breakfast.

Rosebud and I eat together a lot and watch T.V. She's a pretty good friend. We met at my trailer a couple years ago. We said, "We ought to do this again sometime."

Rosebud gave me crap for sliding my chair in the morning. It makes as much noise, if not more, picking it up and setting it back down. I told her I'd quit sliding it for her. She decided to hate it when people slide their chairs (plastic) on the tile floor. She actually listens for it so she can complain. She's going to crap when she reads this, when it's a book instead of a journal.

I'm all into today for some reason. Maybe it's all that sugar. Sugar frosted flakes, a cup of coffee with sugar, and a jelly-filled, frosted doughnut. Oh, and an orange ZINGGG.

Friday. On May 5th, at 8am, is my TEAM. I believe everything is in order. I have a letter saying I have no warrants or cases pending. I also have certificates to show that I'm not wasting my time here. They said I should exercise regularly.

Sunday morning. I'm showered and ready for work in an hour. My dream this morning was really crazy. I dreamed that Fred and his friend from Surplus World were aliens. They were planning on abducting all my boys, Lisa and little Josh, along with me. I told Fred, "I thought you loved us." He got this weird look on his face, and said, "What's love?" I was telling him all the wonderful plans I had of us all being together. Without love, there isn't much to live for. I think they were going to reconsider, as a ship was landing. Then I woke up, thinking I was late for work.

I have two hours to spare. I'm writing this in the dark so I don't wake up my bunkie. She woke me up to start with but I'm not returning the favor. I hope Raymond decides to write me a letter.

Rosebud is teaching me how to crochet for the "Linus Project." We make blankets for babies and children who are underprivileged or orphaned. They gave me a bag of yarn with three colors. It's supposed to be worth 50 community service hours. It's also good towards my

TEAM.

My TEAM is in five days. I'm excited to know my "out-date" and halfway house plans.

Days later. May 5th, TEAM day. I still didn't get my out-date but he did tell me that I get 90 days of halfway house time. That means subtract 3 months from the projected out-date, which would be September 10th.

The blanket I was crocheting is finished. It turned out good. I already gave it to the education department and they told me we'd get a certificate sometime.

The three-day, yearly inspection is finally over. We are all so tired from working to pass the inspection. Also, this is commissary day, and I'm getting a perm. It costs $9.25, and Lori is going to give it to me tonight.

Once again, I m the token person for the dish room this morning. I like to do the first day, morning shift to get it out of the way. We're having fish today so the pans will be easy and I can work alone, which I prefer. Maybe bringing my book will be a good idea, in case it's slow. At 12 cents an hour, I don't believe anyone will complain.

They took a couple more girls to Durango for hanging out in thc T.V. room in the dark, after hours. I'm sure they were homosecting. That makes 6 girls in the last 4 days. These girls need to watch themselves. They say there are snitches, but I think they are just plain stupid and do dumb shit. They act like it's a joke, a pajama party. This is a prison.

Sunday. One more week and it's my 56th birthday. I'm still having a tough time believing I'm over 50. I just got off work and my bunkie is sleeping with the blinds closed, so I had to come outside. "Had to" is a poor way to describe it because it's totally beautiful out here. The breeze is slightly blowing and the birds are singing all around me. There must be 5 or 6 kinds of birds singing and chattering away.

I have an hour or so before I go back to the kitchen, so I figure it's a good time to write my short story for creative writing. "Radio Flyer" is about my first ride in a wagon pulled by my brother, Mike, when I wasn't quite three yet. Lorenzo, the instructor, is a very interesting person. He directs plays and movies. He seems to enjoy sharing his creative knowledge. I certainly appreciate him doing the class for us. Maybe my book will be a good one after all.

They did a shakedown on this whole place yesterday, going through everybody's rooms. They didn't take any of my stuff, so that was cool. The girls are heading toward the lunch room right now, so I'll be back.

I got my two photos from the photo shoot in the visiting room with Johnny, Lisa and Little Josh. Now I have something nice on my bulletin board. I love looking at them.

Rosebud let me know I was on the call-out sheet for Monday at 1pm, for creative writing. My beading class is going well, for only doing one lesson so far. We're making a string of daisies, like a bracelet.

Raymond wrote to me and said he read the book I sent him, and he's going to read it again. He felt that there was an incredible weight lifted from him. The book was "Conversations with God" by Donald Walsh. I let Rosebud read the letter. She said he was a total intellectual. In fact, I think it may have been too deep for her to grasp. Raymond is a very deep person.

Rosebud and I got run out of the T.V. room when the girls changed the channel before our movie was over. Instead, I wrote Fred a letter, and sent him my first draft of "Radio Flyer." There's not enough time to take a nap before I go to work so I guess I'll go and mail my letter.

On my way to mail the letter, Darma was calling me from the other side of the campus, explaining she had some pictures for me. I thought she wanted me to do a drawing but it was doubles of the pictures I had taken at my visit.

Mother's Day. Johnny came to visit me with little Josh again. He called the prison and inquired whether or not they could have a wedding here at the prison so I could attend. They wanted to get married on my birthday. That is the sweetest thing I ever beard. What a wonderful son I have. It's getting too dark to write, so I'm going to lie down now.

Later. As I was getting ready to jump into the shower, they called my name over the intercom to get to the case manager's office. He had me sign papers for the halfway house. The papers were just the agreement to follow all the rules, without incident. I'm so happy! They are shooting for 90 days, but I may only get 60. Whatever they want, I'll get.

When Johnny was visiting me, he told me about Lisa having a boyfriend whose name was Fletch Little, born on my Joshua's birthday. I told him that Joshua, his brother, was working it from the other side. Joshua's nickname in high school was "Fletcher."

He told me he had cheated on Lisa one time, with a friend of Audrey's. Johnny showed up at Audrey's house really wasted. Instead of being a friend and keeping him honest, the friend seduced him. He knows that it was his fault, but his friends didn't help him; they used him. He feels pretty stupid about it now. Lisa is wondering if Johnny's going to do it again, so she keeps Fletch Little on a string, just in case.

Rosebud keeps giving me shit about my hair, but I like it. My hair pretty much says "kiss my ass."

This is May 16th, 2011, the anniversary of my son Joshua's death 13 years ago. It was a Saturday. I got a call from his father in Seattle, at 10:30am, and he said,"I didn't know that Josh was up here!" I said "Oh my God, you found him. I was thinking he was dead or something!" Larry said "Oh my God, Rhonda, he is. He blew his head off with a shotgun!" I kept screaming "NO! NO! NO! NO! NO! NOOOO! NOOO..." and fell on my knees with my face in my hands, weeping.

Larry, his father, flew down from Seattle with Josh's body. We buried him in the graveyard in Patagonia. He had only been gone 8 months. Josh skateboarded to Washington State to be with his girlfriend. She tried to kill herself with pills because of her abusive step-father. She didn't die at that time, but went unconscious, never to return. Joshua went to his roommate's closet, where he found the grandfather's 12 gauge. He took the time to write lyrics to tell me why, before he went into the bathroom and put the gun in his mouth and pulled the trigger. They had to tear the door off the hinges to get his body out. Oh my God, this is difficult to write. I have to go to work now.

May 17th. I just got back from the laundry, and found

out they can't dry my hand washed clothes today, so tomorrow it is.

My "Radio Flyer" short story was a hit in creative writing class yesterday. Now I have to write a story about compassion.

My story, so far, is about Raymond being a mess and feeling like a loser. I need to work on it the next couple of days. My next class is on Thursday.

Last night, Rosebud had this lost look in her eyes. We are all leaving her this year. All of us that love her the most are getting out in a few months. She's already feeling the loss.

I'm going to really hate leaving her here. She's been a good friend to me and I love her. All I can say is she knows where to find me when she gets out.

Johnny finally sent me a letter but it wasn't from him. He mailed me two letters he found from Tink. He never mailed them to me. They are a year old!

Also, there was a photo of me on Halloween when I was Babushka, the Russian prostitute. I was flashing my red snatch hair that matched my wig. I won $100 that year at the Stage Stop Hotel's costume contest. I flashed my crotch at the band, and they quit playing! That was the first time Bryan ever went out with me. He stayed for two and a half years. It's hard to believe how it all ended. I have some cards to do and a couple photo-drawings, so I'd better get busy.

Friday, May 20th. It's a totally beautiful day, here at the camp. I've got a few hours before I go back to work. Thinking about my story of "spirit," to remind me that I once had it, sounds like a good project right now. I started my story in class.

Tomorrow is my birthday again in prison. It's my 56th B-day and I heard that the world is supposed to end tomorrow, again. What a birthday that would be! Wow! SEE YA!

The world did not end. It's June 1stq and I'm still here. This is my first entry since my birthday. It seems that ever since I took that creative writing class, I don't feel like writing. It's not what I was hoping for, as far as learning writing skills.

Yesterday I signed my papers for the halfway house in Tucson, called "Dismas Charities, Inc." on south Richey by Palo Verde, off the freeway (I-10). My release date from here is September 20th, 2011. I told them I'd be living at Dale's house because I have no clue about the status of my trailer. I can always change addresses later.

For several weeks now, I've been having a severe bunkie problem. I think Lynette is schizophrenic or bi-polar. She's been bad-mouthing me continuously around the camp and then not speaking a word to me. Now, all of a sudden, she's talking to me and being nice! I feel like the other shoe is going to fall any minute. No matter what she says or does, I know I'm a good bunkie. She's just a self-centered, fat, two-faced, Mexican bitch, who thinks white people are beneath her. Well I'm leaving˙ in September and she will still be here. Then she can handle her room any way she wants. Really, there is nothing to handle.

Rosebud has been especially depressed lately. It's so hard to hang around someone who hates everything. I think she realized my plight, and started letting up some. She's like a little kid, and she was 50 years old on her last birthday.

My other buddy Michele, from the library, and I sit out front on the bench, and critique the passers-by. Like sitting at the Mall, watching the people while getting a tan in the meantime. I check out a book, and she piles on a few more. She says I'll need them. I've read all the books she's given me so far. I'm learning about different authors.

I mailed a couple of envelopes to Raymond yesterday and a letter to Johnny, letting him know when I'm getting out. I'm sending my stuff home, starting now. It won't take any time at all to be ready to go, when it's time. I have an hour or two before I have to go back to work so I'm going to start another book, "Beyond Reach" by Karen Slaughter.

Wow, what a day! This was the worst day for pans, ever. Nonstop pans. At mail-call today I got two letters, one from Mike and one from Suzie. Mike said that June is his month, according to Peter Popov, the prophet. Mike wants my address and information again, so he can send me money after he wins the sweepstakes.

Suzie says Bryan is doing good at home with his folks. His mom doesn't let him lie around and do drugs. Now he is doing all the things he would have done if we were together. Sparkle Mike asks about me whenever he sees Suzie. He's working for the "Tree of Life." I've always liked Mike a lot. Suzie says I should have a lot of work when I get home. She thinks I'm getting out in December, so I'm going to write to tell her the good news.

It's my day off, June 2nd. So far, I've read a couple chapters of my book and returned another one that I tried to read four times. The author was so descriptive that I couldn't get the point.

Also, I mailed all of my photos from my bulletin board to Ray. I'm going to just keep mailing stuff home until all that's left is halfway house stuff. Next week, if we get paid, I'm going to buy a couple more cosmetic bags and a duffel bag for the halfway house.

I need to go to the R&D open house and find out about getting my packages home. Also, I need a form for Johnny to be able to pick me up. Now that my bulletin board is empty, I feel like I'm leaving soon. Actually, it's 110 days.

Five days later... Monday, June 6th, 2011. This date in 1973 was my high school graduation. I passed on a 3.4 because I missed a lot of the last semester, getting high on mescaline at Dodge Park.

My mom talked the principal into letting me make up all the work that I had missed. I had contracted mononucleosis (the kissing disease) and was sick as a dog! I spent three weeks in bed with books piled high and a really long list of assignments. I had a 4.0 all the way through school until it really counted. That's about the time my father and I started "not" getting along, He was constantly lecturing me or screaming at me, until I left home.

I hitch-hiked across the U.S. four times before I was 21, crazy! I wouldn't hitch-hike anywhere now. My poor mom is the one that suffered the most, God rest her soul. AMEN.

It's hard to believe now fast five days flew by. I hadn't noticed that I didn't made an entry in my journal until today. I finished a book and started another one. Tuesday night we are supposed to give our creative writing presentation at 6pm. I really don't care if anyone comes to it. After the show, we have only 4 more classes to finish.

We all gave Susan (teacher), our stories that we wanted to "polish," so she could proof-read and critique them. This is the part I've been looking forward to. I want to be a better writer, not a performer. Apparently, we are going to give a presentation at the end. Oh joy, joy, and joy. That reminds me, I need to press my good "greens" for tomorrow night.

I mailed Johnny the POV form to pick me up. I told him to bring me a bag of clothes when he comes to get me. I've gotten no response from Raymond since I mailed him a letter saying they will have to check out their place. I sent a picture to Suzie of Johnny, Josh and me on Mother's Day. I told her to keep it for me.

I can't believe how they rip us off. We get 12 cents an hour, and pay full price for everything on the commissary. I bought some shades (glasses) two weeks ago and lost a screw already. They cost me $5. That's a week's pay. I hope they don't make me buy underwear because they are going to throw these away. I need to find out about that.

Well, I guess it's time to go out and read for a while. I'm reading "Indelible," by Karen Slaughter. Maybe I can locate a box to send my stuff home in. I only need a small one.

Tuesday, June 7th, only 104 days left. Tonight is the presentation. I didn't hand out even one program. I'm not looking forward to it at all.

I am so pissed off about how many women are here

that shouldn't be. At least 10% of the girls in here did nothing illegal. They knew someone, or someone knew them. The system is so crooked and the public has no clue until it happens to them. I'd better take a nap and start over, forget about what's really going on.

Wednesday morning, I made it through my creative writing presentation. A lot of people went to it. I almost got choked up a couple of times. I got to read my story after a black woman, Nefertiti Love, who had the audience going to sleep. They appreciated my short, cute story. It's just what they needed to pull them out of it.

I have 4 more classes on Thursdays only. I also start cross-stitching on Friday. Gigi is letting Rosebud and I go to beading on Monday and Tuesday to make up for last night. We missed beading because of the presentation. She let us sign the book as if we were there.

I'm up extra early this morning and I'm waiting to go to work at 5:30am. Lynette, my bunkie, gave me some new boot laces last night, so I replaced them in my boots this morning. I sure could use some coffee right about now.

I almost finished my other book by Karen Slaughter. I think I'm going to try another author. Only 103 more days before I leave this place. All I seem to do is day dream about it now.

Taya is letting me do watercolors on Saturday mornings. I finished one picture and started another. Also, I did another color pencil drawing of Christina Aguilar singing. It turned out real well. That's all I have on my bulletin board besides my grasshopper on a flower.

Walking around the unit this morning, I found the perfect size box to send my stuff home in. I don't have much. After the breakfast dishes I'll probably pack it up, along with getting my greens together for the laundry. I am probably checking out the news before work. See ya...

This is Sunday, June 12th. My knees are having trouble when I go up the stairs. What really bothers me is that I was agile before I was incarcerated. This adventure has taken a physical toll on me. To stand from a sitting position is a chore, also to sit after standing. I am trusting that my condition will improve when I get out of here. I'm wondering what the cause is, maybe because everything is cement or metal. When I first was locked up, there was a long period of inactivity (locked- down for over a month). Enough of that!

Yesterday was my day off and I water colored all day. It was so wonderful. I love to paint. I did an ocean scene on a beach with rocks, and the tide coming in. It looks like an oil painting. I also did a light colored wash and painted foliage in front of it, a nice effect. Then I painted a branch with a blurred-out background. Pretty. Last of all, a hummingbird sipping a honeysuckle flower. Four paintings in a few hours, and I like them all. As soon as I can, I'm going to buy a watercolor set, paper and a few good brushes. I love doing it.

Also ,I love to crochet. It's an excellent way to spend extra time. There will be no reason for me to be idle and unproductive.

Something wonderful came in the mail the other day, a letter from the Santa Cruz County Court (Keith Barth). He said I was clear and had nothing pending in his court.

What a good person he is. We've had our moments in the past, but I have never lost respect for the man. In fact, I'm one of his biggest fans.

Another wonderful thing is, I only have 100 days left in this place. I was just telling Lynette now I can hardly write when I want to do watercolor. Doing artwork is my total passion. I still have about a half an hour before I go back to work again, so I'm going to sketch my next project.

Next day, shit! The girls on the dish crew are getting to me! They keep jumping in and trying to HELP me. They are not helping.

I felt like walking off the job again today. I have 99 days left and I'm outta here! I can't decide whether or not to write Choppa a letter on how I feel. Never mind, I've decided to let it go. I "so" don't want to be here another minute. I'm not going to miss anyone or anything. I think I'll go outside and read until I have to go back to work again. Tonight is beading class at 6pm.

I keep hearing about how much they liked my "Radio Flyer" story. Maybe it's an indication that people may also enjoy reading my book. I'm sure they'll enjoy looking at the pictures. When I looked through magazines, I looked at the pictures, not the stories. My eyesight is part of it, but an outstanding picture might get me to read an article.

This is June 14th, 2011, Tuesday. This morning after breakfast I went to the message center (the camp officer in a booth). I asked if it was OK to go in the visiting room. I wanted to check out my pictures in the display case. I told him I was doing a sequel and I needed to know the background color I used on the original. He told me he didn't know if I could go in there without getting in trouble, so he said, "What if I go in there with you, and there won't be any problems?" What a nice thing to do. He could have been a creep and told me good luck, but he chose to be a total gentleman. I can totally respect that.

It's about 8am and I finished, thanks to the officer. He was a nice looking white guy, young too, a real sight for sore eyes.

What a beautiful day. The breeze is blowing just enough to keep it pleasant but still not blowing my papers away. Apparently, there is going to be an inspection today and everyone is going nuts!

My bunkie cleaned our room yesterday and I swept the floor before I left the room. I had found a couple of sugar packets from the kitchen in my locker and a bag of hot Chitos that I threw away (counter band). They must have missed them on their last search.

Yesterday was kind of strange for me, a day I saw coming many years ago. I have been waiting for it since high school, after reading the book by George Orwell, "1984."

We had to get our thumb prints taken for commissary. We all lined up at one time. They took 4 pictures of each thumb print, which showed on a screen next to our picture. We had to do it without question. This is only the beginning. Soon we'll be doing the same thing on the outside to get groceries. Obama is lost and doesn't know it. I'm wondering how many lives I've lived. It can't be just this one; it's too timely. I'm learning not to get so freaked out and to hold my tongue. At least I appear to be conforming.

I told the officer that helped me this morning that I was thinking of showing him the picture I finished, but he might think I was silly, seeing this is a prison. He said, "Gotta do something to pass the time." What a nice guy.

Pat called me over to look at a pretty yellow bird that fell out of the tree onto the bench. I laid it on a rock and Pat said, "Why don't you draw a picture of it?" I told her I was thinking the same thing,

Looks like the DAP meeting just got out. They are all coming up the hill, at least a hundred of them. They would probably close this camp if it wasn't for the DAP program. That's the rumor via "inmate dot con."

There goes that officer again. He has been all over the place this morning. He sure doesn't sit on his ass. Michele just walked by, heading for the track. She's having me read a book to see how good it is, so she can read it. Michele and her ol' man got 10 years. She's only got a couple years to go. Her goal is to be like GI Jane when she gets out, not fat and dumpy like most of the girls are when they get out of prison. It's like they are trying to eat their way out! She wants to be a real "babe" for her ol' man. Michele is good people. I can say that literally because she is a Gemini, like me.

It feels so good to only have 98 more days left here. I had breakfast with Evelyn, who's leaving right now. I just heard her name called over the intercom to come to R&D. She's going to a halfway house in Phoenix for a while before she goes to Flagstaff to live with her sister. Evelyn has been rolling silverware since I arrived last

October. She's so sweet, not too bright, except for the smile that's always on her face. I'm so happy for her, she doesn't belong in prison. Most of us don't.

There sure are a lot of birds in here. So many different kinds. Their racket is all individual and all over the place chirping, cawing, fluttering, yelling and singing.

Pat called me over to the tree again because she saw something red, like maybe a cardinal. We figured out, it was only a leaf. Amazing how red that leaf was, all by itself on top of the forty foot tree. The rest of the leaves are still green.

This place has very beautiful landscaping. When I get home, I'm going to work on my yard a lot. I see how it can make a difference, in a big way, in my attitude when things are trimmed up and in order. I'm going to simplify my life.

Wednesday, June 15th. Only 97 days. This morning I got up for breakfast and my toe hurt pretty bad, so I took a hot shower and went to sick call instead. My toe is infected again. This time they are giving me 30 days with a soft shoe permit, instead of a couple days. They hadn't given me enough time for it to heal properly, so it stayed chronically screwed up. I'm no longer allowed in the kitchen area without boots. I'm pretty happy about that! No more scrubbing pots, spraying trays, or staying in between shifts. Yippee! Yahoo!

That's what those girls get for messing with me the way they do! I'm a hard worker, and they need two people to cover my spot. One can't do what I can do. I guess I'll go work on finishing novel so I can start the next one.

I went to work this morning and collected trays. Then I went back to work at lunchtime. Mr. Kimball said I couldn't work at all because I couldn't get a shoe on my right foot without injuring myself. He said, "Nothing personal, but see you in 30 days!"

Looks like I need to keep drawing for my commissary. I already finished a drawing job I got this morning. Now that creating writing is over, I can start another one. 95 more days!

It's Friday! I'm unemployed! I'm happy! My foot doesn't hurt! I'm going to write to Fred and ask him for a couple of bucks for the backpack that I want to buy for the halfway house. He keeps offering me money and I kept saying "not yet." Now it's time. It's done. I'm mailing the letter now.

It's been a few days since I wrote in my journal. There are only 91 days left. Every day I am painting watercolor in the mornings. In the last two days, I've painted five paintings! My skill is improving considerably. I told Taya that I've been having trouble painting, thinking of things to paint. She told me that it doesn't matter, just keep painting! I'm going to miss her. She paints with me when she can. She's my teacher, as I am hers.

Rosebud thought she was having a heart attack this morning. They put her on "Idol" for a couple of days. Choppa is on Idol too, with torn ligaments in her knees. The dish crew misses us bad! I don't miss working at all. My day is pretty full. This morning I did two photo drawings before I painted a river scene. I'm getting better at landscapes.

After 4 pm count, I got into the shower. Just as I got my hair sudsed up, they called count again. I had to jump out of the shower wrapped in my towel. I also grabbed Gail's towel that was over the door for extra cover. I barely made it to my cubical in time. My hair was still soapy and Lynette let me stand behind the wall, instead of in the door opening. Everyone got a big kick out of it.

Gail is a really cool, one of my favorite people. She calls me Bozo. One morning we were brushing our teeth and I started to comb my hair. I said, "All I have to do is dye my hair red and I'd look like Bozo." She's been calling me that ever since. "Hey Bozo, what ya doin'?" I say, "Just clowning around!" Ha, ha.

Good morning, world. It's time for a change! Rosebud is off the chain with her negativity and I can't stand it anymore.

I was listening to my radio while I was walking down to medical to get a refill on my pills. Rosebud walked with me, having to do the same. She kept talking really softly, so I had to keep taking out my ear buds to hear her. Each time, she was bitching about something! Her bunkie asked her to take a shower yesterday because of the smell in their room. I'm thinking it's probably her blankets, but now she won't shut up about it! Some people have BO, no matter what they do.

Her Bunkie, Roxy, wasn't being mean. She's a nice girl. In fact, she was the hairdresser at FCC, where I painted the walls. We got talking one day and I had left FCC a month before she arrived. She told me that everyone gets their picture taken next to the 6 foot rose I painted on the wall. It's nice to know that my efforts are appreciated.

Today is my creative writing class. There's only one more after this one. I'm going to read my story about becoming an industrial painter for the presentation. It's a long story, but Susan thinks it's a good one. In the meantime, I'll work on my art jobs so I don't get behind.

Anyway, I still haven't been able to read my story all the way through, as it is so long. It will be like the first time reading it at the presentation. After that, were done with the class. Yippee!

The presentation is on beading night again. I'm going to have to make it up next week, or go before the presentation. We missed beading this week too, because Gigi was on Idol.

Someone is singing Happy Birthday again. Another B-day in prison. Only 89 days left. Time for short-line, later....

Saturday night, June 25th. Only 87 more days and I'm outta here! I painted two paintings today, a Spanish Matador and an archway floral scene. They turned out OK, I suppose. It's obvious that I'm experimenting with different effects. The movies for this weekend I've already watched. I'm seriously thinking of going to bed and it's only 5pm.

Still nobody has written or sent any money; no news there. It's now the 29th of June for about 6 more hours. I'm waiting for my turn in the shower. There were 7 girls in front of me a while ago. I want to lie down real bad, but it should be my turn soon. My bunkie, Lynette, is sleeping already.

Last night the presentation was a hit! The girls ahead of me had the audience in tears, so it was a good act to follow. My story was about becoming a Journeyman Industrial Painter/Sandblaster, in Washington State. They got a few good laughs out of it. They were really enjoying my story. We have one more class and then we get our certificate. I think this class will help me a lot when I rewrite all this.

Today I painted a little girl swimming with her mother, one of my better paintings. Once again, I cleaned off my bulletin board and sent all the artwork home to Ray. The letter I wrote was asking why he hasn't written. Chopped liver? I'll be coming home soon and nobody is writing. I haven't heard from Fred either since I asked him to send me some money. Suzie hasn't written and I sent her a photo. John Russell (Nito) hasn't written and I sent him a drawing of his prom picture. My brother Greg hasn't written since he said he'd send me money for my B-day. I'm guessing he couldn't afford it. I haven't heard from Johnny since I sent him the POV form for him to pick me up on September 20th. He'll be taking me to the halfway house.

Being here isn't so bad since I have thirty days convalescence. My toe is healing finally, and I'm getting a lot of artwork done. I figure it's best to continue painting as often as I can and just keep on doing those photo- drawings for commissary. That may be all I have to lean on.

Days later.... It's 4th of July and Fred sent me $90. What a sweet heart. I painted him a watercolor of a dog lying on a pillow. It turned out beautiful. Also, I painted a "surfer" dude under a wave. Pretty awesome.

It's July 8th, 74 more days! My wonderful son, Johnny still hasn't sent in the POV form. I'm going to Open House to see for myself. If not, I have to send another one and hope he sends it right back. There' only 14 more days before it has to be in. That's my biggest "pet peeve" about Johnny. He doesn't write to me when I really need to know what's going on. He hasn't ever failed me, though! Not even if it's the last second. Usually that's the case. I don't know what's going on with Raymond, either. I keep sending him stuff and no reply. I'm chopped liver!

Every day I paint, sometimes two or more pictures. Only a couple times I did only one. Today I painted a giant cheese burger and a girl eating a watermelon.

Yesterday I painted two little kids playing in a box. I barely got back to the unit, when Vera Hoffaditz said, "Oh, is that ever adorable. You should give that to me." I did. We washed dishes together when I was first here. She's been down for about 8 years now and she's going home on Monday. She and her husband are bikers. She's 61. Vera reminds me of a little Nazi. I mean that endearingly. She's a tough little shit! Her friend, Donna Callipio from Hawaii, is crocheting a blanket for her to have on the bus ride home.

My toe is still not healed yet and I'm supposed to go back to work on the 13th. That means I need to go to sick-call on Monday before my soft-shoe pass runs out. They will charge me another two dollars but it could be worse. I only make 12 cents an hour, so I'm not that crazy about going back to work.

It's Friday already again. Amazing how fast time is flying by. It's almost blowing my hair back! I was thinking about starting a project for Choppa, painting her two boys and her husband. Taya photo-copied the pictures so I could see them better. I'm in the mood, so that's what I'm going to do.

July 12th, 2011, 8pm. I'm waiting to take a shower. I've painted several pictures in the last few days but my free time may be cut short. Tomorrow is the expiration date on my convalescent pass. I'm going to medical in the morning and the doctor will see that my toe is infected again since my antibiotics have run out. I was healing nicely until then.

Hopefully they give me more meds and more time off. I can't wear a shoe on that foot, so I believe they will have to reinstate my convalescence. Going back to work now would be a total drag. The dishwasher is down. They are waiting for a heating element to get here so they can fix it. As it is, they are washing everything by hand, which is a real bitch.

Anyway, enough of that shit. Only 70 more days. Johnny had better get that POV form in. I wrote a letter and sent it to Lisa. She'll get him off his ass! Now that I've showered, I ought to go to bed. 10pm count is in a half hour so I'll have to wait, reading my book until then, envisioning good news tomorrow.

Tomorrow... I went to sick-call this morning and was so blessed to get Dr. Smith again. He jammed a piece of cotton under my toenail to help it drain and to keep the skin away from the nail. He told me to leave the cotton in there for a couple days before I pull it out. I may want to put another piece under there afterward. He put me back on the antibiotic again for 14 days, gave me a soft-shoe permit that's good for a month. What a great day!

After the doctor I went to the art room and painted with Taya and Catherine for a while, until Taya started talking to me about the paper I was using. I have used quite a lot and she needs it for her watercolor class. Mr. Roads, her boss, said I could special order paper to replace it. Taya helped me to figure out what to order. The paper was $10.95 for 100 sheets, from which I'll give them about 30. The shipping is $7 no matter how much I order. One pack costs the same as ten.

I also ordered beads for jewelry. The order could take as long as 6 weeks to get here, and that's just in time to blow this popsicle stand. I'll be able to make beaded stuff that's easy to sell for cash on the street. I'll have the paper, so I'll buy the watercolors when I get out. I'll have 70 pages to paint with or do whatever kind of art I want.

It's been a good day. Thank you, God. I love my life today. I'm going to read my book since there's a couple hour before count.

Doris gave me a duffel bag today for the halfway house. That made me do a little jig!

It's Sunday afternoon in about 15 minutes, July 17th. I missed breakfast to take a shower this morning, in hopes that my son would come to visit. The reason I think he might come to visit is because of the letter I sent to Lisa's address. There was a little bit of cussing in the letter. I'm upset that he hasn't returned the form so he can pick me up. I figurcd Lisa would make sure it got done. This morning I painted a couple more cards for my inventory that I'm leaving with.

When I was dressing this morning I almost tweaked my back. I can feel the achy spot whenever I move. Maybe taking a nap would be a good idea but I don't feel sleepy.

Finally I finished, hopefully my last photo-drawing. This one is for Tracy Burney. She gave me a really nice art book and some charcoal, so I needed to pay her back.

Patty Mendez is getting me another cosmetic bag to put my beading stuff in. Now I have one for my shampoo stuff, one for beading and one for colored pencils. The duffel ought to hold everything just fine. I'm getting excited now, only 65 more days and outta here.

Suzie hasn't written in a long time, so I sent her one of my cards with a little note, asking if she and Grandma Jean are alright. I miss those two the most, besides my kids. I also miss Fred.

Time is flying by. It's Monday again. Raymond's address label keeps showing up everywhere, so I wrote him a letter telling him about it. I'm concerned about what's going on with him. I asked him to stop leaving me in the dark. It's making me crazy! I sent it with a card I had painted, and even made the envelope. It was a wishbone. I'm soaking my foot right now so it gives me this chance to write.

Rosebud's long time friend, Tracy Burney, lost her dad yesterday. Her niece found him on the floor and asked if he was OK. He said he was fine, but when she rolled him over, he quit breathing.

They might not let Tracy go to the funeral; she got a "shot" for missing a "call-out." The call-out was to award her with "room of the week." I can't believe this place. Anyway, I only have 64 more days. Right after she got the news of her father, I gave her the drawing of her and all her kids for the drawing book.

I finished another book, "Darkness" by John Saul, and it's time to go to bed. There was a dust storm earlier and we had to go to our units so they could do a re-call to make sure nobody was missing. They will still do another count at 10pm, usually when I am sleeping good.

At dinner tonight, Vicky gave me her address. She shouldn't even be in here. She reported an accident, hit and run, and waited for the police. They blamed her and gave her two years. Her husband is dying. He's holding on until she gets out, to remarry her so she gets his retirement and the house. She gets out in 21 days. Vicky just lives in Chandler, so I'll be able to visit her when I come to Phoenix to visit Johnny and Lisa.

    We are on lock-down as of now. Ms. Hawthorne just came from the FCI to warn us not to go outside. To do so would mean "Durango."

These girls are not taking it seriously. They are all loud and running around. I imagine somebody will be going to jail before it's over. I'm playing solitaire until count.

It's Wednesday, and I painted four cards before 9am for my inventory.

Tink wrote to me and I got the letter yesterday. She's out of prison and living in Tucson. She sounds good, and still loves art. She got a chance to learn pastels and acrylics while she was in Carswell in Texas. Now she's working at a dry cleaner, and plans to go to the Graphic Art Institute in Tucson. I'd like to do that. I dreamed about us painting together last night. I'm going to find something to do for a while. 62 more days.

Sunday afternoon, 58 more days left. Yesterday I woke up with a headache and threw up. I went back to bed. Rosebud gave me a couple 800mg IBUs. I took them both when the first one didn't help. My headache still didn't go away. I think it was the food, the beef stir-fry. It had some awful sweet-and-sour sauce they put on it. Rosalie said it was probably the MSG, a preservative in the sauce.

Rosebud got a visit yesterday. It was her daughter and her son. The daughter had come to meet her mom before, but it's the first time for her son. It's hard to believe she hasn't seen her kids for 15 years. Talk about being a f#ck-up! Her sister saved them from the system and adopted them because Rosebud couldn't do it.

I've been painting my cards every day except yesterday. I stayed in bed all day and all night. I'm still feeling a little heavy-headed, but I've been able to eat and paint my cards. I had to quit reading my book. My glasses were straining my eyes.

My boys still haven't written to me and I'm feeling unwanted. It's hard sometimes to believe they miss me, or even care, when I don't hear from them at all. I need to get out of this prison. If Johnny doesn't send in the POV form, I'll be taking a bus and a taxi to the halfway house.

I guess the only thing that matters is that I make it there on time. I was hoping to get some clothes from Johnny, but whatever... I've missed so much and it makes me impatient.

My toe is healing and I should be back to work on the 14th of August. That will give me another month's pay before I go. That might help with a taxi! I'm getting anxious and it's hard to calm down. It seems that things are bothering me more than usual because of it. Soon this will all be behind me. I think it's time to check out the T.V. Room. It's cool in there and hot out here, even with a good breeze.

Monday evening. I got a sick headache again today. I

had to leave the lunch line right when it was my turn to go in. I stood in the heat for about 45 minutes while this girl would not shut up! She talked nonstop Spanish, standing right next to me, until I felt like throwing up. Amazing. I thought of taking conversational Spanish until lately. I've decided I don't like the language. The majority of the people who speak it in here are totally rude and self-important. I can't believe all the times that I risked my freedom to help them out. Never again. It feels like they hate white people, and don't let us forget it! Why do the younger Latino girls in here think we whites are such slime?

Only 57 more days! No mail at mail-call and no visits this weekend. I wish my kids would let me know what's going on. Now that I'm feeling better, I'm going to read my book and hit the hay early.

Next day. I'm feeling good today. I did 6 cards, read several chapters in my book, finished what cross-stitching I could do (ran out of thread), took a nap, and now it's time for short-line (dinner). I'm getting bored painting cards, so I got a full sheet of watercolor paper (9 x 12) and sketched a picture of a girl that I have been waiting to paint for some time. I'll paint her tomorrow.

I have quite collection of them now and I'd really like my bead shipment to get here for a change of scene. The only thing about that is I have to send the stuff I make home. We can only keep our finished crafts for 14 days, probably to keep us from selling them for commissary! Only 56 more days.

I wrote a letter to Tink yesterday. I told her my book was on the boring side. I told her I was going to do my best to make it interesting with my imagination on the rewrite.

Both Tink and Suzie wrote to me. I got the letters yesterday, July 27th. Tink told me she lives real close to where my halfway house is. She wants to learn to watercolor and bead. It could be fun.

Suzie told me my brother Mike is living in my trailer now. Garland and Brad Hatfield threw him out of Darrell's apartment. Mike used to take care of Darrell, but Darrell died last Christmas. I wrote Mike and warned him not to talk to my landlord about the rent. If he does, he could possibly screw things up for me.

My brother Greg, in Florida, is paying my rent until April. Mike better not have spilled the beans to Greg, or my landlord, by announcing his presence in my trailer! I don't want to live with him again. He's gross. Yuk!

Suzie says that Bryan is doing good in North Carolina. He's building houses and staying clean at his folk's house. Too bad he couldn't have done that when he was with me. We were destructive to each other, obviously. I sent another letter to Johnny and Lisa, asking for them to tell me what's going on, I really need to know. Only 54 more days. I think this would be a good time to take a nap.

Later. I'm on the last photo-picture for Lydia Brown, of her husband. He's black, big as a house and extremely good looking. That will give me the stamps I need to mail the rest of my stuff before I leave. I also painted a picture of a little boy looking for an egg, for a medium gray T-shirt. I'll wear it on the way out, along with my sweat pants and tennis shoes, with my gray duffel bag. My entire outfit will be gray, to match my hair, except for my shoes and my underwear.

I was outside reading my book and a huge dust storm came up. Looks like I can't wait until tomorrow to take a shower. My hair is full of dirt.

That shower was fantastic. A couple games of solitaire and it's time to wind it down.

Taya keeps asking me about the "sensory deprivation" tank. When I answer her questions, she wants to argue. I didn't say I believed it, either. We almost got into it and I don't want to argue or fight with anyone about anything. I'm going to stay away tomorrow and maybe she will get the point. She needs to leave that one alone, for both of our sakes. I'm sure I can find something to do besides paint tomorrow.

Saturday afternoon. I went to the art room as usual, but I didn't talk and I changed where I sat. I let Taya do the talking, and whoever else showed up.

Taya seems bothered by all the compliments I get on my artwork. She gets them too, but works on large paintings that take her a week and I do little ones because of my situation.

I don't want to spend any money on large paper, or to ship them home. The whole thing is ridiculous. She's the art teacher. Taya took a course at an art institute but never had the passion for it like I do. She chose massage therapy instead.

Apparently, she's learning this stuff as she's teaching it. I have always done art, so I'm a lot faster but that doesn't make me better. I am a big fan of her work, without a doubt, but she sure needs a lot of encouragement. Taya is a little needy in that area. I'm sure she would disagree, completely. She can be any way she wants to be. I support that totally.

I have 52 more days and tomorrow is the last day of July. I'm going back to work in two more weeks, the 14th of August.

The guard woke me up again last night, banging his flashlight on Rosebud's bunk. She keeps hanging stuff up to block out the light, but the guard can't see if she is breathing or not. This is the 2nd time this month. She's got her shit hanging up right now, again. She's such a complainer that she wears me out sometimes. I can only take so much.

I finished a cross-stitch project and a card for Johnny and Lisa. While I was lying awake last night, I figured out what to write in it:

"Always remember to cherish your moments together, and your days will be filled with love and happiness that will last throughout the years."

All my love,

Mom

Sunday morning, 9am. I just painted the coolest card ever. It's an opened can of sardines with torn wrapping and ribbon, with a card that says "Happy Birthday." I had this crush on my girlfriend's oldest brother. He was "way" older but he was nice to me, and funny. Eddie had given me a present that year. I was 13. It was so exciting. He had to like me; he gave me a present. It was 3 cans of sardines in mustard sauce! I had set the gift on my headboard for several hours before opening it. He wrapped it so nice. It took me forever to eat them; they were so special. Bless your heart, Eddie Rick.

Since I go back to work soon, I need to paint as much as possible. The more inventory I have, the better. I got a letter from Tink yesterday. She offered to help me find a job before I get out. I told her to go for it. She is a great friend and I miss her. You can be sure we will spend some time together when I get out. She also offered to get me to the halfway house from the bus, to save me the taxi fare.

I wrote Raymond a letter the other day and told him how much it hurts that he stopped writing. I told him how sorry I was for the way our lives got separated. I wish that I could have hugged him every day of his life and that I loved him, but that's not how it went. The time we have left is the important thing now. I only want to be part of his life, as much as he will let me. My others, too, of course. That's all that matters to me right now besides being creative. I love my family.

Patty Montez just gave me a commissary sheet so I can figure out what I want people to give me for my artwork. Two pictures will cost her two packs of AAA batteries and a cosmetic bag with no handle.

I painted a few cards this morning and did some stationary for Dianna. Lydia just sat down and palmed me some stamps, so I can send home some more stuff for Raymond.

I'm so happy right now just knowing Johnny is picking me up. I guess I freak out too easily. Being in prison gives me a helpless feeling. No matter what's going on out there, you can't do anything except envision the best scenario, pray, write or nothing. Oh yeah, or freak out.

Only 48 more days and they are flying by once again. My toe is completely healed but I still wear a flip-flop on one foot and a tennis shoe on the other. The paperwork says to do that until August 14th. This Saturday evening at 6pm the girls are getting together for a group picture for my book. I love my buddies here. There's no bullshit, just the raw truth with the OGs (old gangsters). That's me; I'm an OG.

I keep thinking about this book I'm writing. Even if it's not that good of a story, there will be a lot of pictures. I sent Johnny a thank you letter for sending in the form. I also sent him a picture of an ant carrying a Cheerio. Pretty cool.

August 5th, Friday. Emma Peabody is here and has my old bunk in the hall. I went to sharpen my pencil in the T.V. room and saw that Emma was using it. I didn't recognize her, but she did me. "You're Raymond's mom, aren't you?" she said. She was just a little girl when I moved to the ranch in Sonoita. She said she was just over at Raymond and Dale's before turning herself in. It's like everyone is going to prison now days. There are a lot of kids here.

Sunday morning, August 7th, 9am. I've cleaned the room, made envelopes for 7 cards, ate breakfast and I'm wondering if I'll get a visit. That would be the ultimate cool thing to happen.

Our group picture consists of Donna Collipio from Hawaii, Patty Montez, Rebecca McMillan (Rosebud), Julie, Taya Sedam, Gail Hopple, Rolina Hadamio, and me. Choppa couldn't be in the picture. She was soaking wet from exercising, and she said she forgot about the picture. We are going to do another one next week.

Taya, Cathrine and I are getting one taken. We spend a lot of time together in the art room. Cathrine is an original "rainbow" person. Save the earth through and through. Her daughter is in here with us too. Cathrine has been beading for 35 years and she's going to show me the ropes. I'll be ready to go into production when I get cut of here.

There's one more person in the group picture, Tracy Burney. She went to school with Rosebud since third grade. She's getting out this year because of the DAP program. Looks like Rosebud has to find new friends because she still has a few years to do. Oh, and let's not forget my bunkie, Lynette.

Days later... Wednesday, August 19th. Only 41 more days left. I painted a chicken and an egg for Fred this morning. I know he loves his chickens. I haven't written to him in a while, not since he put money on my books, and I sent him the puppy painting. I am buying 3 manila envelopes @10 cents each, the big spender that I am.

Johnny came to visit me for a couple of hours and brought little Josh with him. Lisa and Johnny are no longer engaged and they are fighting about money. She just wants what she wants and that's it!

I wrote her a letter asking her to help me save the world by not buying things she doesn't need and not wasting stuff. She is so wasteful. She is helping to use up our resources like a mad woman with her attitude. People have to start being conscious of what they are doing or we will cease to exist. We can't just keep taking and not giving back.

A lot has been going on at home. Mike is on a queen size mattress in the middle of my living room. I wonder if he still feels my place is not worth fixing. Nito (John Russell), my youngest son, is working three jobs and is buying himself cool stuff. He still may get a baseball scholarship for college. Raymond, my middle son, still doesn't have a job and never has. Also, he is talking to God on his computer. I'm glad it's not someone else!

Johnny had to tell me that my grandson, Josh, is not paternal. Lisa has entrapped my son. She knew all along that she was pregnant with someone else's baby when she met my son. What a bitch. She went on letting us believe that Josh was Johnny's son, even giving him Johnny's dead brother's name.

She says she told him, but Johnny said he would remember a conversation like that. I kept telling Johnny that Josh looked just like him, which he did. Josh has blue eyes and blonde hair and is even a little bow-legged like Johnny. Finally my son had to tell me. I was a little shocked, but not too much. That boy will always be Johnny's son and my grandson in my heart. What a bitch! Welcome to the world of deceiving women. To be honest, I'd like to choke her out. Roman Catholic, my ass! She doesn't know God at all.

No longer am I going to get Lisa's car, instead it will be "Camo Dave's" old truck. It's an 81 Toyota pickup with a roll-bar and a camo paint job. It's beat to shit. The hood is held down with a chain. Johnny bought it for $75 because Dave blew it up!

I can't wait to get out of here and start living my life again. It's exciting. It's Friday again already. Only 39 more days and I can sleep in a real bed. This hard bunk does nothing for me. My ankles and knees are swelling up again and are stiff. I'm not retaining water; my arms are as skinny as ever.

I did a pretty cool painting today. Two dogs in a rowboat with oars in their mouths. They are rowing toward a tennis ball floating in the water. I'm sure Fred would love it.

The kitchen crew is totally ready for me to come back to work on Monday. Michele at the library found me another Dean Koontz book. It's a bunch of short stories. I'm enjoying it a lot. I need to take a nap for an hour or two so the swelling in my legs will go down.

August 13th, Saturday afternoon. I did a pretty cool painting of a girl doing the back stroke. I seem to do water scenes quite well. I like the distortion under the water. There's a certain satisfaction that I get I get from "pulling off" such a picture.

Taya gave me a real nice painting of Bob Dylan that she did for me. It's really good. Monique Craft, the photographer, brought me the group picture from a week or two ago. They gave me doubles of each one. I gave one to Patty, Rosebud and Jo, whose name is Joanna Lopez. She's in the picture. Poor Jo is going to be here a long time. I hate to leave her here, and Rosebud, too.

I start back to work in two days. I'm looking forward to it. They say I've been off work long enough to grow another leg. There's not enough time to nap before dinner so maybe I'll play solitaire for a while and put my feet up. Actually, I'll put my whole body up since I'm on the top bunk.

36 more days! I went back to work today. They gave

me a run for my money, that's for sure. Working in the dish room is no joke around here. It's better because I can put my hair up now. It's finally long enough.

It's funny how the job is so fast paced, but in short intervals. I was able to paint a sign for Taya this morning, "No food allowed in the craft room."

Tomorrow it's my turn to work in the morning between shifts. Time is going to fly now, two days at a time. I'll be out of here in no time at all and on to the next adventure. I'm pretty excited about starting a new life again. This is the first day after two months that I'm wearing my boots. The "hillbilly" toe on my left foot is a little cramped but they will break in again.

Wednesday, hamburger day. Only 34 more days, and not a day too soon! I worked my ass off the last couple of days. I forgot how tough my job really was. My ankles weren't as swollen at the end of the day. Inactivity is not my friend.

The girls across from my room are making me sick with their blatant homosecting. I need to get out of here. Flaka is running around showing her stuff, hoping someone will have sex with her. I'm glad she's not on the dish crew anymore. I've been trading stamps for IBU's and I think I could use one now. I feel a headache coming on, and my sore body....

The inmate that teaches the parenting class asked me if I would do face painting for the kids at the end of the class. She asked me in the art room when Taya was there. Taya said, "Why don't you ask me to do it?" That really put the girl on the spot, so she said we both could.

I told her at dinner that I didn't want to do it at all. I told her to let Taya do it. I can't believe Taya sometimes.

She's always there every time I turn around.

I don't really mind since she has given me access to the art supplies I need. I'm not used to someone following me around all the time. I've had to get used to it.

I tried to watch a movie but the girls won't shut up. I went to mail-call instead. I told them to watch whatever they "f#cking wanted."

I have a lot of stamps right now; everyone paid me. I also got 2 shampoos for the halfway house. I hope Johnny can find me some clothes. The time is going faster now since I have two days on and two days off.

Thursday afternoon and it's hot outside. The light is better for me to read by out there. My knee has been bothering me a lot lately so I'm trying to stay off it as much as possible. Maybe I'll take a nap before everyone gets off and starts screaming to high heaven, spanking each other!

Friday. I got a letter from Raymond yesterday and one from Lisa too. Raymond says he hasn't been writing because he is overwhelmed and doesn't know what to say. He's pissed off at the way people keep saying it's the end of the world and everyone is going to die. He's so angry. He's having trouble seeing past it.

Lisa says what I had to say about saving the earth really hit home. She realizes how much is wasted every day and at least understands what I was getting at. She's too important, so it won't change anything.

I'm ready to go now. There are only 28 more days and a wake-up. I'm taking a nap. Maybe later I'll write a few letters and my "special order" finally got here.

A few days later... 25 more. Rolina and Cathrine hooked me up with needles and beading thread. I already made a cool pair of earrings that I gave to Taya for a gray T-shirt. Now I'm all good to go. The only thing left to buy is some lotion for my alligator skin. I got a sewing kit, lotion, and another pad so I could continue to write this book.

They called me to sign my release papers the other day, and told me what time Johnny could pick me up. Also, what time to be at the halfway house. They only give you just enough time. I'm leaving Tuesday, September 20th, 2011, at 9am, with bells on! I hope Johnny can find me some jeans. He already found my boots.

I just finished another book, "One Last Scream" by Kevin O'Brien. Good book.

Wow. I just woke up from an hour nap and my knee doesn't hurt as much. They have been swelling and hurting all the time now. When I get out of here, it will go away.

Friday. Quite an eventful day so far. I painted a real cool picture of the angel Gabriel with his wings outstretched and spiraling, creating a universe of magenta, purple and yellow. I splashed stars on it, flipping my brush with white pearl paint. Very cool.

Rosebud has the day off and she keeps farting in her sleep over there. I'm going outside.

Good morning. It's Saturday and I'm up early. I have to write my brother Mike and tell him what I think of him taking over my trailer.

Sunday evening. My ass is so kicked! I worked really hard today. Also, I did a resume for the job fair on

Wednesday at noon. There will be companies there interviewing us. I'm sure glad today is about over; now it's two days off.

Time here is growing short. Only 32 days left and it's hello, Johnny! I need to tell him, because he's my son, that thanks to him I don't feel so alone in the world. He makes it fun in this screwed up world. All my boys make it worthwhile. I'm feeling a little sappy right now. Even Rosebud hugged me real hard today. She already misses me and I'm not gone yet.

Tuesday. It's a day off and I've been beading all morning. Jolee did such a nice job typing up my resume. It made me cry. Jolee took my rough draft and turned it into a masterpiece. Taya is making me several copies for the job fair. Choppa and I both have to go, leaving Rocio and Cindy to handle the dishes for lunch. Who knows, something neat could come out of this. No matter what, I have the best resume that I've ever had, to use for the rest of my days. God love what she did for me.

It's almost lunch time and I'm pretty hungry this morning. There are only 20 more days and it's a wonder I can eat at all. I slept with curlers in my hair last night for the job fair today. I went to work with them still in my hair. Kimble said, "Nooo way." I said that I need to leave them in or my hair will fall in the steam. He said "All that for the job fair? All you're going to need to know how to say is, can I supersize that?"

Funny guy! Every time he looked at me, he started laughing and shaking his head.

I finished another book, "Killing Spree" by Kevin O'Brien. I think I like him as an author. I'm off to return my book and waste some time.

I am so tired tonight, and work wasn't that hard. Rosebud just woke up bitching from the noise and its only 5:30pm. Of course, she bitches constantly about something 85% of the time. Maybe I'll work on my beaded ankle bracelet. I'm almost done. Then I'm hitting the sack.

Today is Labor Day and I've worked harder today than any day since I've been here. The pans would not stop coming. Walking up from the cafeteria to my unit, I felt as though I was going to fall down. The only reprieve is that we get 2 days off after dinner dishes. Thank God we have a great crew.

Only 14 more days and Johnny will be picking me up. This last week I made a bracelet, earrings and a necklace to match. Maybe I'll wear them out of here.

Its pork chops today. We had chili cheese fries for lunch. Very excellent! Today I did Blue Thunder's portrait; she loved it. Also I did praying hands with roses for Gail Hopple.

While I was reading my book, I kept wondering, what was that smell? I figured it out soon enough. It was my laundry. I opened the hamper and it about knocked me down!

Since going back to work, my boots got wet and my socks smell terrible! I loaded all my socks into my wastebasket, squirted it with dish soap, then took it into the mop closet and washed them in the mop sink. Then I wiped out my hamper and dried my stuff at the laundromat. Now it smells fresh and clean in here. Now the only thing that needs washing is my towel and the bedding. Maybe tomorrow.

I got a letter from Fred today. What a sweet guy. He's afraid I won't like him and I already think he's wonderful. I wrote him back and told him so.

It's Saturday morning, September 10th. Only 9 more days and a wake-up left. I agreed to do one more drawing. The photo had 5 people in it. The faces are real small too.

It's been difficult to fight off the urge to pack my stuff when it's still too early. Next Tuesday is the day. I'm on my last paperback, I'm done water coloring, and no more photo-drawings. I've already been paid my $9.60 for the month so it doesn't matter if I don't show, but I will. Thanks to my careful planning and lack of spending, I'll be leaving here with a little over $100. That will be plenty to cover whatever I may need at the halfway house.

I already have all my hygienic supplies from commissary and I get to keep 5 pairs of underwear, bras, and socks since they throw that stuff away.

Monday. We worked this morning and now they just announced a lock-down. That's sort of funny because there are no doors on our rooms. We have to stay in our units while they fix our electricity. It just went dark but my bunk is right by the window. I can see fine.

Only one more Monday after this one, and I'm a free woman! I've been getting zits lately, must be stress.

Wednesday evening, September 14th. I've had quite a day so far and so has Rosebud. They took her out to a real dentist this morning and pulled 23 teeth! They knocked her out first, but oh, wow! She's pretty happy because they will give her dentures when she heals.

I've done my last portrait today of a baby. Taya leaves

a week after me and Catherine will soon follow. Taya is from Colorado and Catherine is from New Mexico. I just finished my last novel, "Are You Afraid of the Dark?" by Sidney Sheldon.

The laundry service is back on track, so I don't have to wash my clothes by hand. Today they washed my "greens" and tomorrow the "whites," and I'm good to go. That's my last chance to wash them before I go. As soon as I get out, I need to get the skin cancer cut off my neck. There's only a little spot but it keeps bleeding.

Tuesday morning. I have taken a good look at my life. For instance, I felt abandoned by everyone. They all left their stuff for me to deal with, though. So I have this "huge" pile of stuff and nobody left to claim it. I can't wait to re-model my trailer and spend time with my boys. I'm looking forward to sharing my life with them and my friends. I'm no spring chicken and it's time I start having fun with the life God gave me. I also hope to find a job at a resort or fancy restaurant. It doesn't really matter that much. I just need to pay my bills, buy gas and food.

My artwork and beading is cash under the table, and small sign stuff. Everything will work out fine. I can't wait to see Nito and Raymond. I have to remember to get phone numbers from Johnny when he gets here. This is it! I'm outta here!

10.

Hello, Johnny!

It's Wednesday morning at Dismas Charities Halfway House. I've already met a real nice guy that's fun to be around. Right now, Mario is seeing if we can get a pass to go to the Swap Meet, just down the road. I still haven't talked to a counselor yet and so far, I socialize with mostly guys. I don't really relate to women, as I have mentioned many, many times. Everyone here seems to be pretty cool. I was just showing Mario my watercolor post cards; he loves them. He gave me ten dollars for a baker's dozen.

I didn't sleep at all last night, lying there thinking about what Johnny asked me in the truck on the way here. He asked if his dad had a problem with commitment. He seems to think he gets it from his father. Lisa has convinced him he has a problem with commitment, while she is sleeping with another guy several nights a week, leaving Johnny home with his "son." It's driving Johnny crazy. I need to tell him that he doesn't have the problem. She does!

She led everyone, in the beginning, to believe she was pregnant with Johnny's baby. My son, being the wonderful man that he is, stepped up to the plate and has been doing the "right" thing. He's been by her side through thick and thin, and does whatever needs to be done. He loves little Josh like only a father could. They are so good together. Now Lisa has let him know he's not the paternal father.

She lied the whole time and now accuses him of not being able to commit because he hasn't married her. Thank God. Now she says that's why she has another boyfriend. For Johnny to ask me about his dad shows me how willing he is to consider that maybe he is the one at fault. God love him.

She sure saw him coming. He had sucker right on his forehead, and he thought she loved him. Poor Johnny's heart got stomped on right out of the gate. He still wants to be the best father to his son. It seems to me that Johnny has his priorities in order and is committed to what is important, that being that little angel from heaven. I am so proud of him and his big loving heart. He is so forgiving.

Johnny is truly deserving of better than that. He doesn't need to be tied to a manipulating, lying, self-absorbed little girl who loves to create chaos and pain for others. I don't know what she will do when she gets pregnant again. Maybe expect Johnny to father it too, as she looks for the next victim? I imagine he would for the kid's sake. God bless them.

Since I feel like moving forward right now, I'll have to recoup the last days of the Federal Prison Camp and my journey to here another time.

Right now I'm sitting here watching Mexican T.V. I'm not sure what's going on but it's entertaining. I called Raymond and Nito, but they didn't answer so it cost me a dollar each to leave a message.

The monsoons are coming in and we just got sandblasted by the wind. The smoking area is in the parking lot in back of the building. It's like a sandbox with a table in the middle of it. There's a small awning but that's it. Now it's starting to rain. While I'm thinking about it, it's time to write Johnny a letter.

Next day. I woke up with a cigarette hangover. My head hurts and my eyeball felt too big for its socket. When I went to bed last night I had a sore throat. Today I'm not going to smoke anymore cigarettes.

This morning a nice Native fellow, Freeman, asked me where I came from. When I told him FCC, he said his sister is there and is getting out soon. When I asked him what her name was, he said, "Deborah." I asked, "Antone Thomas?" He said, "Yeah!" I told him she was my bunkie!

There's another young white guy, "Roy," who's from Sonoita. His mom, Sharon, knows me. There are some real nice people in here. Lurleen still hasn't found a job but she goes on job search every weekday. She's been here for a couple of months. I remember when she left the camp. She's going downtown by Congress Street, where my son Joshua used to live.

My heart still hurts when I remember those times when my son was a young man living in his first apartment. Josh and his buddies, Dan and Shannon, shared an apartment in Tucson. He sure didn't mess around growing up. I miss him so much.

I remember a time when I bought him a new pair of shoes. He was wearing this pair of faded out, tore up, red converse high tops. There was so much duct tape on them you could hardly tell that they were red. When I came back to visit him a week or so later, he was wearing his duct tape shoes again. "What the heck, Josh?" I asked.

Dan told me they were cruising around downtown and this guy was sitting on the sidewalk, barefoot and out of luck. Joshua gave him his new shoes and walked home barefoot. God, I miss him!

I imagine the counselors will be calling me sometime today to let me know what is going on. I still haven't talked to anyone about what they expect of me. I called Ray again last night and he confirmed that my stay with Dale and him would be temporary. I told him, "Of course!"

I have to find a job and fix my trailer. Maybe I ought to write my brother Mike a letter so he understands what's going on. He can decide to help me or not. I just mailed letters to Suzie and Mike, also to Palo Verde Signs requesting they give me a job, or at least consider it. I put in a request to go to Wal-Mart on Speedway and Kolb for tomorrow. If they accept my request, it will be the first time to really be free.

Alfred gave me a Dean Koontz, "Odd Thomas" book. Mario gave me a couple of books, too. My headache is subsiding now so maybe I could read for a while. I'm going out to read in the sun. It's cold in here. The natural light is better on my eyes.

I just read all the goodbyes in the card Rosebud gave me when I left. It seems everyone gave their regards. I was surprised by how many girls signed my card. There are three pages, two sides!

I often think about Mr. Swift. Ol' Swifty put a mustache, Go-T, and horns on my photo on my "merry-go-round" paper. That's the paper everyone has to sign before I can be released. He asked me not to give his real name in the book. It already sounds fictitious. I'm going to get in line for lunch.

Sunday, September 25th. I went to church with Mario, "Our Lady Queen of all Saints." It was a Catholic service, all in Spanish. We took communion and the wine was real, which freaked me out. We have to blow a breathalyzer when we come back to the halfway house. Thank God it didn't blow dirty!

I wanted to go to the dollar store. That's why I went. I had to read the flier in order to know what the service was about. We had to fill out a paper saying what the sermon was and the name of the Padre. The girls were asking if I "got some."

Later I found condoms under my pillow. They took my pad away on Friday because I left it on my bed. They gave it back today. They let me go to Wal-Mart on Saturday and I took a bus for the first time. There are some pretty creepy people riding the bus.

They gave me a bus pass for church but we walked. The pass is good for all month. I can use it sometime when they don't give me one, but send me out anyway.

The girls keep telling me that "Bob" really likes me. He's a real nice guy and funny, too.

I finally got my work detail, cleaning the women's bathroom before 9a.m. It only takes me about 15 minutes to do it, and that includes sweeping and mopping.

I started smoking cigarettes again, only half at a time and only a couple times a day. I don't want to get sick again. After church today I was going to change into some shorts since it was so hot, but I lay on my bed for a minute and passed out for a couple of hours.

We were just watching "The Transformers," the last

one. It was pretty cool. Now I think I'm going to go to bed, even though it's early. The mattress on my bed feels like a cloud instead of a sidewalk.

Monday morning, 8am. Last night, one of the girls said they needed an artist at a tattoo shop on Speedway. I thought I would write a letter to them today. Also, when I was riding the bus to Wal-Mart, this guy got on the bus wearing a "Philly's Finest" T-shirt. That's where my son worked before he took off skate boarding to Washington. He never even picked up his last check, which I had my father cash for me to help bury him. I had to call his boss and let him know why Joshua hadn't showed up for work. That was back in 1998.

There seems to be only one in the phone book, so I'm going to write them a letter. Maybe they'll give me a job.

Tuesday, September 27, 2011. I wrote letters to Johnny and Dale. I asked Johnny to loan me 10 dollars and asked Dale to call Mark Kane to see if he still wants to buy my Airstream trailer. I mentioned that I'm going to need help with getting my truck registered and insured, once Johnny finishes fixing it. I asked Dale to write back but I don't think he will. Right now I'm finishing up a beaded bracelet that maybe I could sell.

Wednesday morning. Last night I went to my first AA meeting. A guy, Alan, gave me the 12 steps to read, so I read it to myself. Then I asked this other guy, John, what to do with it. He let me know they wanted me to read it out loud to everyone. Pretty funny!

This morning I had a hell of a time doing my detail, the girl's bathroom. Those girls just take the place over! I could hardly get to the sink to brush my teeth. When I opened the door to go in a stall, there was another girl in there. Now they left for "job search," so I went in and the sink I just cleaned was full of crap. There was even a bra hanging from the door. There's an inspection today and everything has to be in order. I cleaned out the sink again but she may have to lose the bra.

I got a letter from Johnny yesterday with my driver's license enclosed. He said Lisa and he have broken up and she's moving in with her boyfriend. Johnny now has to find a place to live and they will switch off, week to week, having my grandson. Poor Johnny, he always has to deal with adversity. He said he may have to couch surf, and maybe sleep in his truck for a while. I feel bad asking to borrow $10 from him. If I can sell my Airstream, I'll split it with him.

Next day. I filled out job-search paperwork today for tomorrow: Gulf n' Stuff, Monster Signs and a couple pizza places. I hope I can make it to all of them. John Gwinn gave me some numbers for assistance, like medical and possible home repair. I called an 800 number to get an AHCCCS medical application. They will be mailing it to me. Maybe it will save me a trip; it's hot out there. All I have to wear is jeans and a T-shirt for job-search. It will have to do.

Days later... I'm going home on Saturday. I'll be on "home confinement," which means I have to call a lot and come back to UA. I also have to bring them paperwork every week. They will fill me in on how it all works before I go. Fred said I could stay at his house until Grandma Jean can put a land-line in my trailer so I can go home.

Last night they woke me up at midnight to UA. It took me 3 hours to go because I am dehydrated. After the third unsuccessful try, I started to cry. Finally they gave me a second cup of water. I took the pen that was lying on the counter to doodle some roses on my styrofoam cup. When I finished my masterpiece around the rim of the cup, I wrote "everything's coming up roses..." La, La, La.

When I finished, I was able to drop. Alice said she was going to have to write me up because it took me more than two hours. Later, after I went back to sleep, she woke me up to tell me she wasn't going to. It's a class one violation and could send me back to prison.

This morning they woke us up with a fire drill. We had to go outside and line up in the parking lot to be counted. I'm pretty tired today, so a nap is in order later. The only thing about sleeping during the day is you can't get under the covers and they keep it cold in here. It's freezing all the time.

The guys in here are pretty funny. Mr. McKinney, "Big Mac Daddy," is a real character. He looks sort of like the penguin in Batman. Then there's Mr. Turner. He's the fellow that checked me in and gave me the 25 cent tour. He's a really big dude, nice as can be. In the afternoon, Rayus comes in. She's a Mexican Nazi! She lives to mess with people. She lies in waiting for someone to break the rules so she can bust their balls!

Looks like the tobacco Mario gave me when I got here is finally running out. Mario, Frank and I are watching Bonanza. Frank, at one time, had 427 classic cars. A real interesting guy.

Well, I'd better start a drawing of a dog that I said I'd do for Lurleen. I finished it and put it under her pillow. They still haven't called me to let me know the rules of home confinement.

It's been a while since I've written. I ran out of paper. As you can see, problem solved. I have decided to stay here at Dismas until my release date. Fred should be getting the letter I wrote him by now. I apologized for being so freaked out. Maybe after this is all over, a couple years from now, I'll be well. I'll probably receive a letter from him soon.

Yesterday, October 12th, I was on job search. I have already filled out approximately 120 applications before this. The manager at Wendy's, about a mile from the halfway house on Palo Verde and Irvington at the Chevron station, said he would call me. It was his first day as manager at that store and he needed to get his bearings first. His name was Thomas, a nice guy. He asked me if I was looking for a manager position. I told him, "No, I just want a job."

The people around here at the halfway house are really cool. The staff is great, especially my counselor, Mr. Wilson. He has gone over and above to help me through this adventure. I consider him a friend. He has a good friend in Patagonia, David King. They worked together for years in the BOP (board of prisons). Before I was arrested, I had painted a sign for David and his wife, Katie, for their bed and breakfast place by the high school. Coming here to this halfway house, I realize once again how small the world really is.

This morning they called Sammy and me to UA. The only problem is that I had just gone to the bathroom before they called me. We only have 2 hours before they write us up if we can't produce a urine sample. We get one small cup of water. Sammy was able to go in about an hour. I had 7 minutes left when I finally dropped.

While we were in the bathroom, Gabby, the director, told me that Annie, from Red Mountain Foods, called for me. Gabby let me use her phone to call back. Annie said she was sending a photo of their new building, along with some ideas, so I could design a sign along with an estimate. Annie also said she would do whatever to get me a work furlough to do her building. I'm pretty jazzed!

Apparently, I forgot to sign in when I came in from outside. Mr. McKinney came in the T.V. room and put his clipboard down on the coffee table, and let me know. It made me jump! He's a character. In fact, he's the main character in this movie.

There's supposed to be two new girls coming in today. I'm wondering if I am going to know them.

I think about a lot of things that I don't write down. Maybe on the re-write, or maybe I'll just keep those to myself. Doing all this writing has helped me to keep my sanity, and kept me from getting things out of context. I try to see things for what they are.

It's Wednesday and I work the closing shift at Wendy's. Bob Napper, my buddy, got the lock off the bike that was chained to the bike rack in front of Dismas. It's only a 22 inch bike, but better than walking. The repaired tire is still holding air. I'm smoking my last cigarette that I made from butts.

This place is really filling up. One guy is going back to prison sometime soon. He went to the hospital yesterday and they gave him Percocet. He ate one. They gave him a class 100 violation and called the Marshals.

I need a couple of lights for my bike. I could get a ticket riding without one at night. If I got a ticket, I'd probably have to go back to prison.

On the news the other day, they found a woman's body in a ditch by the I-10 overpass and Palo Verde, right down the street from where I work. Hopefully, lightning won't strike twice. They will probably have me putting the sandwich orders together again at work. I'm pretty stressed out about it. It's too much to remember.

Two more girls are here today. One's half black and half Mexican, and the other is Asian.

I've been thinking about my son Raymond a lot, I hope he's OK. Maybe I should write him a letter.

I'm going to back-track a little. I forgot a few things I wanted to mention regarding job search and what not, the time before Wendy's.

I was sitting on a chair in front of the "bubble" Mr. McKinney sits in, waiting to UA; I was imagining fish in a tank. I needed to write my name down for a sack lunch for job search. The lunches they give us are the worst in the world! The bread is about a week old. Thank God they give us a bottle of water to wash it down with.

They also give us an apple that I don't eat. I don't want to loosen my bottom front teeth. The dentist in the prison loosened my teeth when he cleaned them and they are just now tightening up. I cried when it first happened, thinking I'm going to lose my front teeth. That's terrifying! My mouth caving in like a mummy.

I think I'll go outside for a while, and listen to my radio, now that I feel more comfortable.

Gabby wants me to paint something to put on the walls around here. Robert Lee was telling me that

Dismas has an interesting meaning. When Christ was crucified, the thief's name next to him was Dismas.

A couple people got jobs today. John Gwinn is a cook at the Ajo Cafe. He said he would help me remodel the bathroom in my trailer for my Volkswagen Bug that belonged to my son Joshua. That's only if Johnny says it's a good trade. It really belongs to him.

William got a job at Beer & Burgers, right by Wendy's. Lurleen just got back from job search and was waving through the window at me. Things are looking up around here. They just put the baseball game on, so it's time to go outside.

Many days later, October 24th. I've been working at Wendy's for 5 days now, and today is my first day off. I already got a warning for not calling when I got to work. If I forget again, I'll be written up and that's not good.

There are a couple of people that keep smoking up my tobacco. There's not much I can do about it. I know how it is to be without. The only thing is, I'm out of money. Hopefully, someone eventually pays me back. Well, I guess I'll go smoke one of the two cigarettes I have left.

Saturday, October 29th, 2011. Johnny is going to stop by today on his way to Patagonia. He's hauling his Z car to my place. He can't keep it parked where it is now. He said he's going to pick up a "Power Wagon" at his dad's that he bought to fix the "Fletch Mobile." John Gwinn is going to talk to Johnny when he gets here to see what radiator I need to buy for my truck. Johnny said he put pressure to the system and it was leaking like a sieve. John knows a guy who owns a radiator shop here in Tucson.

We had a great conversation on the phone yesterday,

about 45 minutes of laughing! Johnny sang me a rap song he wrote about his "Whiskey Dick." He's something else. What a kick!

This is where I stop writing my journal. I stayed at the halfway house until December 16th, 2011. Johnny came to pick me up and had his new girlfriend with him, Isis. (I'm getting away from rewriting "Laundry Day" to mention, in present time, that I love Isis with all my heart. Now, back to the story.) He was towing my Toyota truck behind him.

After leaving Dismas, we went downtown so I could meet my probation officer, Susan Calderone. She seems like a real straight up kind of person. When I told her I didn't need any counseling, she said "Ok." That was really cool. My biggest nightmare was having to go to the counseling, when I didn't need it. After leaving her office we headed for Patagonia by way of Rio Rico. We stopped at Dale and Ray's on the way to Fred's. Ray gave me all the stuff that I had sent to him to save. We all went through the artwork I had done. Ray never showed anybody what I was sending him, so they were all amazed, even Dale.

When we got to Fred's, Johnny changed out the radiator in my truck while Isis and Fred were talking, getting acquainted.

I stayed at Fred's for about three weeks. My friend Josh would bring me into town about every day, in the morning. When I had to walk, it was 45 minutes from town. Everyone was glad to see me back. Irma at the Market asked me if I was working. I told her, "Not yet." She asked, "Could you repaint the lettering on my store?"

My answer was, "Of course."

That was my re-entry into the working community. From there I painted the gas station signs for Charlie. Then it was the Creative Arts Center, the Gathering Grounds, Long Realty, Red Mountain Foods, and on and on....

My probation officer, Susan, had me going to UA once a week from December through August. Then she put me on "random." I have a clean record and I continue to work. I have to report monthly using a computer and continue to do what I am supposed to be doing.

I would like to thank the community of Patagonia for all the love and support they have given me through the rough times and the good times. I hope God blesses everyone. AMEN.

If anyone is interested, I've written another book, "Rhubarb Pie and Ice Cream for Breakfast." I wrote the book while sitting at the Gathering Grounds coffee shop, looking out the window, eating rhubarb pie and ice cream with my coffee. A much better way to start the day than doing laundry!

About the Author

I was born May 21, 1955, in Pontiac Michigan. My father was 22 and my mother was 23. When my father married my mother, she had a four year old son, Michael, from another marriage. We lived behind the engineering department of Pontiac Motors' parking lot, on Third Street. We lived there until I was four. I remember the rhubarb patch in the back yard. We used to dip the stalks in sugar and eat it like celery.

We moved to Pleasant Lake Woods, on Pleasant Lake, Michigan where I lived until I was barely 18. I hitch hiked across the United States four times before I was 21. I finally landed in Phoenix, where I lived about 10 years. I moved to Seattle for a while and became a Journeyman Industrial Painter. My son Joshua was about three at that time. I had three other sons, Johnathan, Raymond, and John (Nito) Russell.

I have been the town sign painter since the early 90's, and was also a bartender at the Big Steer Bar for eight years. I was the manager of the Hot Stuff Pizza/Smash Hit Subs at the Texaco in Sonoita, Arizona for 3½ years.

I reside in Patagonia, Arizona where I am still the town sign painter and local artist. I have lived in the same trailer for 20 years. This is where I plan to live out my days. My boys will always be able to come back home, as long as I'm alive.

Rhonda Brew

Made in the USA
Charleston, SC
20 November 2013